T0305244

The Crisis of Risk

To Kimberley, Alexa, and Jackson

The Crisis of Risk

Subprime Debt and US Financial Power from 1944 to Present

Scott M. Aquanno

Assistant Professor of Political Science, Faculty of Social Science and Humanities, Ontario Tech University, Canada

 Edward **Elgar**
PUBLISHING

Cheltenham, UK • Northampton, MA, USA

Published by
Edward Elgar Publishing Limited
The Lypiatts
15 Lansdown Road
Cheltenham
Glos GL50 2JA
UK

Edward Elgar Publishing, Inc.
William Pratt House
9 Dewey Court
Northampton
Massachusetts 01060
USA

A catalogue record for this book
is available from the British Library

Library of Congress Control Number: 2021939213

This book is available electronically in the **Elgar**online
Political Science and Public Policy subject collection
http://dx.doi.org/10.4337/9781800370838

ISBN 978 1 80037 082 1 (cased)
ISBN 978 1 80037 083 8 (eBook)

Printed and bound by CPI Group (UK) Ltd, Croydon, CR0 4YY

Contents

Preface

This book offers a different perspective on the subprime crisis by examining the intimate relationship between mortgage-backed securities and the international bond market's base on US Treasury bonds. This entails rethinking how debt markets operate and developing concepts that have so far only been touched upon. It also involves investigating the deep institutional roots of key markets and their connection to the imperial dynamics of modern finance. The analysis rests on a particular understanding of financial demand, one no doubt strongly shaped by my (brief) career in the world of high finance. This conceptualization cannot be demonstrated in any straightforward way, though the ensuing historical analysis brings into light certain foundational trends. It is rather a 'conviction animated by attachment, scholarly contemplation of history and the present, and argument, nothing more' (Brown 2015: 11).

This book suggests that financial markets – investment patterns, the strategic orientation of firms, the process of buying securities – rest on common sense constructions of risk, and that the special credibility of US bonds since the beginning of the postwar period has been sustained by a semiotic ensemble simplifying the complexity of financial exchange. It examines how this belief has been rooted in the material basis of US imperialism in this era from the time it was initially given expression by the Bretton Woods Accord at the end of the War. After the breakdown of the fixed exchange rate system in the 1970s, it was reinforced by the Volcker shock and a new monetary system. Moreover, the book argues that this conception of risk has been cradled by US regulators in the Federal Reserve and Treasury Department, who have actively managed the international bond market.

Apart from its general importance, this view challenges conventional interpretations of the subprime crisis by drawing attention to its deep historical roots. In some cases, these historical connections are more or less out in the open, as with European demand for dollar denominated mortgage bonds. Others are obfuscated and more complex: the development of a transatlantic hub-and-spoke financial network based around Wall Street. Others still are distant and probably less meaningful: financial innovation and engineering. Yet, in one way or another, these mechanisms and processes were influenced by US risk power, as the credibility of dollar denominated debt spiralled outwards through the post-Second World War era.

In many ways, this is an unpleasant conclusion, for it shows how different core aspects of the financial apparatus pivot around embranded constructions densely linking risk to capitalist exploitation and domination. This indicates the difficulty of utilizing the financial system to mobilize investment for non-capitalistic projects, or non-reformist reforms, and is a huge obstacle to emancipatory change. Such political issues, however, are not covered by this book, only hinted at. Likewise, little time is spent assessing 'deep' material economic relations – things like the realization of surplus value, the accumulation of productive capacity, investment trends, patterns of class struggle, the growing primacy of the financial sector, and so on. These are important analytically and have bearing on the argument, but are outside the scope of this study, all the more so since they have been taken up effectively elsewhere. Instead, the key aim is to trace the historical interconnectivities discussed above, linking the 2008 crisis to hidden patterns of financial power and imperial domination, and showing how key financial relations and contradictions were themselves triggered by the pervasive demand for US Treasury debt. This alone is a tall task and involves digging into the bowels of the financial system and international bond market.

The idea for this book was originally formulated in the mid-2000s. Even before the crisis, it seemed clear that the bond market's base on US Treasury debt was mixing unfavourably with neoliberal class domination, and creating important contradictions. Yet these at the same time did not appear to threaten the Treasury bond market, as many were predicting. In fact, Treasury markets seemed to be creating new stable conditions for international investment. The subprime crisis magnified these tensions and spurred new questions.

From these beginnings, the book developed through my doctoral and post-doctoral studies at York University and the University of Toronto, and took shape as the subprime crisis ravaged global markets and eventually reinforced US financial power. It benefited immensely from countless conversations with Leo Panitch and Sam Gindin, whom I have long considered close friends and mentors. Consciously or not, my most creative ideas reflect theirs. I also owe a debt to Stephen Maher, Greg Albo, Martijn Konings, Lou Pauly, Dick Bryan, Alfredo Saad-Filho, David Wolfe, Ann Porter, Gus Van Harten and Randell Germain: their spirit of inquiry, feedback on earlier drafts of this manuscript or related works, and vast knowledge, greatly improved the ideas in this book. At Ontario Tech University, I have benefited from the constant support and strong interest of many colleagues and students, only a few of whom I can mention here. Particular thanks go to Shanti Fernando and Alyson King in the Political Science Program for their encouragement and cheerful help, and to Tanner Mirrlees for his always stimulating observations. Barb Perry, Peter Stoett, Shahid Alvi, Thomas McMorrow, Olga Marques, Carla Cesaroni, and Tyler Frederick also deserve special mention. In the closing stages of this project, I received valuable feedback and support from Caroline Kracunas, Katia Williford, and the team at Edward Elgar Publishing. To all, and especially Caroline for your strong interest in publishing this book, my sincerest thanks.

Finally, I am ever grateful to my family – Mom, Dad, Jim, Sharon, Kimberley, Alexa, and Jackson – for their endless patience as this project took different turns and developed through bits and spurts. It is to my wife and two kids, whose loving support and sacrifice made this project possible, that this book is dedicated.

Scott M. Aquanno
Toronto, December 2020

1. Subprime markets in global capitalism: history and contradictions

For the last decade or so, progressive intellectuals have been determined to understand the 2008 financial crisis. Immediately following the crisis, attention focused on the contradictory nature of neoliberal accumulation and the faulty and fraudulent risk management practices and financial innovations that destabilized core markets and crippled bank balance sheets. This literature got overly side-tracked declaring the speculative nature of financial accumulation, but nonetheless revealed the class origins of the crisis (Foster and Magdoff 2009; Baker 2009). Moreover, it recognized certain points of contact between the accumulation of US mortgage loans and the global savings glut in Asia. Even though this connection was frequently conceived in the narrowest terms, the contextualization offered by this view reflected a further attempt to see beyond surface events.

More recent perspectives have moved in a different direction, holding that the international transmission of US subprime mortgage debt reciprocally impacted US and European markets (Tooze 2018). Recognizing the transatlantic dimensions of the crisis, and its impact on the wholesale funding channels forming the nerve centre of global capitalism, this new literature shows that European banks used international money markets to accumulate risky mortgage bonds, and that this sustained and underpinned the dysfunctional conditions leading to the collapse (Aliber and Kindleberger 2015).[1]

Yet though these contributions highlight various scales of financial power, and important contradictions, their tendency to focus on the period immediately leading up to the collapse has produced only a partial accounting, one that strains against viewing deeper historical connections. Subsequently, the crisis has been detached from the Bretton Woods financial system and the perceived safety of US Treasury bonds. With this, an important opportunity has been lost to develop critical research, and avoid falling back on vague ideas that fail to grasp the complex forms of power centring financial markets. Developing this literature requires reframing the crisis and addressing the deficiencies in financial scholarship that obfuscate reality.

This book encourages readers to explore the *long* history of the subprime crisis through an approach to financial risk that challenges conventional understandings: it links both the crisis and its management to a new type of abstract risk launched in the post-Second World War era. This view takes issue with the common IPE (International Political Economy) account of financial rationality, which sees actors and institutions as risk takers, unconcerned with volatility, and contributes to the critical scholarship on the subprime collapse, both the older literature which emerged in the immediacy of the crisis and the newer literature which has surfaced over the last few years. At the same time, it offers new insight about the development of financial markets and US financial power.

By exploring the intersubjective meanings shaping the popularity of US debt, and the historical development of subprime markets, I take seriously the *cultural turn* in political economy, and resist attempts to explain financial flows in purely material terms. This is to argue that constructions of risk exist *inside* financial markets and that base-superstructure approaches, which separate semiotic orders from economic practice, erase many key forces and mechanisms shaping demand. The approach adopted by this book therefore addresses a slightly different set of questions: How did the postwar credibility of US financial instruments imprint on US and global financial markets? And most importantly: What is the relationship between conceptions of risk in the international bond market and the 2008 financial cloudburst?

This book also endorses the *institutional turn* in political economy. In the following pages we will notice that US risk power was constituted in specific institutional relations at the international level and acted through different policy decisions, which structured a certain type of outcome for financial firms, markets, and regulators. Moreover, we will see that these institutional properties influenced the historical path of the financial system, shaped the nature of US financial risk, and fashioned the particular trajectory of the subprime crisis.

FRAMING MARKETS, STUDYING FINANCIAL POWER

This book departs from what I have earlier called an institutional Marxist (IM) framework,[2] and builds on the cultural political economy (CPE) tradition associated with Sum and Jessop (2013). It thereby adopts 'tools from critical semiotic analysis' and identifies institutional formations as important 'entry points' for studying the social world (ibid.: 140, 38). Such an approach also situates cultural and institutional forces within wider material relations, given that both IM and CPE build from the concept of *emergence*[3] associated with critical realism,[4] and offer a stratified view of the social world.

Cultural Turns in Critical Political Economy

CPE highlights the semiotic (meaning making) nature of all social relations as well as the 'emergent non-semiotic features of social structure[s]' (Jessop 2014; 2015). It views the production of meaning as a necessary 'condition of going on in the world', since real life events cannot be grasped in all of their complexity (ibid.: np). This explains why meaning systems evolve – beyond the simple observation that humans are sentient, reflexive creatures – and centres the wider and deeper structural components of reality. CPE identifies three primary semiotic stages. First, before particular discourses are picked 'for interpreting events, legitimizing actions and ... representing social phenomena', the social landscape is characterized by a wide variation of 'construals', as actors draw on their own subjective experiences and agential powers (Sum and Jessop 2013: 185). Following this moment of *variation*, the *selection* of discourses occurs as individual construals are funnelled through extra-semiotic practices. This amounts to a process of structural selectivity as discourses are chosen, in part as agents interact with the generative mechanisms of wider strata. Finally, there is the retention of discourses involved in the 'enactment of meaning systems in organizational routines ... institutional rules, material and intellectual technologies' (ibid.: 185). This process of *sedimentation* leads actors to forget the 'contested origins' of semiotic meaning systems, giving 'them the form of objective facts of life' (Jessop 2015).

From this, Sum and Jessop distinguish between semiosis on the one hand and imaginaries on the other. The former refers to the production of shared meanings, the latter to a semiotic 'ensemble' that configures 'various genres, discourses, and styles around a particular conception of the economy and its extra-economic conditions of existence' (Sum and Jessop 2013: 165; Jessop and Oosterlynck 2008: 1158). Imaginaries frame 'individual subjects' lived experience of an inordinately complex world', but are not defined by their semiotic characteristics alone; they include the structural and institutional supports giving them force to shape the world and are thereby the 'creative products of semiotic *and* material practices' (Sum and Jessop 2013: 165, my emphasis). They are inherently durable and play a 'central role in the ... reproduction or transformation of the prevailing structures of exploitation and domination' (ibid.: 165).

Imaginaries 'exist at different sites and scales of action', and have 'more or less performative power', for they support a range of structural and institutional mechanisms, each with very different functions and organizational features (ibid.: 165). This focuses attention on the role of *hegemonic* imaginaries, which develop as social forces 'try to make one or another imaginary the ... dominant frame in particular contexts', and brings Sum and Jessop close to Gramsci's view of ideology (ibid.: 171). Yet the intentional manipulation of consciousness professed by Gramsci is not at work in the same way. This is what Sum and Jessop (2013: 170) mean when they say that 'imaginaries are based on different entry-points and standpoints' and do not necessarily 'privilege some entry-points and standpoints'. Though imaginaries can evolve into ideologies when material interests elevate their views to the level of common sense truth, they allow for a greater degree of openness and social learning, and are less intentional in their formation and ongoing reproduction.

This focus on the dialectical emergence of semiotic processes weds Sum and Jessop to critical realist social philosophy. At the same time, it extends the work of Bhaskar, Creaven and Collier by opening up the 'transitive' (theoretical, ideational, discursive) construction of knowledge and the layered process of meaning making. A key contribution is to show how imaginaries consolidate domination by structuring common sense everyday life patterns and are grounded in capitalist power relations.

However, the CPE model has its own lapses and problems to contend with. There is first a tendency, stemming from its incorporation of Jessop's Strategic Relational Approach, to trivialize and discount the wider structures that shape meaning systems. Indeed, Jessop argues that the dialectical relationship between different social strata relativizes the basic properties of real structures. This means that even the core features of capitalism – competition, exploitation, and for-profit production – can be altered without social struggle and changed unintentionally. Such a view denies the influence of capitalist social pressures 'in the last instance' and is in all essentials wrong.[5] As a result, the CPE approach is valuable only insofar as it accounts for the durability, although not immovability, of real existing structural relations. This is to recognize, as Wendy Brown (2015: 76) has shown, that 'capitalism has drives that no discourse can deny ... to grow, to reduce input costs, to search out new venues of profit, and to generate new markets, even as the form, practices, and venues for these drives are infinitely diverse'.

Second, the CPE model fails to work out the relationship between institutional systems and social imaginaries. Its claim, that institutions are one part of the diffuse extra-semiotic landscape that sets cognitive frames and guides collective action, is empty of content: it is difficult to know whether institutions are important features of the non-semiotic social structure, and to what degree they sediment discursive frameworks to produce economic imaginaries. By contrast, *institutional Marxism views the unfolding of objective history through institutional forms of organized power*. This defines institutional rules and norms as concrete manifestations of the relationship between structural pressures and agential forces (their 'combination' in CR terms) and calls attention to how institutions sediment semiotic meaning systems.

A third problem arises from its narrow application. The CPE model has been used to explore semiotic practices, though not in a way that amends the separation between economic and discursive power. One of the major contributions of post-structural scholarship has been to recognize the always partial treatment of cultural systems within traditional base-superstructure research. By denying 'the separation of symbols/discourse/culture from material/structure/economics or culture/ideology/theory from politics/economics/practice', post-structuralists have opened 'technical and depoliticized practice to political scrutiny' (Peterson 2006: 120; de Goede 2006: 7, 14; de Goede 2003; 2005).[6] Thus rather than simply viewing the emergent properties of cultural systems, we need to understand how certain economic relations are themselves formed through, or anchored in, discursive meaning systems. This is not to deny the existence of wider material practices – as in much post-structural research – but to acknowledge that intersubjective meanings function as emergent strata *within* the economic 'base'.

Institutional Turns: CPE and IM

Beyond attributing institutions a role in the structuration process, CPE sees them as important in the selection of social construals, since they narrow options and privilege certain 'interests, activities and organizations' (Jessop and Oosterlynck 2008: 1156). This stems from a neo-institutionalist interpretation of the path-dependent and path-shaping characteristics of formal and informal institutional rules, norms, and codes of conduct. Borrowing from the work of Skocpol,[7] Hall and Taylor (1996), and Thelen (1999), institutions are seen as providing 'a framework in which relevant actors can reach and consolidate agreement' (Sum and Jessop 2013: 62). The major point is that they 'stabilize the cognitive and normative expectations of ... actors by shaping and promoting a common worldview as well as developing ... the predictable ordering of various actions' (Jessop 2001: 1231).

Through this, CPE distinguishes between structural and institutional mechanisms. As 'path-dependent and path defining complexes of social relations' that are 'connected to specific forms of power and domination', institutions are given both 'microfoundations and macrocontext': they are 'sustained and instantiated in individual, organizational and interorganizational activities but they are also embedded ... in a complex ... societal formation' (Jessop 2001: 1217, 1222). This recognizes three important points: (1) that institutions sediment the relations established by structural mechanisms and 'assume the structures which operate through them'; (2) that 'institutional analysis occurs prior to action even if the action subsequently transforms institutions and institutional contexts'; and (3) that agents have the 'capacity to engage in learning and to reflect on institutional context, institutional design, etc.' (Maher and Aquanno 2018: 40; Jessop 2001: 1230). More generally, it draws attention to institutions as a 'complex emergent phenomenon', relatively autonomous from structural and agential forces (ibid.: 1230).

Unquestionably, this view of institutions furnishes an important break with core approaches to structural analysis, which have been hampered by the tendency to either ignore institutional properties altogether, or subsume them into wider structural ensembles. In the latter case, institutional rules are treated as structural accessories before being boiled down to the condensation of structural relations. This inhibits understanding of the dialectical interplay between structural relations and institutional rules, and robs institutions of any autonomous force: as passive carriers of structural logics, they cannot 'obey laws other than the structural laws within which [they] are rooted' or 'do things that could not be predicted from an analysis of the underlying structure' (Collier 1994: 116).

Yet CPE offers only a provisional starting point for understanding the ontological significance and emergence of institutions, as it provides no more than a blueprint for the formation or relative autonomy of institutional forces. Institutions and structures are all too often blurred together and the analytical basis for their separation is insufficiently explained. IM addresses these problems, pushing forward the institutional turn within CPE, by mas-saging Marx's base-superstructure framework into 'a thesis about vertical explanation' (Collier 1994: 48). Even if the economic structure is basic to the politico-ideological superstructure, the emergence of social mechanisms means the latter is somewhat autonomous from, and capable of acting back on and shaping, the former. This provides a narrower basis for understanding the totalizing logic of the economic base and brings the emergentist perspective close to Thompson's view of 'history as process' (Thompson 1978: 9). The effect is to substitute a teleological assessment of capitalism, in which the inner laws of production lead automatically to fixed outcomes, for recognition of the complex contingency, immense variety, and *openness* of capitalist social organization. If the economic structure exerts certain basic 'pressures' or 'sit-uational logics',[8] it does not issue structural laws which lead in 'monocausal fashion to social effects' (Thompson 1978: 9; Creaven 2000: 238, 275).[9]

From this stratified and vertical perspective, IM offers a more thorough understanding of institutional power and formation. It sees institutions as emergent properties that develop from the subjectivity of human agents and the objective conditions within which they are embedded – including, above all, the transfactual properties of capitalist social relations (Maher and Aquanno 2018: 36). This view, that institutions arise from the dialectical relationship between objective and subjective forces, recognizes the casual efficacy of agents and acknowledges that the 'moment of choice' is itself a 'structurally localized conjunctural element embedded within hierarchical causal relations' (ibid.: 36). Moreover, it sees institutions as the specific organizational manifestations of capitalist structural relations.

All this is to say that institutions profoundly shape the social landscape and are themselves constantly evolving. Institutions are key nodes of power because they constrain action, as in the traditional neo-institutional account (ibid.: 38). Yet, by drawing together different social resources and privileges and constructing organizational forms that allow struggles to be carried forward, they also form the 'very positive conditions that make possible the realization of foundational mechanisms' (ibid.: 38).

IM subsequently argues that institutions need to be placed 'at the center of the search for an explanation of the making of global capitalism', and that state capacities have been *restructured*, not absolutely eroded, with the liberalization of markets (Panitch and Gindin 2012: 1; Maher and Aquanno 2018; Konings 2011). This provides the basis for questioning the use of such concepts as embedded and disembedded liberalism, and views state/institutional power as separate from, but intermeshed with, economic power. It also problematizes the 'state versus market' approach characteristic of IPE scholarship, that sees neoliberalism and financialization undermining state institutional capacities.

To summarize and draw together the above content: this book works from within an institutional Marxist framework and draws on CPE to highlight the critical role of intersubjective meanings and institutional practices in the historical development of postwar financial markets. At the same time, it seeks to overcome certain weaknesses in the CPE framework by advancing three central arguments:

1. That institutions are emergent properties which evolve and develop through the combination of durable economic structures and discursively embedded human subjects;
2. That institutional formations, by both constraining and enabling action, shape the dynamics of economic change and development;
3. That institutions express and sediment discursive constructions that operate as cognitive locks and influence financial demand.

THE LONG HISTORY OF THE SUBPRIME CRISIS

With this outline in mind, we can pass back to the issue at the heart of this book. The present work is separated by its focus on the deep history of the subprime crisis.[10] Here it is argued that the origins of the crisis are only poorly understood if we perceive the collapse of US mortgage debt separate from, rather than linked to, the specific evolution of *abstract risk* in the international bond market (IBM).

This entails paying close attention to the IBM and stitching together data from the Organisation for Economic Co-operation and Development (OECD), the Bank of International Settlements (BIS), the US Treasury Department, and the US Federal Reserve, as well as other public and private organizations, to examine issuance and demand in this market since the 1940s. The book defines the IBM somewhat unconventionally as consisting of three central trading posts: the market for *domestic-international* bond issues; the *foreign* bond market; and the *offshore* market.[11,12] Posing the history of the subprime collapse in this way also requires acknowledging the complex constitution of financial demand and its relation to risk. This book views financial demand in terms of the stratified vision presented by critical realism, cultural political economy, and institutional Marxism. It argues that financial markets are organized by diffuse, imperially constituted definitions of risk that have their basis in, but cannot be reduced to, material economic relations. This abstract form of risk is expressed as a financial common sense, offering a cognitive lock which reduces the complexity and uncertainty of financial exchange. The concrete forms of risk that we are much more familiar with – the forms which are quantified, measured and weighed against rates of return to construct investment portfolios – are emergent from, and subordinate to, this deeper system of financial control. I will argue that this view of abstract risk helps us understand why international demand for US debt has always vastly exceeded the United States' share of global GDP (Figure 1.1).

The approach taken by this book finds support in Keynes' position that popular social norms influence financial valuations. It is also connected to Weberian scholarship on the social relations of money, in so far as it sheds light on the ideational constitution of financial markets. Likewise, IPE studies of the global financial marketplace have done well to reveal the social and political basis of demand, filling some of the gaps left by Weberian-inspired theories of money and finance. Using what can be called a *Political Economy of Monetary Relations Approach*, IPE scholars have shown that financial markets rely enormously on state institutional resources and are configured by monetary systems developed at the international level (Block 1977; Helleiner 1994; 2003; 2009; 2010; Pauly 1997; Hall 2009).[13] At the same time, these studies have focused on the unique international credibility of the dollar in serving US financial hegemony. IPE scholarship has been able to connect financial demand to state power and socially constructed ideas of credibility, and recognizes that norms of market confidence have primarily benefited the US dollar in the postwar period.

There are, however, a number of problems with this literature. Apart from simply asserting that market actors have special faith in the dollar, the most severe problem is that it neglects the emergent nature of financial ideas within the institutional channels of capitalist organization. The concept of *risk imag-*

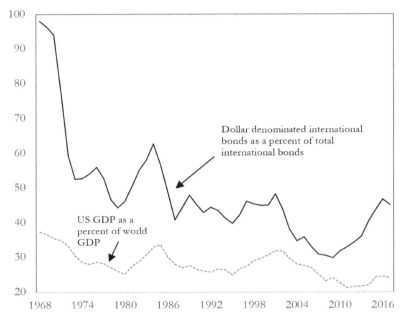

Note: International bonds exclude the foreign-domestic component of the US market.
Source: BIS; World Bank.

Figure 1.1   *Dollar denominated international bonds and US GDP*

inary is presented to animate the stratified forces shaping demand and show how key state and international institutions sedimented and reproduced US risk power. I argue that the Bretton Woods Accord formalized a new common sense around financial risk, ushering in a long period of US risk hegemony in the international bond market that reorganized wide swathes of the global financial system and set the conditions for the 2008 crisis. I argue, moreover, that financial branches of the US state formed a critical part of the institutional ensemble sedimenting US risk power. Developments in US state capacity underwrote the stable reproduction of the international monetary systems underpinning the credibility of US debt, and financial regulators mediated its particular expression by opening and closing opportunities, while at the same time acting to support and manage global debt markets. The approach adopted by this book therefore links up with IPE literature, but extends it by appreciating the power-laden definitions of risk penetrating debt markets.

Here we should push forward an obvious question which has bearing on the direction of the analysis: what is the special nature of the IBM that makes it important for studying the subprime crisis and exploring US financial power?

First, it must be recognized that the choice to explore the IBM is not arbitrary but rather reflective of the specificity of the crisis. It is necessary to remember that US mortgage-backed securities (pools of individual mortgages linked together and sold as single debt obligations) are simply bonds, and that the accumulation of these issues in Europe and Asia marked a specific form of internationalization. If we set aside some of the instruments that turbocharged and extended volatility, and the short-term money markets through which these instruments proliferated, the crisis was rooted in the US mortgage bond market, and especially the international extension of this market. It was, as we will see, a crisis in the domestic-international branch of the IBM.

This last point is critical and deserves specific attention, for the crisis is still all too often treated as 'made in America'. It is indeed well understood that the crisis had global manifestations, yet this is typically seen apart from the initial catastrophe, often as a ripple of the decline in US consumer spending. This story is premised on a fundamental misreading of the global financial system, one that obscures the international extension of the US mortgage bond market. Framing the crisis in terms of the global circulation of debt – that is, the inter-national bond market – connects it to the institutionalized forms of abstract risk that have governed financial markets from the 1940s. It also draws attention to the hub-and-spoke relationship between US and European markets. As we will see, European banks were drawing on dollar-based money markets as part of a decades-long strategy centred around the accumulation of dollar denomi-nated bonds. It is this that sent global debt and wholesale markets into a sharp tailspin as defaults began echoing through the US subprime market.

By studying the IBM one also uncovers how global debt markets pivot around US Treasury bonds and private dollar denominated issues. Each segment of the market in fact reveals different dimensions of US risk power and offers insight into the institutional channels supporting international demand. The dominance of the Yankee bond market in the foreign section of the IBM shows that foreign banks and corporations were eager to acquire US dollars, and issued bonds in the US market as a way of obtaining dollar holdings. The historical development of the offshore Eurobond market further demonstrates strong demand for US dollars, but as Eurobonds were issued outside the US domestic market, it also more clearly shows foreign interest in dollar denominated bonds. In this respect, the prominence of the Eurodollar bond market (the dollar segment of the Eurobond market), especially as it was used by private US issuers to raise funds, laid the tracks for the US MBS market: it brought European investors into dollar denominated debt, and reflected strong European demand for US dollar placements. For its part, the US domestic-international market shows that international investors both sought bonds for their linkage to dollars and consistently demanded bonds backed by the US state, directly or indirectly. The private and public sections of this market further demonstrate trends in the Yankee and Eurodollar bond market, while showing that bonds backed by the US state have long been uniquely attractive to foreign investors.

The IBM thus offers an important perspective on the post-Second World War evolution of financial demand and the trajectory of the global financial system during this period. It shows that international investors have long been drawn to public *and* private US debt placements as a way of accumulating US Treasury obligations – dollars *and* bonds; and that the accumulation of US MBS by European and Asian investors, which brought the financial system to chaos in 2008, actually reflects a historical modelling of risk with roots in the evolution of financial markets during the 1930s and 1940s.

THE VALUE OF RISK

The historical-empirical analysis carried out by this book represents an essential extension of the critical scholarship, given its tendency to examine the crisis in terms of the dysfunctionality of capitalism and finance.[14] The subprime collapse has often been viewed from the perspective of intertwined accumulation problems, of which tendencies towards over-production and under-consumption, the decline of the US empire, and the irresolvable contradictions of financialization are major traits.[15] Yet for all its contributions, most of this work spends too little time understanding the crisis at the level of financial relations and its interconnectivity with the European 'sovereign debt' crisis. Of greater importance, this work ignores the deep seated patterns of control within the financial system that reinforce rather than undermine US imperial power.

Indeed, the connection between US financial power and US risk power has so far only been touched on. The critical political economy literature has tended to view financial markets in opposition to risk management, as a part of the inherently speculative nature of financial accumulation. This makes it very difficult to understand how the financial system is underpinned by imperial constructions of risk that shape financial demand, and leaves the literature with a vaguely conceived (and non-emergentist) view of financial 'credibility'. Moreover, US financial power is frequently linked to the rise of neoliberal globalization in the 1970s.[16,17] Distinguishing the pre- and post-Bretton Woods period in this way ignores how US financial power has always been anchored in the liberal international institutions developed immediately after the Second World War. The collapse of the Bretton Woods system no doubt led to new forms of financial control. But this did not occur in opposition to the hub-and-spoke relations already conncecting US and European markets. Rather, it took shape from the institutional and discursive patterns established in the 25 years following the war, which placed US Treasury bonds at the centre of the financial system. Here it is shown that the institutionalized forms of risk developed in the 1940s have always been part of the mechanisms underpinning US financial hegemony.

OUTLINE AND CHAPTER OVERVIEW

Chapter 2 works through the relationship between financial markets and financial risk.[18] The argument takes issue with the standard way of viewing and calculating financial risk, which merely stacks up different quantitatively determined market uncertainties: credit risk, liquidity risk, interest rate risk, currency risk, repayment risk, and so on. Moreover, it contests the common image offered in the critical scholarship, which sees investors as speculative, irrational, and insensitive to risk and volatility. Against these narrow views, I argue that international debt markets operate through abstract conceptions of risk tied to imperial power. Chapter 3 builds the concept of risk imaginary from this understanding of abstract risk, working with IPE literature. It argues that the Bretton Woods international monetary system developed in the 1940s, like the dollar standard which followed in the 1970s, formalized a broad understanding about the risklessness of US debt obligations that acted as an interpretive framework for global firms and investors.

Chapter 4 starts the second part of the book and begins to trace the postwar development of the international bond market, as a way of exploring the deep history of the subprime crisis. Focusing on the period from 1945 to 1978, it shows that the abstract formation of risk laid down by the Bretton Woods system supported demand for US debt precisely because these issues could be tied back to the credibility of the US state. It also starts to unfold the complex interplay between US financial institutions and the postwar risk standard in showing how policy decisions influenced the concrete expression of financial demand. Chapter 5 continues this historical account, tracing the development of the IBM from the end of the 1970s to the mid-2000s. It reveals a similar pattern of demand across all three sections of the IBM, showing again that the evolution of financial markets involved both institutional and intersubjective forces coming to bear on the demand for dollar denominated debt. This overview clarifies how the evolution of the IBM set the tracks for the global expansion of US mortgage debt in the late 1990s and early 2000s. Chapter 6 traces the institutional ramifications of US risk power in the international bond market. Standing as the pivot of the IBM, US Treasury debt set down the conditions for a transatlantic hub-and-spoke financial system centred around Wall Street. As this system developed in the 1960s, key European financial circuits became tied into short-term dollar funding markets, and firms in London and across the continent stockpiled US debt obligations, both for their own portfolio and to sell to their clients. Chapter 7 examines the supervisory mechanisms which sustained US risk power in the period leading up to the 2008 crisis. It argues that US financial regulators played a key role managing the IBM throughout the post-Second World War period, and did so in a way that strengthened the dollar basis of global debt markets.

Building on this backdrop, Part III looks closely at the subprime crisis, specifically in terms of the financial relations and conventions underwriting the development of subprime finance, and how the US state managed the operation of critical market channels. Chapter 8 shows that global demand for US mortgage debt developed from a series of portfolio transfers within the IBM, as investors continued to privilege US public and private debt placements due to their perceived risklessness. It also shows that the crisis unfolded out of the institutional legacies and practices that took shape from the development of the IBM in the post-Second World War period – that the expansion of US subprime debt relied on the very same hub-and-spoke financial system that emerged through the accumulation of US debt in the 1960s and 1970s. Chapter 9 extends this discussion with focus on how US financial regulators managed to prevent the crisis from completely destroying the global financial apparatus. We see that regulators managed the collapse of US subprime and MBS markets not only by manipulating the credibility of US bonds, but by drawing on the lessons they previously acquired supervising demand in the IBM in the post-Second World War period. At the same time, they managed the subprime crisis in a way that extended US risk power, repeating previous actions and further internationalizing dollar denominated bonds. I conclude the book by drawing attention to the political underbelly of US risk power, speculating on the future of US financial hegemony by looking at the post-crisis evolution of financial demand. Specific focus is given to the institutional level transformations occurring at the Federal Reserve and their ability to contain key contradictions.

NOTES

1. From this perspective the subprime collapse resembles a typical foreign capital inflow banking crisis (Aliber and Kindleberger 2015).
2. See: Konings (2008; 2011); Panitch and Gindin (2005; 2006; 2012); Maher and Aquanno (2018).
3. The concept of emergence also describes the relative autonomy of internally connected structures (Archer 1995: 14). By granting the separation or uniqueness of each stratum against the inescapable rootedness of more complex structures in less complex aspects of reality, it captures the social world as a 'differentiated totality' characterized on the one hand by the 'directional logic' and 'constitutive role' of wider structures, and on the other by the 'totally novel power within each layer' (Creaven 2000: 34, 59, 41). Subsequently, while the generative mechanisms of emergent strata exert unique effects on concrete reality, by nature of their different form and function, deeper structures have a long-run tendency to 'assert

their movement as necessary' (ibid.: 9). However, neither the evolution of higher order objects from lower level mechanisms, nor the boundedness of the former in the latter, implies a one-way relation of connectivity: because 'the parts are not pure functions of the whole, but go in their own way as well', the unique causal powers of higher order objects are 'capable of reacting back' on their constituent lower level mechanisms (Collier 1994: 117, 110, 113; Archer 1995: 9). This dia-lectical interplay further designates the complexity of real objects, necessitating spatial-temporal analysis of emergent properties and signifying the dynamism and fluidity of structural tendencies.

4. Developed prominently from the work of Roy Bhaskar (1978; 1986; 1989), critical realism (CR) argues that social outcomes are the product of 'relatively enduring structures' (ibid.: 16). As Bhaskar notes, a strong realist position directs both explanatory and emancipatory focus to the social structures which 'pre-exist ... (but nevertheless depend for their reproduction and are transformed by) the indi-viduals who enter into them' (Bhaskar 1989: 4). In this sense, CR presents a deep view of reality that 'looks beneath the course of events to the mechanisms that generate it', and argues that social realities are intransitive and structured (Collier 1994: 50). This ends up separating between three domains of reality: the empir-ical, the actual and the real. Whereas the empirical is 'defined as the domain of experience' and individual observation, the actual refers to experiences and unob-served events (ibid.: 44). It is only at the third level of reality that we encounter the organizing structures of natural and social existence (Sayer 2000: 11; 1992). This conception of structural depth can therefore be expressed in the explanatory primacy acceded to the domain of the real, since the focus on deep structures is well founded only if 'real world events are comprehensible in terms of underlying structures and attendant generative mechanisms' (Creaven 2000: 26). Yet this does not simply mean that the causal powers and generative mechanisms of under-lying structures are transparently displayed in the actual and empirical realm. In noting the counter-phenomenality of knowledge, CR argues that 'the deep struc-ture of something may not just go beyond, and not just explain, but also contradict appearances' (Collier 1994: 7). The work of science in understanding reality and constructing theory (the transitive dimension) subsequently involves moving from the socially mediated realm of the concrete and complex to the abstract and simple layer of deep mechanisms and antecedent structures (the intransitive dimension). This in turn leads to a retroductive method of argumentation, whereby analysis advances 'from a description of some phenomenon to a description of something which produces it or is a condition for it' (Bhaskar 1986: 11). From this view, the domain of the real is in fact a 'hierarchically ordered world of distinct strata governed by causal relations of ... determination', where less complex layers of reality are assumed within and condition more complex layers of reality (Creaven 2000: 29). Though this views higher strata as 'governed by different kinds of laws,' their emergence from less basic strata lays the foundation for a truly strati-fied view of nature (Collier 1994: 191). For Bhaskar, higher order strata are 'new phenomena' which emerge not from the conscious or deliberate workings of lower order strata, but rather from the 'specific interaction or combination of generative mechanisms internal to those objects or structures which exist ... immediately basic to it' (Bhaskar as quoted in Creaven 2000: 31).

5. Jessop's Strategic Relational approach therefore leads us away from critical realism and towards analytic individualism. See Jessop (2001).

6. See also: Hasselstrom (2000).

7. See Evans et al. (1985).
8. The extent to which Creaven endorses this view is a little uncertain. While he recognizes the contingency of societal pressures, his analysis also hints at the persistence of certain capitalist logics (i.e., over-production and under-consumption). As a result, his point seems softer than Thompson's: that laws exist but are not necessarily activated. For Thompson (1978), there can be no understanding of certain laws within real existing capitalism due to the dialectical evolution of capitalist social and economic relations and the force of human agency.
9. Emergent Marxism balances against the extreme contingency view offered by Jessop's Strategic Relational Approach which, if pushed to its logical end, relativizes even the basic properties of capitalist organization. The potential of this project to relativize even the basic class relations of capitalism has made it a popular tool of non-Marxist scholarship looking to add a deeper structural aspect to their work without advocating the primacy of capitalist social organization.
10. It is important to emphasize that the deep history of the subprime crisis has been neglected in the critical scholarship. This is at least partly because the financial practices immediately responsible for the meltdown – securitized subprime mortgage debt, shadow banking, credit default swaps – are themselves relatively new.
11. The domestic-international segment consists, most notably, of the foreign branch of the US Treasury bond market. The foreign bond market can itself be sectioned into a series of distinct bond markets, the most notable of which are those of major industrialized nations, particularly the United States, Japan and Switzerland. The offshore market consists of the Eurobond market and the global bond market.
12. This is not a common definition of the international bond market. Most studies view the IBM in much smaller terms, as either including the foreign bond market and the offshore bond market, or just the latter. The problem with these definitions is that they fail to see how more traditional bond markets engender international linkages between buyers and sellers. In this sense, common definitions create a distinction between traditional national/onshore markets and newer non-national markets. Yet, national markets also have distinct international features. This book defines the IBM to include the foreign owned segments of onshore markets as these reveal patterns of international demand in exactly the same way as foreign and offshore markets.
13. Other IPE scholars who have made similar important contributions, noting in particular the relationship between financial markets and state power, include: Versluysen (1981); Gowa (1983); Frieden (1987); Hawley (1987); Henning (1994); Eichengreen (1996); Burn (1999); Underhill (2003); Langley (2002); Porter (2005); Sinclair (2005); and Best (2005).
14. In particular see: Brenner (2008); Wade (2008); Blackburn (2008); Foster and Magdoff (2009); Harman (2009); Kliman (2008); Lapavitsas (2009); McNally (2008); Nesvetailova and Palan (2008) and Balakrishnan (2010). Also Nesvetailova (2007) has presented a very good analysis of financial crises in contemporary capitalism.
15. Studies on the subprime crisis have also focused on the irrational behaviour of global traders and US homeowners (Muolo and Padilla 2008; Goodman et al. 2008; Shiller 2008; Cohen 2009; Posner 2009; Zandi 2009), patterns of inequality within the US mortgage market (Dymski 2010), and the wider cycle of financial accumulation and growth that supported subprime issuance (Schwartz 2009a).
16. That financial flows not only following the Second World War but up to the present reveal and reinforce US imperial power is a position clearly at odds

with the frameworks offered by Arrighi (1994), Moseley (1999), Brenner (2002; 2004), Callinicos (1999; 2006), Kliman (2008), and Foster and Magdoff (2009). These scholars tend to argue that the US balance of payments deficit, as well as deepening speculation in US capital markets, is a symptom of a wider crisis of accumulation and profitability.

17. In presenting the major notable critique to this scholarship, Panitch and Gindin (2005; 2012) argue that it is precisely because this scholarship finds weakness where it should find strength that it pushes aside sequences of power that unite the period following 1944. In suggesting that patterns of financial risk problematize views that chronicle the fissure of US imperialism and indicate instead that neoliberal financial relations have also been consolidated along the lines of US power, this study can be seen to build from the critical insights offered by Panitch and Gindin, especially their very strong research on the productive and economic dynamism of the US economy following the 1970s. In particular, this book asserts the presence of a post-Second World War risk imaginary on the basis of the wider structures of US postwar imperial capacity made clear in Panitch and Gindin's *The Making of Global Capitalism.*

18. This chapter draws on and develops an article I previously published in *New Political Science*, titled 'Institutional Power and the Risk of Finance' (42:2, pp. 139–54). The sections that have previously been published are reprinted with the permission of Taylor & Francis, through their open access copyright licence.

PART I

Abstract risk and US financial power

The novelty of this book is that it links the near universal drive to acquire US mortgage securities to the institutional and cultural aspects of the post-Second World War financial system. This part turns to the key methodological and theoretical positions allowing for this interpretation, and argues that important points are missed if we utilize conventional models of financial credibility and risk calculation. The argument takes issue with the orthodox view of financial risk, which reduces analysis to the process of stacking up different quantitatively determined market uncertainties: credit risk, liquidity risk, interest rate risk, currency risk, prepayment risk, and so on. Such an approach, grounded in the methodological individualism of neoclassical economics, robs markets of their institutional and qualitative content and thereby ignores how meaning systems, ideas, and interpretative frameworks influence collective action.

The conclusions reached in the following two chapters also reveal strengths and limitations in the critical political economy literature. Though it makes key inroads, this work rests on a narrow view of institutional organization that gets in the way of thinking about US risk power. The challenge is to understand how the actual purchase and sale of debt instruments is institutionally and culturally conditioned. This involves taking proper account of abstract financial risk and how international monetary frameworks construct options by setting certain foundational conditions.

2. Risking finance

This chapter works through the relationship between financial markets and financial risk: it seeks to understand how markets are constructed through abstract understandings and calculations of financial risk and how these shape investment decisions and strategic priorities. In doing so, it departs from the common tendency to view risk as a property of exchange and measurable variable. So too does it problematize critical approaches, which view financial markets as lacking a socially desirable relation to risk management. Both views miss the point that power-laden intersubjective meanings shape the activity of financial institutions and actors. The chapter shows that risk is a 'central coordinating mechanism' within the financial system and itself an embodiment of imperial power (Green 2000: 78).

CORPORATE GOVERNANCE AND THE RATIONALITY OF FINANCE

According to IM, the basic properties of capitalism only shape history by influencing the organizational systems embedding human subjects. Agents design institutional formations and always have power over their reproduction, but these nonetheless configure subjective boundaries, leading similarly placed actors to common economic preferences and motivations.[1] The difficulty is that both mainstream and critical political economy have a long track-record characterizing actors according to their interpretation of financial markets, and beyond the mediating role of institutions. This fetishizes wider organizational systems and categorizes actors as either narrowly rational or narrowly speculative. While such representations have been unable to capture more than a bird's eye view of the relationship between risk and finance, they have powerfully shaped perspectives on financial rationality. This has led to a shallow view of financial reason that at one end denies abstract forms of risk calculation and at the other confuses the relationship between finance and risk aversion altogether.

Risk and Reason in Neoclassical Theory

In formulating the philosophical premise of neoclassicism in the nineteenth century, Bentham, Senior, Bastiat, and Jevons argued that consumption preferences are private and driven by the compulsion to maximize pleasure and avoid unhappiness. In this view, market transactions reflect the sacrifice of less total utility between a 'specified increase in wealth' and a 'quantity of goods previously produced' (Bernstein 1996: 110). This occurs according to a hierarchy of pleasures that are 'as various as the differences in individual character' (Senior 1938: 27). Thus Bentham's position that 'the quality of pleasure being equal, pushpin is as good as poetry', finds equivalence in Walrus' central postulate in *Elements of Pure Economics*: 'From other points of view the question of whether a drug is wanted by a doctor to cure a patient, or by a murderer to kill his family is a very serious matter, but from our point of view it is totally irrelevant' (Walrus 1984: 82).

The key aim of this framework is to reinforce capitalist property and power relations. Yet the principles of atomistic individualism and calculating utilitarianism also produce a specific understanding of economic reason and risk. This is because they atomize the preferences influencing market participation and situate the laws of supply and demand against the marginal utility theory of human motivation conceived by Bernoulli, according to which price and probability 'are dependent on the specific circumstances and calculations of each individual actor,' and vary because 'human beings differ in their appetite for risk' (Bernstein 1996: 110, 112). This ties economic action to the figure of the risk-taker involved in balancing 'satisfaction … derived from each successive increase in wealth' against the 'disutility caused by a loss', and dismisses the cultural and institutional forces influencing action (ibid.: 112).

These central assumptions are untouched by neoclassical financial theory, which stresses that actors are driven by the impulse to maximize profitability, but only in relation to their individual risk tolerance (Tobin 1958; Markowitz 1959; Black 1976; Miller and Scholes 1978).[2] As Weston (1981: 6) summarizes, modern finance departs from utility theory and focuses on 'interactions of individual preferences' as they relate to the essential characteristics of financial assets. Following this, financial action becomes a product of two interacting patterns of risk: the risk threshold of individual investors and the measurable risk within financial instruments. Put differently, demand occurs where there is a match between the risk aversion of the investor and the concrete properties attached to the instrument itself (Markowitz 1959; Weston 1981).[3] Therefore, while financial risk has both a measurable and subjective quality, it is detached from the web of social power and knowledge influencing the financial system: actors respond more or less instantaneously to new information, participate in markets as secluded, solitary characters, and are concerned to avoid risk in classical utilitarian terms. Modern portfolio theory's emphasis on diversification and correlation is not an exception to this, but rather represents an attempt to calculate aggregate portfolio risk on the basis of the risks attached to each individual investment.

Financial Reason in Critical Political Economy

The mainstream view of financial risk is a key subject of critique across heterodox political economy, including in the IPE literature on global financial markets. Much of this has bearing in the work of Durkheim, Veblen, and Keynes, who trace the 'collective effervescence', 'malady of the affections', and 'animal spirits' influencing financial trends. It is also very much tied to Weber's sociological analysis in *Die Borse*, which uses the term *Spielsucht* – meaning 'mania' or 'compulsive gambling' – to portray financial rationality and action (Aliber and Kindleberger 2015: 55; Martino 2018: 467–8). There is also a Polanyian tone framing the literature, as phases of financial liberalization are contrasted with phases of market embeddedness governed by 'the world of real value, work and production' (Konings 2018: 42). On this reading, finance represents the 'world of fictitious profits' and is thus unhinged from the conditions regulating the productive side of the economy, which suppress the 'accelerating multitude of transactions' that naturally inhere in open financial markets (Martino 2018: 471).

As a result, the critical scholarship tends to present financial reason in terms of the specific characteristics of financial markets, with speculation seen as 'an irresponsible bet on the future ... unwarranted by fundamental values' (Konings 2018: 11). This conflation between financial reason and economic irrationality offers a very different vision of financial markets, as unstable and crisis-prone, and influences how moments of intensified financial control are represented and contested. As Konings (2018: 11) notes, the speciation view of finance:

> has always been an important element of the heterodox critique of capitalism, but it has become its centerpiece during the neoliberal era ... Where mainstream economic theory often discerns little more than self-correcting deviations from an equilibrium state, critical and heterodox perspectives find irrational forces that are responsible for the periodic build-up of unsustainable, top-heavy structures of fictitious claims. That dynamic, they argue, must sooner or later come to a halt when foundational values reassert themselves and overleveraged financial structures begin to unravel.

This view marks a double rejection of the neoclassical rational expectations thesis: financial reason is cast in terms of the waves of mania that overcome investors, and the marketplace is seen in social terms, as impacted by collective sentiment and irrational exuberance (Nesvetailova 2007).

Both Strange and Kindleberger show how the speculative approach to rationality is applied. For her part, Strange (1998: 96) argues that 'there is a tendency, inevitable in a system dependent on the activity of banking institutions, to overbanking – that is, to the imprudent expansion of credit with increased profits to the banks but increased risk to the system of financial panic and collapse.' This view is devoted to one side of the financial system, and is detached from the other. All the institutional mechanisms and practices designed to control volatility, which paradoxically emerge from the same competitive pressures incentivizing speculation, and often lord over them, are cast into the darkness. The upshot is that financial actors and institutions are shamed as risk takers, eager to substitute instability for profit, whatever the consequences. Unlike neoclassical financial theory, which views markets as efficient and actors risk averse, Strange rejects the efficiency of markets and affirms their sociological function, yet does so through a one-dimensional approach that obfuscates key dynamics and their relationship to accumulation.

Kindleberger uses aspects of the rationality model, while identifying speculation as a 'biological' feature of financial operation (Aliber and Kindleberger 2015: 20). He argues that the neoclassical view violates 'insight from financial history', which shows expectations do not automatically cohere to new information and ongoing calculations, but 'change slowly at some times and rapidly at others' as investor mindsets switch 'from confidence to pessimism' (ibid.: 105). He sees markets driven by sentiment and periods of economic euphoria where the 'quality of debt increases because lenders and investors become less risk averse and more willing … to make loans that had previously seemed too risky' (ibid.: 88). This basically repeats Minsky's analysis of the credit system, which identifies three distinct periods of credit creation – hedge finance, speculative finance, and Ponzi finance – and argues that periods of euphoria dramatically recalibrate investor risk thresholds, making the financial system vulnerable to destabilizing credit expansions.

Yet market volatility does not equate to irrational investment decisions. Rather, Kindleberger sees financial reason as socially determined and thereby discards the static interpretation favoured by neoclassical theory. This allows him to separate the 'mob psychology of the market' and the prudence of individual investors: '[historical] examples show that despite the general usefulness of the assumption of rationality, markets have on occasions … acted in ways that were irrational even when each participant in the market believed he or she was acting rationally.' Nevertheless, this animates the prevailing view of financial reason in the critical scholarship. That individual investors regularly 'succumb' to the hysteria of the market, thinking their actions are prudent, means their mode of reason as market actors is speculative (ibid.: 57). Put differently, the sociological view Kindleberger utilizes ultimately subsumes financial reason to the irrationality of the market (ibid.: 55).

The Kindleberger–Minsky model therefore identifies financial markets as inherently crisis-prone on the basis of a socially informed conception of rationality that sees investors as periodically driven by forms of 'feverish speculation' and 'blind passion' that, despite their irrationality, appear utterly rational (ibid.: 55). Like Strange, neither Kindleberger nor Minsky specify the terms of this financial reason, yet the cautious, calculating, risk averse figure drawn up by neoclassical theory is abandoned as a universal constant. In problematizing the power neutral equilibrium model of finance, and accounting for the volatility and panic-stricken nature of markets, a different image appears, one defining investors as speculators, or even gamblers, subject to mob psychology.

FINANCE AND ABSTRACT RISK

This book advances a very different view of financial reason. It sees actors as constantly concerned with limiting financial risk, and human action shaped by prescribed institutional boundaries, formed as subjects contend with wider structural forces. It argues that critical scholarship downplays how banks, asset management firms, broker-dealers and other financial firms seek to control and limit risk. This also means rejecting the very narrow and self-serving understanding of risk calculation offered by neoclassical theory, which denies the complex forms of organizational power and class domination framing financial relations. While neoclassical theory identifies risk as a central category, it 'wants to understand the laws of capitalist society through the analysis of exchange as a purely private act' (Hilferding 1905: 371). In the face of this, neoclassical theory can acknowledge none of the structural-institutional pressures identified by institutional Marxism, and is left emphasizing only quantifiable forms of risk.

For one thing, building such a viewpoint entails analysing the channels within financial firms developed for mobilizing, investing and accumulating capital, and how these create organizational logics emphasizing risk mitigation. The sociological literature on risk is foundational in this respect – it situates actors within established patterns of control and investigates the historically-evolved corporate governance strategies developed to manage financial accumulation.[4] A key starting position is that 'much of the critical literature on international financial markets is predicated on a set of myths' that wildly diverge from the actual organization of financial institutions (Clark and Thrift 2015: 231). Such myths feed a vision that firms practise high-risk processes of profit-making, and scantly recognize that all major firms, even the least cautious, are built around 'a bureaucratic process of risk management that is dependent upon assessing dispersed knowledge about market conditions' (ibid.: 229, 230). These procedures shape organizational priorities precisely because accumulation occurs 'through the creation and exploitation of … financial risk' (Christophers 2015: 6). Thus, while each profit strategy requires some risk, firms develop internal practices emphasizing the safest possible mixture. This often means restraining capital gains accumulation, since it presents the greatest overall risk (ibid.: 9–10).[5]

The same priorities shape trading practices and organizational hierarchies. Despite extending systemic risk, derivative markets serve a 'risk management' function, as they bring 'hazards under control and allow banks to forge systemic plans for the future of their firms and clients' (Zaloom 2004: 365, 370). They provide 'the opportunity to avoid the effects of risk' and generate the 'opportunity for making a living by taking risks' (ibid.: 365, 370). Though speculators often 'exploit rather than ally risks' and 'create a public definition of themselves' by 'perform[ing] risk taking', their action is always overseen by 'risk managers and executives' who 'have access to the full picture of risk taking' and 'monitor the company's exposure to loss' (ibid.: 371). Such considerations demonstrate that speculative trades only take shape through 'the eye of the risk manager', and that the 'social typology of the pit and the ambitions of the traders' are constituted through a broader pattern of 'risk surveillance' (ibid.: 372).

Crucially, investment strategies are intertwined with, and shaped by, deeper operational rationalities. These act as integrative frameworks or strategic forms of control, influencing procedures through formal and informal infra-firm learning strategies, 'codes of practice', and an 'authoritarian management hierarchy whose task is to manage risk on a global scale' (Clark and Thrift 2015: 241, 234, 240).[6] Such attempts to measure all aspects of risk are registered in the emergence of powerful new managerial positions within financial firms, such as the Chief Risk Officer, and in the rise of shareholder value, inasmuch as financial institutions push corporations to 'manage their stock price' (Power 2015: 254). They are also intimately rooted in value-at-risk (VAR) modelling and data collection techniques that have allowed the calculation and assessment of different forms of risk. This obsession with 'measurement-based' risk management has also fostered 'control-based' governance models that serve to complement VAR-based testing, such as 'risk communication', and formalized audit committees (ibid.: 258, 251, 263). In conjunction, these risk management approaches comprise a new enterprise management system (EMS) that has become a 'world cultural model' (ibid.: 260).[7]

This all shows that the governance strategies firms utilize to manage operations prioritize risk control, and further that these create a 'normalizing logic' influencing the action of financial agents (Christophers 2015: 4).[8] Set against the IM framework, which places institutions in relation to the transfactual properties of capitalist social organization, we can see that financial accumulation creates distinct pressures to manage and mitigate risk that tend to invoke particular, though not uniform, patterns of institutional design.[9]

Second, we must be careful not to see the behaviour or logic of firms merely in terms of calculable and measurable risk. These named forms of risk (liquidity risk, transferability risk, insolvency risk, political risk, counterparty risk, etc.) are front and centre because they are immediately visible. Yet they are themselves emergent from deeper systems of control. The distinction between concrete and abstract risk is vital in this regard, since it acknowledges the wider risk ontologies objectified in financial institutions and products. As Lipuma and Lee (2004: 55) explain, concrete risk 'derives from the natural sciences ... and is especially appealing because it allows for the use of mathematical statistics which, in turn, allows the financial community to price derivatives precisely.' However, this 'natural science view elides the social ontology underwriting its objectification of risk': it brackets 'the social embeddedness of risk and the process by which agents construct risk as social facts' (ibid.: 54). For Lipuma and Lee, financial instruments, namely derivatives, are thus 'based on a notion of *abstract*, monetized risk that organizes ... circulation and pricing' (ibid.: 55, emphasis added).

In this reading, the cultural and economic characteristics of financialization 'cannot be separated' because the various forms of risk objectified and unified in a financial instrument render it a 'socially imaginary object', subject to the 'classifying powers of language' (ibid.: x, 24). This not only establishes the qualitative forms of quantifiable risk, it constitutes risk itself as a power relation and opens to an understanding of *risk power* in the world of finance. Lipuma and Lee argue that the social ontologies associated with abstract risk 'embody the perspectives and promote the interests of Euromerican capitalism', as they rest on basic representations of the sociopolitical world formed from imperial imaginaries of different localities: 'the culture of the financial markets, animated by Western ideology, turns each of the circulated images into a universal icon of a certain space or locality' (ibid.: 55). It is these 'summary images', they argue, that are developed to quantify different forms of measurable risk, meaning that the analysis of financial circulation must always be 'both socio-structural and technical to grasp the necessary relationship between surface and underlying forms' (ibid.: 58, 64). From this perspective, concrete, measurable risk is informed by abstract risk and joined to all the political and economic entanglements constituting culture and Western ideology. This links risk not only to financial demand and firm behaviour, but to hegemony and imperial power.

As crucial as it is, this stratified view remains frustratingly underdeveloped in Lipuma and Lee's framework, owing to how it is narrowly tied to derivative instruments. Moreover, Lipuma and Lee offer a purely cultural view of abstract risk and do not capture the underlying institutions and state agencies organizing markets. Abstract risk is somehow unmoored from political mechanisms and institutions – detached from material relations and juxtaposed to concrete risk in this way: whereas the latter is managed within the elaborate sphere of the firm, the former has no broader organizational properties. The management of abstract risk, if it occurs at all, is affixed to the management of concrete risk, in a way that the two categories blur together.

This book endorses the approach to risk offered by Lipuma and Lee, with some important clarifications. It sees financial demand formed from overlapping calculations of risk influenced, most widely, by the abstract classification tied to imperial power. Though the relationship between risk and finance is revealed at the firm level in familiar classifications – liquidity, counterparty, reinvestment, political, interest rate – it also has a much broader facing, one that is not overtly measured and calculated, but nonetheless generative. Yet I argue that the abstract conception of risk formed in the postwar period is best viewed as an economic imaginary – an institutionally and structurally configured semiotic order that draws together different financial discourses, market genres, and investment styles. Hence, rather than seeing abstract risk in strictly cultural terms, I argue that it has an institutional location and is furthermore supported by key state agencies. This book politicizes and institutionalizes Lipuma and Lee's concept of abstract risk, connecting it to CPE and IPE literature and underlying investment practices, in search for a deeper understanding of the subprime crisis.

SUMMARY REMARKS

This chapter argued that risk mitigation is a central feature of financial practice and therefore acts as a 'model of economic conduct' within financial institutions and markets (Brown 2015: 34). This view bumps up against the common image offered by critical scholars, which constructs investors as speculative, irrational and more or less insensitive to risk and volatility. There is indeed an important tension between the view offered here and the portrait of casino capitalism advanced by Strange. As the critical scholarship has failed to centre risk, so it has ignored the diffuse and abstract forms of risk shaping financial action, as well as the forms of financial organization designed to mitigate the volatility of markets. As we will see in the next chapter, this has led IPE literature into a narrow reading of financial confidence and credibility that fails to see how international monetary systems shape abstract risk and structure demand.

NOTES

1. On this reading, consideration is opened to what Brown calls the 'distinctive form[s] of reason' that take shape through historically-evolved institutional patterns (Brown 2015: 34).
2. The central pillars of neoclassical finance theory include the capital asset pricing model, mean-variance portfolio theory, arbitrage pricing theory, and state preference theory (Weston 1981; Ho and Lee 2004). All of these models 'follow from the application of utility theory' and similarly emphasize the role played by individual preferences (Weston 1981).

3.	Behavioural Finance represents a significant improvement on neoclassical finance as it largely accepts the market inefficiencies and looks to explain price movements through the mental attitude of investors. In general, market actors are thought to weigh information differently due to the social nature of the decision-making process, creating over- and under-reactions to market events (Barberis 1997; de Goede 2005; Sewell 2010: 5). At times, behavioural theorists have come quite close to the position of Keynes and Minsky (see Selden 1912; Shiller 2000), but the tendency is to endorse the individualist components of neoclassicism. Indeed, for most scholars, the goal is to provide a more sophisticated interpretation of neoclassical finance theory, one which studies the influence of psychology on market practitioners. As de Goede (2005: 23) says, 'behavioural finance shares with mainstream finance the assumption that human aspects have a disturbing and distorting influence on economic fundamentals.' In this way, the conceptual tools and classifications employed by behavioural theorists are also very much grounded on autonomous individual understandings of gains and losses, and hence are also sociologically suspect.
4.	Still, this work must be applied selectively, if it is to be used to understand corporate power systems and to build an alternative view of financial risk. This is because it detaches institutions from broader ensembles of capitalist control and affixes them to a dizzying collection of socio-cultural forces. This makes it unable to grasp the wider forces pressuring firms and actors to assume this posture, or the contradictions associated with such strategies. The transfactual properties of capitalism are accordingly abandoned in the institutional analysis offered by Power (2015) and Zaloom (2004) and replaced with references to Habermas, Foucault and Beck. This links institutional and corporate power to a nebula of cultural forces, detached from the class relations and contradictions shaping financial accumulation. This considerable limitation leaves the sociology literature without a theory of institutional formation capable of accounting for the stratified forms of control organizing intra-firm relations and corporate governance strategies.
5.	See also Ayres and Braithwaite (1992) and Banham (1999).
6.	Notably, Power (2015: 251) shows that financial firms have adopted 'risk-based concept[s] of control focused on the risk quality of earnings.'
7.	From these practices of risk mitigation, Power comments on the politics of financial re-regulation: he argues that 'the emergence of EMS makes a certain regulatory style possible, one that increasingly relies on the self-organizing resources of banking organizations' (Power 2015: 261–2). Key regulatory shifts, including Basel's internal risk-based rating system, thereby develop out of the financial industry's obsession with controlling market risk. Yet far from expressing a new financial disposition, the development of EMS through the 1990s expresses the 'fundamental' rationality that 'returns on assets are always relative to risk' (ibid.: 254; Doherty 2000: 9–10).
8.	It is no doubt the case that as the space at the centre of the financial system is taken up by large institutions concerned to exploit risk management practice, other institutions exist within their shadows and practise a different type of financial exchange.
9.	Due to the contingency of institutional design highlighted by IM, this is distinct from the claim that there is some fixed experience with risk in the financial system, or an inner necessity towards risk mitigation that claims all subjects.

3. The power of debt

This chapter develops the theory of risk imaginary presented earlier, showing that financial markets are shaped by institutionalized patterns of abstract risk. In what follows, international monetary systems are presented as centralized nodes of financial power. These systems 'facilitate the exchange of goods, services and capital among countries' through 'official arrangements that regulate key dimensions of the balance of payments' and establish the basic architecture shaping international reserves, capital movements, and exchange rate valuations (Mohan et al. 2013: 4). More than this – at a deeper level – they structure the base sensibilities underpinning markets. While many authors refer to the importance of these systems, most do not capture how they set expectations and preferences, and configure amazingly static relations of power between different currencies, expressed through intersubjective meanings about risk and confidence. The impact and importance of the Bretton Woods Accord is also considered. Building from heterodox scholarship, the chapter argues that this framework organized debt markets around dollar denominated bonds, making them the centre of the IBM, and giving way to a long period of US risk power. A third point underpins the analysis. The chapter argues that financial markets are inherently social – their complexity compounded by the abstract relations of trust mediating exchange, which comprise the connective tissue intermeshing diverse markets and actors. This represents a further challenge to neoclassical finance theory and other such mono-causal interpretations of financial demand.

THE UNDERSTRUCTURE OF FINANCIAL DEMAND

Quite apart from modern finance theory, heterodox scholarship captures some of the social forces constituting markets: it shows that financial flows are mediated by conventions of credibility/confidence and that US Treasury bonds have enjoyed special status in the post-Second World War period.[1] At the same time, these approaches give short shrift to the type of structural and institutional patterns identified by IM. Moreover, the tendency has been to ignore the link between financial risk and demand discussed in the previous chapter.

Keynes, Weber and the Sociology of Money

In describing financial markets as beauty contests, Keynes (1936) argues
that financial asset values fluctuate with investor sentiment. He argues that
the accuracy of financial wagers is determined by their general acceptance,
meaning that financial fundamentals – determined to be fundamentals by
social orientations – ultimately underpin financial flows. Minsky's Financial
Instability Thesis is based around the same idea that financial markets are
creatures of psychology. Minsky (1992) argues that the movement from hedge
to Ponzi borrowing is born out of the optimism accompanying periods of
economic expansion; as growth accelerates in the general economy 'borrowing
experiences [become] increasingly positive' and 'expectations of business
profits' increase, leading to a shift in 'system behaviour' (Minsky 1992: 7;
1972; 1980; Kregel 2008: 5). What changes is not so much the evaluative
criteria used to determine creditworthiness, but the notions incorporated into
these models: the movement away from hedge financing reflects new ideas
about repayment risk emanating from the social climate enframing markets.
    This focus on financial ideas and intersubjective beliefs describes critical
aspects of Max Weber's analysis in *Economy and Society*.[2] Weber (1978)
makes the basic distinction between the formal and substantive validity of
money. The former derives from law and administrative state action and
expresses the calculability of money as a numerical form; it is independent of
the final value money takes in commodity exchanges, as it expresses the the-
oretic legal standing of an accepted means of payment (Eisen 1978: 64). The
latter embodies the concrete attractiveness of money and rests on the social
'ability to authenticate a promise to pay' (Seabrooke 2001: 28). This detaches
money value from the established form of legal tender and affixes it to social
and political conditions generalizing faith in exchangeability.
    The sociological component of money laid down by Weber has received
more recent treatment in the work of Glyn Davies (2002), Viviana Zelizer
(1997), and, most notably, Geoffrey Ingham (1996; 2001). For Ingham, any
attempt to understand money and credit must address the social conventions
constituting credibility. The common problem in neoclassical and Marxist
interpretations is that 'they confuse the specific form taken by money ... with
the generic social relations of the system of the promises to pay,' creating
a false 'opposition between real forms of money and fictitious credit' (Ingham
2001: 307; 1998: 7). This means that 'a conceptual scheme for the measurement of value ... lies behind any particular form that [money] might take'
(Ingham 1998: 9). Accordingly, capitalist bank money is 'no more nor less
than a social relationship'; a 'promise to re(pay) ... that represents neither
actual real savings nor real commodity money' (ibid.: 8). Materialized money,
Ingham's pre-capitalist money, also hides deep sociological settlements, since

its origins are found 'in a much earlier stage of communal development' (Ingham 2001: 310). As Ingham (1998: 9) notes: 'if money is essentially an abstract measuring system, then all money is virtual, including not just modern or even post-modern money as some social scientists have recently suggested.' A similar viewpoint is detectable in post-structural studies of finance. These argue that trading activity reflects 'practices of ... knowledge' that construct and constitute 'the material structures of financial markets' (de Goede 2005: 21, 24).[3] According to de Goede (2003: 81), 'financial practices do not exist prior to, or independently from, ideas and beliefs about them': 'money, whether in the form of coin, paper, stock or electronic transfers, takes on value only through a social and discursive network which underpins the expectation that the monetary instrument retains its value over time and space' (ibid.: 81).[4]

All this no doubt connects to Lipuma and Lee's findings discussed in the previous chapter. We do not have to accept all aspects of the social relations of money view embodied in these accounts to acknowledge that ideas and norms of trust are key properties of money and debt, and influence their attractiveness on the open market. Yet this often comes with an important paradox, found in the view that financial markets are governed only *intermittently* by popular sentiment. Such reasoning asserts the cultural form of markets in the speculative activity of financial agents, and has difficulty appreciating the discursive properties organizing 'normal' financial flows as part of their incubation in emergent institutional and cultural formations tied to the apparatus of global capitalism. Moreover, in some of these accounts it is not only financial assets that are shaped by ideational and normative templates, but every key feature of the financial system. This gestures towards a financial apparatus where ideas exist above and independent from non-discursive social forces, and severely confounds matters.

IPE Contributions

This sensitivity to ideational forces is also at work in IPE literature on money and finance. Yet this is combined with an institutional analysis of the financial system emphasizing key monetary and political arrangements. Cohen's work is a prime illustration. It argues that monetary relations take shape through social 'conventions and norms' and depend on patterns of regulation established to manage the movement of capital, including the tacit monetary frameworks established at the international level that structure relations between currencies (Cohen 1977: 3). In this account, changes in international monetary standards are tied to shifts in attitude, and the functionality of money rests on its 'intrinsic value', or the '*confidence*' in its forward 'value and usability' (Cohen 2004: 4, 39, emphasis added). Cohen takes these points further in *The Future of Money*, arguing that confidence in the forward value of the dollar relates to the stability of the US political apparatus and has been conditioned through the Bretton Woods monetary system (ibid.: 4, 15).[5]

Such views have in fact become a touchstone for many IPE writers. Though they disagree on the relative importance of other market-based factors, James (2009) and Helleiner (2009) claim that market confidence bolstered the international position of the dollar in the postwar period, and that the dollar is likely to remain the most attractive currency because of its 'reputation' and 'perceived safety' (James 2009: 35; Helleiner 2009: 75). Moreover, both explain the central position of the dollar in relation to the Bretton Woods system. James begins his account of dollar hegemony with the 'agreements of Bretton Woods' that fixed the par value of other currencies to 'either gold or US dollars', showing this created a financial 'architecture' which encouraged the accumulation of dollars leading up to 1971, and also informed market behaviour following 1973 (James 2009: 25–6).[6] Helleiner follows this view by confirming 'the strength of the restrictive Bretton Woods financial order' in shaping policy outcomes and market behaviour in the early postwar years (Helleiner 1994: 77).[7]

Porter also strikes close to this mark. He utilizes an institutional approach to show how markets are implicitly constituted and governed (Porter 2005: 25). One key finding is that financial flows are shaped by formal and informal 'knowledge-derived rules' that coordinate action through 'voluntary compliance' (ibid.: 176, 24). Porter argues that the international monetary system has always served as a key component of this, due to how it sets 'social practices' regarding uncertainty and volatility that 'effect the choices … actors make' (ibid.: 168). He emphasizes how 'British hegemony under the gold standard created a system of rules through which states fixed the value of their currencies to gold, thereby reducing the risks of currency fluctuations', and insists that the Bretton Woods system similarly devised a set of rules to 'address uncertainties with regard to the supply of gold and to shield countries from the risks associated with international trade and currency volatility' (ibid.: 168). Crucially, Porter indicates that these rules shaped the development of international securities markets, since their re-emergence in the postwar period depended on 'the confidence that was instilled by the strength of the dollar backed up by the power of the US government' (ibid.: 74).

Perhaps the most prominent example in this area comes from the work of Barry Eichengreen (1996; 2008). In *Globalizing Capital* he examines the evolution of financial markets through the framework configured by the Bretton Woods system, showing how different balance of payments crises, as well as such critical political programmes as the Marshall Plan and the European Payments Union, expressed the conditions of dollar dominance it both promoted and reflected. He further explains the instability of the Bretton Woods system in the late 1960s, and its eventual disintegration in 1971, in terms of diminished 'confidence in the dollar', essentially repeating his claim that the gold standard collapsed when shifts in the sterling market 'undermined confidence in other currencies' (Eichengreen 2008: 122, 82).[8] Eichengreen (2011) repeats this position in *Exorbitant Privilege*, insisting that the dollar's 'supreme reign' through the postwar period only started to waver in 1965 when investors began to lose confidence in its relationship to gold, due to changes in the US economy and its leading role in international trade. This ties the confidence influencing demand for US assets to a deeper set of material conditions. It also explains the dollar's continued dominance after 1971 in terms of lacklustre international competition, haphazardly linking neoliberal markets to the retreat of international and state-based institutions.

McKinnon and Duncan offer very similar accounts, but distance themselves from Eichengreen's view of the post-Bretton Woods period. Arguing that international monetary orders establish 'rules of the game' that are 'generally discernible – even when not written down or formally codified', McKinnon (1993: 1, 2) shows that the period following the collapse of par values saw the development of a new monetary order based around US dollar hegemony. The so-called dollar standard set eight central rules for international monetary transactions based around the development of a floating rate currency system, capital account liberalization, and the dollar as the main intervention currency (ibid.: 29). This system further set up the dollar as the main international standard of payment, unit of account, and store of value and thus retained 'the conventions for using the dollar as international money for official and private purposes' developed previously under the Bretton Woods order (ibid.: 26). Duncan (2003: ix) offers a nearly identical account of the current dollar standard, arguing that it evolved out of the Bretton Woods order largely 'without formal agreement or sanction' and further elevated the dollar's international prominence by freeing it from the constraints of gold.

Overall, then, IPE scholarship has connected demand to the inner workings of the international monetary system, and recognized that socially constructed ideas influence market relations and have primarily benefited the US dollar in the post-Second World War era. This contribution cannot be understated, for it draws attention to the way confidence becomes standardized within financial markets and ends up reproducing particular political and power outcomes. Moreover, it presents a valuable methodological orientation that explains financial processes and outcomes in terms of the institutional dynamics and elemental properties of the international monetary system.[9] Although one would not want to ignore other political forces, or how these organize international standards, this *political economy of international monetary relations approach* offers an analytical tool that in no small measure accounts for the forces shaping demand.

Yet this literature only scratches the surface of these patterns of confidence and their relation to the monetary system. The knowledge templates influencing financial relations are not examined in any meaningful way, let alone extended into a broader, more stratified theory of financial risk.[10] The effect is to reduce both the Bretton Woods system and the dollar standard to their stated goals – establishing or removing par values and capital controls etc. – with the implicit, non-codified rules and norms sedimented within them, which is what Ruggie (1992: 566) refers to as the 'substantive or qualitative' dimensions of multilateral regimes, therefore being either ignored or downplayed. The common sense understanding of financial confidence, which, above all, designates the dollar as a riskless asset, is treated as something apart from the rules governing monetary relations. This deinstitutionalizes US financial confidence, and over-exaggerates the breakdown of monetary relations in 1971, as it emphasizes shifts in par values and capital controls at the expense of wider patterns of financial common sense – the 'principles of ordering relations' attached to these frameworks (ibid.: 567).[11]

By extension, the IPE literature struggles to understand the role states play in formulating and managing monetary systems. Indeed, despite acknowledging the political origins of monetary agreements, the relationship between these and developments in state capacity are not always explored. Moreover, IPE literature has not been able to understand the integral role states play in reproducing monetary settlements during moments of non-radical change, let alone how such episodes impact the overall shape of the financial system. These problems are especially pronounced in discussions of the post-1970 period, as the assent of neoliberalism is frequently seen marking the release of markets from their state institutional supports and the subsequent loss of state capacity. This all makes the limits of IPE literature abundantly clear: though it offers crucial methodological guidance and identifies key patterns of credibility and confidence, it is insufficiently aware of the institutionalized practices and mechanisms upholding such patterns and their impact on financial relations.[12, 13]

THE POST-SECOND WORLD WAR IMAGINATION OF RISK

As we have seen, it is misleading to look at the safety or future worth of debt instruments merely in terms of assessments of international rating agencies or financial firms. These calculations are not simply the product of investor expectations and past credit relations, or a firm's discounted cash flow. Rather they reflect wider conceptions of risk and financial common sense that cannot be quantitatively measured.

Within the context of institutional Marxism and CPE, this makes deep financial networks and objective conditions visible, and points to a different mode of analysis, whereby demand is constituted through risk orders (or imaginaries) linked to systems of organized power. The work of Weber, Eichengreen and McKinnon adds a further point: that *the postwar monetary system institutionalized a broad understanding about the risklessness of US debt obligations which acted as an interpretive framework for global financial markets.*[14] This theory of risk imaginary develops and situates the concepts of credibility and confidence – these become specific styles or genres of classification belonging to a broader assemblage of perceptions rooted in abstract risk – and offers a more fine-grained understanding of the institutional context incubating markets, linked to the methodology discussed above.[15] At the same time, it obliges consideration of the interaction between institutionalized concepts of risk formed through the international monetary system on the one hand, and national-level state institutions responsible for the formation and ongoing management of these standards on the other: as risk imaginaries include both the international and state institutional formations sedimenting and routinizing their operation, they are subsequently conditioned by the interaction of the institutions within this ensemble.

The theoretical framework offered by this book therefore requires situating financial markets within the complex patterns of control erected by the postwar monetary system and the broader structure of US *risk power.* An additional point is required given the discrepancy between the Bretton Woods period and the longevity of US risk power. As we will see in Chapter 5, the collapse of this system and the movement towards a pure dollar standard in the early 1970s marked a significant, though far from radical, augmentation of the postwar system. This condition of the reproduction of US risk power similarly acted as a conditioning framework for global financial markets – a new institutionalization of the same risk convention. So while the institutional systems sustaining the credibility of US debt instruments have been recalibrated over time, there is a basic continuity in the way market outcomes have been influenced by tacit systems of knowledge informed by patterns of imperial power.

On the Material Basis of Risk and the Global Risk Anchor

Evident in this rendering of risk and political control are three important issues which we must address before concluding the chapter. It is necessary, first, to refer to the distinction between the concept of risk employed here and the idea of value used in traditional Marxian scholarship. Marxian political economy treats value as reified labour power – the socially necessary labour time embodied in commodities (Marx 1867). Surplus value stems from unpaid labour inputs, or the appropriation of labour time by owners of the means of production, as expressed in the difference between the exchange value of labour and its use value. This book discusses a different set of social processes and shifts the focus along two related planes: from the production sphere to the circulation sphere; and from the contradictory class relations between workers and owners to the institutional categories shaping the credibility of debt.

Marxian scholarship has mostly stayed away from such issues: it has focused on the *generalities* of capitalist organization and avoided the *particularities* and singularities of supply and demand that Marx himself was eager to abstract from (Marx 1894).[16] It is one thing to offer a rich analysis of class power and the relationship between financial and productive circuits of accumulation. But quite another to navigate the institutional politics of credibility and the inner workings of financial flows at the level of risk. Moreover, the commodity view of money creates certain complications, namely it struggles to explain how credit instruments, in the form of US Treasury bonds, have themselves emerged as hybrid world money.

The most notable exception to this is Lapavitsas' work on the historical relations of credit and money. Lapavitsas starts from a traditional Marxian view, seeing money as the basis of credit relations and as an equivalent form of value rooted in the contradiction between use value and exchange value. He nonetheless gives considerable attention to the social relations conditioning credit flows. In reconsidering the 'essential economic relations among capitalists', he argues that forward transactions require 'trust in the counterparty making the requisite transfer of value in due time' and that money markets are structured by promises made between lenders and borrowers (Lapavitsas 2003: 68, 70–71). The capacity of securities instruments to act as credit money 'rests on a sum of private assurances given by individual capitalists' and their credibility 'depends on the ability to persuade others of the validity of the original promise to pay ...' (Lapavitsas 2003: 77). This improves the understanding of credit transactions offered by Marx, which is set largely in terms of the independence and autonomy of borrowers and lenders – in fact, Marxian analysis has basically assumed 'that capitalists approach each other as foreign entities' within the credit system and that understandings of forward repayment emerge through 'regular production and trading contracts' (ibid.: 70).

This brings us, second, to the relationship between abstract risk and economic power. In the end, the Bretton Woods system, like the dollar standard after it, was prefigured by deeper patterns of material domination, as well as the capacity of US regulators to manage the forward worth of US Treasury obligations. In other words, the postwar monetary system and subsequent reproduction of US risk power resulted from the strength of American capitalism (see Panitch and Gindin 2004; 2005). Risk power is tied to economic power in this way because future claims on state revenue can only be realized through the appropriation of surplus value, as public debts are paid through revenue captured from the productive circuit. As a liability of the state, created (and held) by central banks against interest-bearing state bonds, paper money is similarly a form of state debt; it officially stands in relation to government bonds and always represents a state obligation, unwound only by the transfer of future revenue streams in the form of state backed debt. As fiat money is stored as a claim on future economic surplus and held as a unit of exchange, and is not in itself a store of labour time, its utility inexorably depends on the demand for commodities to which it provides access.

Neither can risk power be reduced to economic power. As relatively autonomous, emergent properties, institutions can follow a rhythm of their own, although the more basic structure will in the end always express its directional logic. There may in fact be a temporary disjuncture between material power on the one hand and institutional conceptions of risk on the other, where a new regime has not yet been consecrated. Similarly, the demand for money and its value on the open market, reflects not merely trade or productive power – demand is always forward looking and hence grounded in the type of expectations captured by abstract definitions of risk. From this, we can say that the risk and value forms basic to financial transactions reflect separate but interdependent forms of power, with the former ultimately subordinate to the latter.

Finally, the reader will note that debt obligations are not constituted under a uniform pattern of social trust – that different types of debt correspond differently with the properties erected by systems of abstract risk. To this extent, the basic risk chain in debt markets has to be disaggregated into its constituent elements. To put it slightly differently: there is a functional difference between US dollars ($\sum_0$) as simple debt obligations of the Treasury Department, and US Treasury bonds ($\sum_1$) as repayment promises based on the return of underlying dollars at a specified rate of interest. In the strict sense, Treasury bonds are the composition of two layers of social trust. There is similarly a difference between Treasury bonds and US corporate or private debt issues ($\sum_2$). While the credibility of a corporate bond also has two layers – in this case the risk of default attached to the corporate issuer as well as the perceived risk associated with the underlying currency of denomination (i.e., dollars) – these are structured by different social actors, and thereby reflect different abstract components. Neither the corporate issuer nor the Treasury Department is fully responsible for the debt. In the following equations can be seen the social basis of different debt obligations, where TD_1 and TD_2 signify the Treasury Department's guarantee of currency debt and bond debt respectively, and CI the guarantee provided by a corporate issuer.

$\sum_0 \text{risk } f(TD_1)$

$\sum_1 \text{risk } f(TD_1 + TD_2)$

$\sum_2 \text{risk } f(CI + TD_1)^{17}$

Returning to the differential application of US risk power, it is important to think through the contrasting promises comprising different instruments. In this respect, it is helpful to draw on the so-called Uno method of analysis (associated with the work of Japanese Marxist Kozo Uno), which sees the financial system as a complex pyramid of elemental credit relations. For Uno and his contemporaries, including Lapavitsas, debt instruments form a chain of 'interconnected promises to pay – rising from the simple to the more complex – [that] mutually sustain each other in generating social trust and validity in the credit system as a whole' (as translated and interpreted by Lapavitsas 2014: 123). Both Lapavitsas and Uno are more interested in understanding the basic properties of different financial assets, especially the temporal characteristics of debt, than in examining the systems of risk reified in debt obligations. Subsequently, they focus on trade credit, banking credit, money market credit, and central bank credit as the different components of the credit pyramid. Nevertheless, the conception of a financial pyramid of trust in debt markets remains the same when the focus is state-based conceptions of risk.

If we substitute the credit proprieties identified by Uno with the risk chain discussed above ($\sum_0$ to $\sum_2$), the debt pyramid reflects different *tiers* of financial credibility. Figure 3.1 expresses this view in reference to US risk power. The first tier of the pyramid, representing the most basic pattern of social trust, consists both of US dollar obligations and US Treasury assets. The unity between the two is realized by their common dependence on the perceived credibility of the US Treasury Department; that there are different layers structuring each obligation does nothing to change their common relationship to the US state. The second tier is composed of dollar denominated corporate/private debt. The credibility of these obligations is partly achieved from the perceived risk of Tier 1 placements, as they are linked to the private issuer guaranteeing the bond as well as the forward worth potential of US dollar debt. This informs three conclusions: (1) the overall risk of corporate dollar placements will tend to ebb and flow roughly in parallel with US Treasury obligations; (2) the popularity of US corporate bonds is buoyed by the conceptions of risk tied to Tier 1 debt, making private debt placements *carriers* of US risk power; and (3) the collapse of corporate risk in any segment of the market can occur separately from the collapse of US risk power, despite their co-evolution. The third and final tier is composed of non-dollar denominated private issue bonds. These obligations have no immediate link to the Treasury Department and are not directly constituted by abstract risk. Yet, however frayed, there is a connection here to the bottom tier of the pyramid, given the centrality of US Treasury debt to global markets. In this respect, a shift in the social worth of Tier 1 debt may impact valuations in the Tier 3 market.

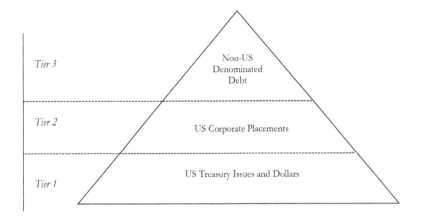

Figure 3.1   Financial risk credit pyramid, non-temporal

It is important to note at this point that the debt pyramid framed in Figure 3.1 is not indicative of overall credit risk in the global economy. The special attractiveness of Tier 1 US Treasury debt does not mean that Tier 2 US corporate bonds are more attractive than, say, Canadian sovereign bonds (GC_1) or money market instruments. Concerning corporate placements, only the following law can be applied: within the context of US risk hegemony and with all else being equal, including the maturity time of the debt, the promises underlying US denominated corporate bonds will be more credible than those underlying Canadian denominated corporate bonds due to the fact that $TD_1 > GC_1$.

SUMMARY REMARKS

This chapter identified strengths and weaknesses in the IPE literature on financial markets and presented a different way of understanding financial demand, one linked to the cultural and institutional turns discussed in Chapter 1. It argued that the Bretton Woods international monetary system developed in the 1940s, like the dollar standard which followed in the 1970s, institutionalized a broad understanding about the risklessness of US debt obligations that acted as an interpretive framework, or common sense, for financial firms and actors. The outcome of this has been a hierarchical configuration of Tier 1 and Tier 2 bonds, which anchored the global financial system to US Treasury debt and functioned as an objective force within financial markets. As we will see in the next part of the book, this has been a main driving force in the development of the financial system, pulling firms and investors into dollar denominated bonds, and paving the way for new institutional relations of dependency.

NOTES

1. Heterodox scholarship tends to use these concepts interchangeably.
2. The intellectual tradition handed down by Keynes and Minsky has been continued more recently by Kindleberger.
3. See also Callon (1998), Preda (2001; 2002), Aitken (2002), and Hooper (2001).
4. Anthropological studies on finance similarly demonstrate the importance of social networks and discursively constructed meaning systems in the interaction between investors (Abolafia 1996; Hertz 1998; Maurer 2002; Arnoldi 2004). For example, Hasselstrom (2000) shows that financial flows are deeply embedded in relations of trust and security between market actors.
5. Cohen argues that the postwar international monetary system helped to create a hierarchy of world money, with the greenback 'the most esteemed of international currencies' (Cohen 2004: 14; 1998).
6. Despite this, James (2009) sees the dominance of the dollar in the post-Bretton Woods period largely in terms of global savings, and much less in terms of the international monetary system.
7. Likewise, Schwartz (2009a; 2009b) links US differential growth between 1991 and 2005 to low interest rates generated by the unique attractiveness and popularity of the dollar. This cycle of financial arbitrage, whereby US firms borrowed at low rates of interest and invested at high rates, depended on the full range of the dollar's market-based advantages, and was inexorably drawn from the international monetary regimes of the post-Second World War period and the financial norms these created (Schwartz 2009a: 23). In *States Versus Markets*, Schwartz goes so far as to link the 'centricity of the US dollar' to the global financial system established 'through both Bretton Woods and the subsequent international monetary regime' (Schwartz 2019: 207).
8. See also Eichengreen et al. 2018.
9. Summarizing the typical IPE account of the international economy after the Second World War, Strange notes that 'the Bretton Woods system … plays a leading role in the story' (Strange 1998: 103).
10. To some degree, this limitation has been addressed within the IPE field by Kirshner and Seabrooke, though neither has shifted focus to the complex verticality of postwar financial flows. In *The Study of Money*, Kirshner (2000: 408) reviews Cohen's analysis and concludes that 'while the role of ideas is an important implicit foundation of [his work he does not] take on the issue in a systematic way.' The main problem, he argues, is that Cohen identifies the role of trust in credit relations without ever considering 'what is the source of this acceptability of others' (ibid.: 422). As he states: this failure is 'ubiquitous and emerges at critical moments' in Cohen's analysis (ibid.: 422). Unfortunately, Kirshner's own framework emphasizes the 'role of ideas in money' only in so far as they 'skew the ways in which policymakers understand and react to problems' (Kirshner 2003: 655). As a result, he only considers how ideas 'harden into an ideology' at the level of policy and the way this shapes and influences the political options available to states (Kirshner 2003: 655; 2001). Seabrooke's analysis proves more helpful because it is not tied to the issue of policy change. Noting that IPE scholarship has basically stayed away from the intersubjective meanings surrounding money, he references Keynes and Minsky to insist that social relations and conventions shape financial markets (Seabrooke 2001: 22, 27). However, these social foundations are

important not because they lead to encompassing knowledge systems, but rather because they influence state capacity and, above all, impact modes of behaviour within low-income communities. In *The Social Sources of Financial Power*, Seabrooke (2006) argues that positive state intervention creates relations of trust and confidence that bolster the financial participation of lower-income groups and enhance domestic financial capacity. As a result, Seabrooke's analysis of money and finance deals with popular sociology and stays away from the broad systems of financial risk addressed by this book.

11. The consequences of this approach are on display in Strange's influential analysis of the postwar financial system. Strange (1998: 103) argues that the standard vision of the post-Second World War international economy actually 'overrates the importance ... of the Bretton Woods system' as it fails to understand how 'credit creating mechanisms' structured the financial system through the postwar period. For her, the Bretton Woods system influenced international behaviour but only operated on the basis of 'a series of supporting measures taken by governments of the major trading countries that sustained the outflow of private capital and stabilized exchange markets' (ibid.: 105). From here, Strange advocates a narrow international monetary relations approach that distinguishes between the institutions of the Bretton Woods system and the structural power the US derived from the elevated role of the dollar following 1944. When put in context of her larger argument, that credit control associated with structural power is achieved 'in the last resort' on 'the basis of reputation on the borrower's side and confidence on the lenders', Strange's analysis feeds into a decontextualized view of financial credibility that politicizes credit and debt relations merely in terms of their management by state officials (ibid.: 28). This fails to explain the political and institutional origins of postwar financial confidence and separates the discursive constitution of risk and credibility from the stratified system of US hegemony. Strange's failure to do more than just state the importance of financial confidence leads her to a shallow view of the Bretton Woods system as well as a narrow understanding of the semiotic and institutional basis of US financial power.

12. Underlying this are two related problems: a tendency to insufficiently examine the exploitative characteristics of capitalist social organization; and a common impulse to separate institutional forms of organizational power from wider capitalist pressures and dynamics. This essentially repeats the problems associated with neo-institutionalist scholarship discussed in Chapter 1.

13. As a result, abstract risk is experienced as a distinct pressure in financial relations that is often expressed through long-term ideas of confidence and credibility.

14. Sum and Jessop (2013) note the presence of different economic imaginaries to highlight the complexity of semiotic constitution and the fragmented sources of power and influence conditioning lived experience. This point draws attention to the way ideologies differ from imaginaries in their purposeful connection to the power bloc. Yet Sum and Jessop (2013) also argue that hegemonic imaginaries structure and condition lived experience. In expressing the Marxian roots of cultural political economy, this point draws attention to how certain constructions emerge as economic struggles are resolved and transmitted through different organizational apparatuses. This shows how dominant conceptions of risk institutionalized in the global monetary system drive expectations of future worth and influence financial demand internationally; at the same time it places emphasis on key institutional practices that lay the basis for relations between national currencies and forms of debt.

15. We can say that the abstract concept of US financial risk forms the core of a post-Second World War economic imaginary shaping and constituting global debt and financial markets. As a semiotic order or ensemble, this imaginary networks and webs together different financial practices and discourses – it is expressed in conceptions of financial credibility, in feelings of investor confidence, in intersubjective meanings about asset safety, in investment styles, in comparative assessments about political and country risk, in views about state capacity, and so on. The postwar imaginary shaped and rearticulated these practices, discourses and styles around a particular base conception of risk.

16. Using the theory of abstract risk, this book shows that financial demand is not random and subject to individual-level motivations – that it too is driven by underlying logics and material processes.

17. This formulaic expression borrows from, and is inspired by, Lapavitsas' work in *Profiting Without Producing* (2014).

PART II

The deep history of the subprime crisis

By 2007, after over a decade of growing demand, global markets were overflowing with US originated mortgage-backed securities (MBS). With this, and the collapsing value of these obligations impacting derivative contracts and wholesale funding markets, the US mortgage crisis immediately overwhelmed global markets. This makes it all the more imperative to examine the *internationalization* of US mortgage bonds and to clarify the relationship between these and the global debt system that emerged after the Second World War. To some extent, widespread demand for securitized US mortgages grew from low Treasury bond yields and the liquidity of the US market, and reflected how these issues were clothed to appear safe. Yet such points provide no more than a preliminary accounting, for they suppose a rather vulgar understanding of the financial system.

In the previous part of the book we explored the abstract properties organizing global debt markets using insight from IM and CPE. This part explores the institutionalization of abstract risk in the aftermath of the Second World War. It shows that key branches of the US state supported the development of US risk power through European and global markets, leading to the development of a hub-and-spoke system of accumulation centred around US public *and* private debt. A key point is that this system developed from the complex interplay of relatively autonomous institutional forces, and was not in fact the teleological outcome of abstract risk.

The analysis in this part is thus historical and institutional. Chapters 4 to 7 trace the postwar history of the IBM and offer two general findings: (1) that the Bretton Woods system influenced demand for dollar denominated debt and forged new organizational alignments and dependencies traversing and intermeshing national markets; and while the officials 'burdened' with the responsibility of managing globalization did not always act consciously, (2) the formation and reproduction of US risk power depended on key regulatory branches of the US state (Panitch and Gindin 2012: 142). To be clear, the goal is not a strong causal argument – piecing together the fragmented development of the three branches of the international bond market cannot itself prove US risk power, though the popularity of US debt instruments can undoubtedly be seen in the evolution of these markets. The depth view of reality presented by critical realism demonstrates the multiplicity of interactive but autonomous forces influencing concrete social processes, and the limitations of empiricism. In short, the existence of causal mechanisms and generative forces can neither be validated nor invalidated by the presence of predicted outcomes, due to the variability of structures and conditions influencing observable events. This makes the ensuing discussion 'empirical but not empiricist' (Maher and Aquanno 2018: 41).

The following historical anthropology is thus rather more about offering insight into the origins and evolution of US financial credibility, and tracing how the institutionalization of abstract risk developed out of the continuous interplay of state and market forces and came to reside in – but also well beyond – the US Treasury bond market. Through this, we can observe the reach and influence of the Bretton Woods risk compromise, its broad impact on the global financial system, and view the subprime crisis as part of the complex and contradictory evolution of global debt markets *tout court*, rather than as something outside of history.

4. International bonds and the Bretton Woods era

Though IPE scholars all too commonly pronounce the decline of the dollar, very few ignore its historical prominence and the unquenchable thirst for US Treasury bonds. Yet with focus on the dollar's reserve status and the foreign purchase of US Treasury bonds, rather than the international bond market more generally, the special credibility of US debt has been viewed myopically, if at all. The perceived risklessness of Treasury bonds and the impact of this across debt markets, including the interconnectivity between private placements and US risk power, remains a black box. By contrast, the framework developed above shows that dollar denominated bonds have long anchored and integrated global debt markets. This is not a matter of saying that policy changes or corporate decisions were irrelevant in the development of these markets. It is about properly situating such actions within the institutional conditions set down by the international monetary system, and recognizing how the interaction of different organizations stabilized and shaped abstract financial risk. Grasping this entanglement of forces and mechanisms, we can locate US subprime and MBS markets in the long-term credibility of dollar denominated bonds, both public *and* private.

This all requires piecing together the fragmented history of the IBM and working with an understanding of this market that captures global interconnectivities. Starting briefly with the inter-war period leading up to the Bretton Woods system, this chapter and the next (Chapter 5) bring together a wide range of empirical data and literature on the postwar international bond market, albeit in a way that remains somewhat schematic – given the complexity of instruments, the variation in measurement styles, and the availability of information.[1]

THE PATH TO BRETTON WOODS

As noted, US risk power actually developed around two different international arrangements: the Bretton Woods standard and the dollar standard. Prior to the development of the Bretton Woods system in 1944, international demand for US dollar debt was strong, but intermittent and unstable. As Eichengreen et al. (2018) have shown, the growing strength of American capitalism through the early 1900s stimulated foreign demand for dollars. The scale of this came to the foreground in the late 1920s when demand for dollar debt outstripped that for pounds, and the dollar became the dominant global currency. But if the dollar's international assent had strong material foundations, it also had very specific state institutional origins, following as it did the development of the Federal Reserve system in 1913. Key here was that the Federal Reserve took on the responsibility of 'develop[ing] a market in trade credits denominated in dollars' (Eichengreen et al. 2018: 33; Broz 1997). With this, and the Fed's move to discount bills of exchange, the global financial system became ever more linked to the dollar. Thus, even though the US overtook Britain as the world's largest economy in the late 1800s, the dollar's gradual assent awaited developments in US state capacity.

These state institutional shifts interacted with, and were amplified by, the collapse of the international gold standard in 1914, which established the pound sterling as an international store of value and the Bank of England as the most credible grantor of future worth. Even though most industrial countries tentatively re-established gold par values in the 1920s, on the basis of an overinflated pound sterling (which the Federal Reserve sustained through low domestic interest rates), the period from 1914 to 1939 was anything but stable.[2] The slow collapse of the gold system, which itself emerged out of changing patterns of control in the capitalist world system, eroded 'confidence in the sterling's convertibility to gold', and created a certain amount of space for the growth of US debt markets (Eichengreen et al. 2018: 22). Underpinning this were persistent 'doubts about the ability of the Bank of England to maintain convertibility' (ibid.: 50). By 1931, 45 per cent of global foreign public debt was denominated in dollars, compared to 51 per cent in pound sterling. Excluding bonds held by commonwealth countries, US denominated debt reached nearly 60 per cent in the early 1930s (Chitu et al. 2014; Eichengreen and Flandreau 2009).

Yet even against these shifting institutional compositions, the dollar's ascendance was only partial and sporadic. Following the collapse of the global economy in the 1930s, foreign demand for the pound again skyrocketed, as investors sought increased financial safety and accepted the discipline imposed by the Bank of England (Eichengreen and Flandreau 2009). Moreover, as two-thirds of dollar denominated foreign issues defaulted, which was about double that of pound denominated debt, New York underwriters pulled back from issuing foreign bonds. The high default rate of US foreign debt reflected a number of factors, but was strongly associated with the inexperience of US underwriters compared to their British counterparts (Chitu et al. 2014; Eichengreen and Portes 1990).

After its brief triumph in the 1920s, the dollar share of the international currency market fell to about 30 per cent (Eichengreen et al. 2018). With the gold standard already in a shambles by this time, growing international demand for pound denominated debt reflected long-standing financial sensibilities and the lingering effects of a defunct system. But the dollar's return to secondary status also had much to do with the institutions of US financial management. Prior to 1935, the Federal Reserve's influence was blunted by its overt politicization, as the Secretary of Treasury and Comptroller of the Currency wielded direct control over its lender-of-last-resort functions. Moreover, the Fed lacked the institutional tools to support the dollar and reinforce its emerging international status. Depression era reforms changed this – they greatly enhanced the Fed's capacity to manage market fundamentals in the interests of the long-term stability of the dollar. The 1932 Reconstruction Finance Corporation Act added Section 13(3) to the Federal Reserve Act, giving the Fed wide-ranging emergency powers, and the Glass–Steagall Act (1933) further bolstered this authority by granting the Federal Reserve Board power to temporarily advance funds to member banks, so long as such transfers were 'secured by satisfactory collateral' (Sastry 2018: 18). The 1935 Banking Act set out another profound elaboration, namely it gave the Fed 'capacity to conduct discretionary monetary policy by varying reserve requirements and selective credit controls' (Panitch and Gindin 2012: 59). As Panitch and Gindin (2012) correctly argue, it was the development of these state institutional capacities in the 1930s, out of the chaos of the Great Depression, that laid the groundwork for the Bretton Woods system in the 1940s.

Thus, far from marking only a temporary deviation in the dollar's teleological climb to hegemonic status, the re-ascendance of the pound in the 1930s reflected unresolved institutional problems that were only addressed through political compromise. The period leading up to the Bretton Woods Accord helped reset expectations, and saw the development of institutional cables supporting a new financial common sense. However, it would take the US state overcoming inward looking and protectionist impulses, and committing to deploy its new institutional capacities, before this could be fully realized.

The framework established at Bretton Woods reinforced and stabilized international monetary relations around these new state capacities. Under the terms of the agreement, the dollar was tied to gold at the price of $35 per oz, and all other currencies were linked to the dollar at set par values, while the newly created International Monetary Fund was tasked with supporting these monetary relations. The system required member central banks both to redeem their currency on demand for US dollars and to maintain a fixed price for their currency against the dollar. At the same time, it transferred into the dollar the abstract credibility of gold, which had been developed through the classical gold standard, effectively making the dollar a gold substitute and US Treasury debt a 'riskless asset' (Grabbe 1996: 12). This sedimented a new financial common sense and moved the world financial system away from the volatility of the antebellum period and towards a long period of US risk power, even though, as we will see in the next chapter, a similar type of instability temporarily emerged in the 1970s, leading to the re-institutionalization of dollar credibility in the dollar standard.

INTERNATIONAL BONDS AND THE BRETTON WOODS ERA

If the inter-war IBM was characterized by fluctuating definitions of credibility, its development after the Second World War followed a much different path. As the new Bretton Woods Agreement mixed with old institutional settlements and evolving expressions of state power, international bonds were increasingly denominated in US dollars. In fact, while total foreign public debt was still held mainly in pounds at the end of the Second World War, this quickly changed as US markets asserted their dominance and investors scrambled to obtain dollar obligations. This was registered by the changing composition of global foreign exchange holdings: whereas about 75 per cent of foreign exchange reserves were held in pounds in the mid-1940s, already by the early 1950s US dollar holdings exceeded 50 per cent of the world total. By the start of the 1960s they exceeded 90 per cent (Eichengreen et al. 2018). While this would drop through the 1960s and eventually level off at around 60 per cent, the dominance of the US dollar and demand for US dollar debt was increasingly unmistakable.

The development of the IBM during the postwar period therefore principally involved the outward expansion of US debt, across new international markets. Most of this occurred in Europe as these economies recovered from the devastation of the war with the assistance of US aid programmes, and under the umbrella of US-led multilateral institutions. Yet while foreign ownership of US public debt expanded considerably, especially following the early 1960s, this was only part of the story. From the beginning, US risk power involved the foreign purchase of US Treasury debt and likewise centred around private dollar denominated bonds – it was neither explicitly public nor private. And these trends were mutually reinforcing, especially since the former fuelled the expansion of offshore dollar holdings (Eurodollars), enabling European banks and investment firms to offer dollar bonds outside the US market. As we will see in Chapter 5, this in turn laid the foundations for the further expansion of dollar debt following the 1970s, as US risk power increasingly penetrated Asian markets and developed through corporate and agency bonds as well.

These developments took shape through specific institutional channels, themselves conditioned by state regulation, as the IBM evolved not as a single market, but as the collection of three interlinked markets: the offshore market, the domestic-international market, and the foreign bond market.[3] Crucially, each market developed in conjunction with the institutional articulation of risk expressed first by the Bretton Woods system and then by the dollar standard – meaning that the dollar component of each segment was far and away the main source of growth and liquidity. The special credibility of dollar denominated debt was therefore expressed along three separate axes: (1) through the dominance of Yankee bonds amongst foreign bond placements; (2) through the strong demand for Eurodollar bonds relative to other Eurobond placements; and (3) through the asymmetrical foreign demand for US domestic-international bonds (including, but not limited to, Treasury bonds) vis-à-vis other internationally oriented domestic placements.

Far from remaining on the sidelines, state institutions were crucial spearpoints in this process, elaborating and reproducing financial norms in all three markets and playing a major role in their formation and operation (Maher and Aquanno 2018; Konings 2011; Panitch and Gindin 2012). It is central that this institutional Marxist view of states, as integral to market formation and capable of conditioning and enabling action, be emphasized, for it helps us understand the historical dynamics of the IBM and the dialectical evolution of the institutions composing the postwar risk imaginary. Let us now turn more specifically to these patterns of market control and their institutional coordination.

The Yankee and Eurobond Markets

Prior to the Second World War, the pound headlined international markets, due to its special credibility. But with the Bretton Woods Accord, things changed: investors became more confident in the forward worth of dollar denominated debt, and the Yankee bond market became a key destination for international investors. To be sure, the expansion of the Yankee market did not simply occur as US investors stockpiled foreign dollar denominated issues – this was one dimension, but it was certainly not enough to spur the rapid growth of Yankee issues, especially because US investors were not as familiar with the European companies placing bonds. From the beginning, the growth of this market involved 'European investors attracted by dollar denominated investments for familiar names' (O'Malley 2015: 14). While these investors were typically blocked from US markets, they were able to access Yankee bonds *indirectly*, as New York issues were placed in Europe through 'discretionary accounts' managed by European financial institutions, and later 'listed in Paris, Brussels and Luxembourg' (ibid.: 14). The development of these investment channels occurred as European firms raced to meet demand for US dollar backed corporate bonds. Yet while this stimulated the postwar redevelopment of major European centres, it did so on the basis of US financial power. *This meant that the Yankee market immediately nurtured the development of transatlantic financial networks founded on the credibility of US Treasury debt.*

Based on these emerging institutional forms, which themselves served as a harbinger of coming trends, the Yankee bond market grew rapidly through the 1950s, and was given further boost with the removal of convertibility restrictions on major European currencies in the late 1950s (Evans 1992: 30). Between 1955 and 1962 the Yankee market grew to over $4 billion, easily outstripping the combined size of the remaining foreign markets (Mensbrugghe 1964).[4] This alone alleviated the so-called dollar shortage. However, the explosive growth of Yankee issues in the early 1960s really turned the tide: while in 1960 'USD 850 million of long-term loans and bond sales by foreigners flowed from the United States', by the first half of 1963 issuance had nearly doubled, exceeding $1.5 billion (Fisher 1979: 17–18).

One consequence of this new form of association between markets was tighter capital controls. Aware that European banks had already developed the institutional capacity to raise dollar funds offshore through so-called Eurodollar markets, and that demand for dollar backed private debt inside Europe was growing, the Kennedy administration imposed an interest equalization tax (IET) on foreign borrowers to stem the outflow of capital from the US foreign bond market and protect the dollar–gold link (Walmsley 1991: 32).[5] The tax, which increased the cost of foreign borrowing by about 1 per cent, was the Treasury Department's rather explicit encouragement to 'Europeans to raise finance in their own market rather than borrow in New York' (ibid.: 32). The IET did not take long to divert capital flows and hollow out the Yankee market: already by the end of 1963 things looked very different – new sales had collapsed and issuers had set up shop in emerging offshore markets, following the Treasury's guidance (Hayes and Hubbard 1990: 32).

It is in this way that the investment patterns burnished by the Yankee market, established over some 10 years of close integration, set the tracks for the European offshore market. Yet far from separating European and US markets, the IET actually strengthened the interconnection, considerably advancing the transatlantic linkages fostered by the Yankee market's earlier development, though on terms that dramatically extended US power inside Europe.

The Eurodollar market was key to this and played a special role in the evolving system. A form of Eurocurrency, Eurodollars are 'offshore dollar deposits held primarily in European banks and redeposited by such banks' (ibid.: 28).[6] This market developed in the 1950s when London merchant banks, hampered by restrictions limiting speculation on the pound, started using offshore US dollars 'for both deposits and loans' (Grabbe 1996: 15).[7] Eurodollars internalized the new risk standards and reflected the credibility and popularity of US debt. They also fell beyond the jurisdiction of any national authority, and were attractive for lending because they were free from exchange controls or restrictions on reserve deposits and interest rates (Fisher 1979: 19).

In effect, the Eurodollar market provided the 'pool of internationally mobile funds' necessary for the Eurobond market (Hayes and Hubbard 1990: 29; Walmsley 1991: 182).[8] At the same time, it allowed banking syndicates to currency match issues placed in European markets – both to raise the dollars necessary for syndication and to be paid in US dollars – and thereby eliminated the currency risk which otherwise would have accompanied offshore instruments (Hayes and Hubbard 1990: 29). In no uncertain terms, the Eurodollar bond market required the prior development of the Eurodollar market. As Walmsley concludes: 'The basic link between the Eurocurrency market and the Eurobond market … is this: no Eurocurrency, no Eurobonds' (Walmsley 1991: 187).

It is only in this sense that the IET was a turning point for the Eurodollar bond market. With the Yankee market closed and European investors unable to meet borrowing needs inside the US, they experimented in dollar financing in their home market, building on the institutional channels already established through the Yankee and Eurodollar markets (Clark 2002: 453). After Autostrade set the blueprint in 1963, with a $15 million placement, offshore issuance exploded, reaching $680 million by 1964 (Fisher 1979: 27). Over the next 15 years, prior to the Volcker shock, the Eurobond market grew rapidly,

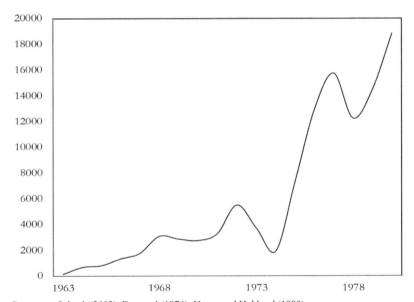

Source: Schenk (2002); Emanuel (1976); Hayes and Hubbard (1990).

Figure 4.1   *Eurobond new issue volume 1963–80*

led above all by dollar denominated placements, which on average accounted for about 60 per cent of total issuance volume (Figure 4.1; ibid.: 27).

The Eurobond market consolidated US risk power, serving as a conduit for its accelerated expansion, because it improved access to dollar denominated debt, and let international investors bypass US onshore regulations. At the heart of the Eurobond market was a renewed process of financial liberalization, owing to the unique structure of offshore bonds. As these were both issued in bearer form and in markets outside the currency of denomination, they too were unregulated. And while it would have been easy to control the market, this would have required a new institutional framework, one that neither the US nor Britain were willing to consider (Helleiner 1994). Subsequently, the market developed as 'the most liberal international financial environment that private market operators had encountered in several decades'; a centre where 'transactions could be made in non-local currencies, especially dollars, completely free of state regulations' (ibid.: 82).[9]

While state policy influenced the specific manifestation of US credibility, passing US risk power through European markets, the opening of new offshore segments – including the Euro-French, Euro-Dutch, and Euro-Luxembourg markets – did little to disrupt the Eurodollar bond market. In fact, demand was so great that even with a large store of hard currency in the form of Eurodollar placements, the supply of new issues remained persistently deficient.[10] This was partly addressed through the voluntary and mandatory restraints placed on US overseas direct investment following 1965. The Voluntary Restraint Program encouraged corporations to 'grow export markets and repatriate dividends and provided strong impetus to the rate of growth of … new international money market[s]' (Grabbe 1996: 13; Fisher 1979: 26). Similarly, the Mandatory Restraint Program (MRP)'s mandatory quotas required that US corporations seek foreign outlets for the financing of international operations (ibid.: 28). These regulations directed US multinational companies to the Eurobond market for capital financing, and gave further form to the evolving transatlantic financial system by linking the Eurobond market and the postwar risk system on the one hand and the growth of American industrial and commercial capital on the other. Following the MRP, the volume of Eurobond issues by affected companies increased from $527 million in 1967 to $2 billion in 1968 (ibid.: 28). During the five years the programme was in operation, 'US corporations floated a total of 271 Eurobond issues aggregating USD 6.978 billion or nearly 33 percent of the entire market over the period' (ibid.: 28).[11]

POSTWAR INTERNATIONALIZATION BEYOND THE EUROBOND MARKET

For all these changes, the US onshore market remained an international flagship. Again, the IET was a crucial condition of this, as certain countries and international organizations were exempted from paying the tax penalty (Fisher 1979: 21). Due to the nature of abstract risk attached to US Tier 2 debt, these qualifications alone facilitated internationalization, and lent a unique dynamism to the Yankee market.[12] From 1963 to 1974, when the IET was finally removed, non-government foreign issues offered for sale in the US market ranged from $504 million to a high of $1.8 billion, with issues by foreign governments representing far and away the largest share (ibid.). This was the case even though total issuance fell increasingly behind the standards set by the offshore Eurobond market (ibid.: 31). When capital controls were lifted in 1974, the Yankee bond market quickly became a more significant outlet for US risk power, but this hardly marked a sharp break with the previous 10 years, as many had predicted. While issuance exploded in 1974, easily outpacing growth in the Eurobond market, which saw new issues slump to 1967 levels, this reflected an unsustainable boost of excitement, rather than an emerging trend. By this time, in fact, the transatlantic financial linkages fostered by the offshore market were already deeply rooted. Subsequently, if the Yankee market became even more central to the foreign issues market, its subordinate international status was increasingly unmistakable. Between 1974 and 1978 the total amount of capital raised in the Yankee bond market reached $33.4 billion, roughly $16.6 billion less than the new issue volume in the Euromarket (Table 4.1). In important respects the two markets remained segmented. After 1974, issues from previously excluded entities increased tangibly, reaching $118 million in 1974, $1.5 billion in 1975 and $1.9 billion by the end of 1978 (ibid.: 165). But underwritings of IET-affected borrowers represented only a fraction of the total Yankee bond market.[13] This speaks to the importance of the cross-border institutional linkages formed through the early development of the Euromarket.

The US domestic-international bond market (capturing US placements issued domestically but purchased by foreign buyers) was similarly constrained in the 1960s and 1970s, as federal regulations on the issue of securities to foreigners blunted internationalization. Prior to 1984, interest payments to non-residents purchasing corporate bonds in the US market were subject to a 30 per cent tax withholding. While the same also applied to US companies issuing Eurobonds, this could be avoided if the issuing company was a subsidiary which generated at least 80 per cent of its income from non-US sources. These regulations encouraged US corporations to 'utilize foreign financing

Table 4.1   Foreign government and international securities offered for
              sale in the US domestic market, 1950–74 (USD million)

Year	Foreign Government	International Non-Corporate
1950	162	101
1955	150	–
1960	395	109
1965	460	201
1968	900	461
1969	683	162
1970	447	342
1971	1400	425
1972	926	259
1973	1160	–
1974	1200	–

Source: US Census Bureau (1976).

subsidiaries' and resulted in the growth of the Eurobond market at the expense
of the US onshore market (Grabbe 1996: 274–6). If this expanded European
markets, it again did so on specifically US terms: enhancing the interconnectivity between US capital and European financial circuits, and expanding the
latter's use of, and reliance on, US denominated debt.

By contrast, US government securities were exempted from the 30 per
cent withholding tax as well as the interest restrictions attached to Regulation
Q. This was an attempt to balance the advantages of foreign debt holdings
against the disadvantages of persistent balance of payments deficits within the
context of the dollar-based Bretton Woods system. Nonetheless, the Treasury
bond market faced numerous obstacles. These included the volume of US
government debt, restrictions on the convertibility of European and Japanese
currency, and interest rate differentials with respect to the Eurobond market.
Furthermore, there is reason to believe that the growth of the market required
a more mature institutional base in the form of an internationally oriented
assemblage of primary dealers and selling groups capable of distributing issues
globally. Above all, the financial stability triggered by the Bretton Woods
system meant less demand for risk-free instruments. It is revealing that the
international Treasury market began bursting at the seams only following
Nixon's decision to de-link from gold, alongside the intensification and privatization of currency and interest rate risk. In this way, the special conception of
risk attached to US debt was not fully expressed in the domestic-international
market until 1971. In the historical role of the postwar monetary system we

can therefore find an opposition between its constitution and containment of US risk power.

This is different from saying that the Treasury market played no significant role during this period. Far from it. If the resurgent liberalism of the 1970s and 1980s turned out to supplement demand, the Treasury market was already the central nervous system of the IBM. As the issuance of US Treasury securities expanded following 1945, reaching $369 billion by 1970, the internationalization of Treasury bonds followed suit. By the start of the 1970s, the Treasury market was larger than the Eurobond market, making it the world's leading international debt market: whereas the aggregate value of Eurobonds outstanding in 1970 totalled roughly $13.5 billion, foreigners held $19.8 billion in US Treasury securities by the end of the same year, or 8.6 per cent of outstanding privately held securities (Figure 4.2). Aside from a general loosening of restrictions, part of the reason for this was that interest rates rose above Regulation Q ceilings in 1966, causing some trouble for European money-centred banks holding dollars, as investments were switched out of time deposits into assets

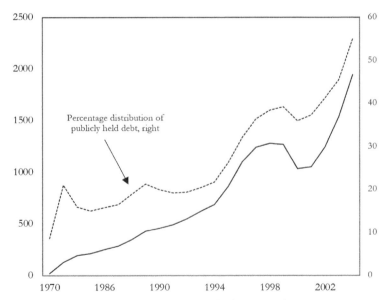

Note: Public debt is total federal debt minus Federal Reserve and government accounts. Foreign ownership as a percentage of total federal debt is thus lower.
Source: US Census Bureau; US Treasury.

Figure 4.2 *Total foreign ownership of US public debt securities by private investors, 1970–2005 (USD billion)*

for which there was no ceiling. Yet paradoxically, by driving a different form of dollar-based financialization, oriented around public borrowing, this made US debt more, not less, important to European markets and in fact enhanced dollar financing through Eurodollar and Eurobond markets.

SUMMARY REMARKS

The growth curb of international bonds from the 1940s to the 1970s emanated from the Bretton Woods Accord, and the material forms of domination it represented. If international demand for US bonds grew through the inter-war period, following the war a new investment terrain quickly took root. Even before convertibility in 1958, the perceived risklessness of the dollar registered in the Yankee bond market and created the conditions allowing the IET to dramatically affect offshore markets in 1963. That the European offshore bond market centred on dollar placements meant that international demand was now increasingly expressed outside the US domestic market, ostensibly beyond the regulatory jurisdiction of the US state. But while new issues entered the Euromarket, the trends initially expressed in the Yankee market continued to be plainly apparent. As the regulatory landscape continued to change, a very similar pattern unfolded in the foreign bond market. And all the while Treasury bonds were far and away the most popular domestic-international placements.

Underlying this were intermeshed improvements in US state capacity and an entirely new financial common sense, itself defined by the risklessness of US dollar debt. Political compromise was also part of the story, as regulations on the movement of capital augmented the size and growth of different markets at different times, but this too was shaped by wider forces and part of the perennial relationships forged in the 1940s. The institutional level shifts associated with such measures as the IET and MRP served to mediate the specific expression of postwar risk in a way that laid down new transatlantic financial connections and deepened the saturation of US risk power. This shows the interaction which occurred within the ensemble of institutional forces composing the risk imaginary, and how this shaped the composition of post-Second World War financial markets. Yet if US and European markets now pivoted around dollar debt, this marked only the beginning of US risk power. As we will see, the opening of new markets, coupled with the further expansion of existing markets and ongoing liberalization, greatly extended the internationalization of US debt, setting the stage for the 2008 financial crisis.

NOTES

1.   Different organizations and US government agencies measure bond and debt markets differently. Moreover, these criteria themselves often change. Some

calculations distinguish between long- and short-term debt, others do not. Where possible, this book focuses on long-term holdings, as these are technically bonds. Issues with a short-term maturity structure (under one year) are considered notes. Organizations also use different data collection methodologies and do not sharply distinguish between foreign and international ownership. For example, even the Federal Reserve and US Treasury department publish different figures.

2. The actual value of gold and silver metals appears to have deeper sociological and geophysical orientations relating to the relative abundance of the earth's natural metals – particularly in the geographic zones where complex market relations initially prospered – and the habit to conflate worth and scarcity. Further, the 'ornamental attributes' of copper, bronze, gold and silver dating back to the Stone Age have helped to construct the worth of these precious metals (Davies 2002: 45). At any rate, risk and credibility have long been derived from the metallic substance of coins in circulation. The attractiveness of gold and silver has historically influenced the exchange potential of state/communal money so that variations in metallic content have generally yielded oscillations in worth (Wilsher 1970; Ingham 1998; Davies 2002). Only where an entrenched social commitment to money is present have shifts in the metallic base of coinage not had noticeable effects on market value, and then only when the alterations were marginal or infrequent (Davies 2002). Moreover, the value of precious metals has been frequently harnessed by political authority, and linked to the civilizational strength or imperial capacity of the political organization counselling demand in this way. In this sense, the making of money under Greek, Roman and British hegemony concerned persistent state intervention with regard to the intrinsic worth content of money (Wilsher 1970; Davies 2002). Often this entailed extending the uniform application of currency and ensuring (perceived) stability in metallic content, but it also took the form of political appeals to mythology and state capacity (Davies 2002).

3. These markets engendered extra-national ties between creditors and debtors as a product of their functionality. We can consider domestically placed debt securities (i.e., onshore issues) international bonds when they are purchased or held by foreign investors or underwriters. A more complicated definition would include those issues brought to market by an investment syndicate (i.e., the complex of primary dealers, underwriters and selling groups) that is itself internationally organized. This book works from the former definition given limits on the available data. A foreign bond is a debt security issued and traded by a foreign company or government in a jurisdiction outside its domestic market. Foreign bonds are usually denominated in the currency of the jurisdiction they are issued in and are labelled according to their place of issue. A bond issued by a Japanese company in the United States in US dollars would be titled a Yankee bond, while a bond issued by a US company in Japan and denominated in yen would be classified as a Samurai bond. Each issue is subject to the discipline of the securities regulator of the country of issue and distributed according to domestic bond standards. The placement of foreign debt securities is typically limited to a single country. Eurobonds are simultaneously issued in several countries and often brought to market by an international syndicate of investment banks. The internationalization of the issue depends on a broad spectrum of investment banks as the issue can only be brought to a domestic market through a selling group licensed in that jurisdiction. As opposed to global bonds, which are simultaneously issued in Europe, Asia and North America, 'Eurobonds are issued in countries other than the country in

which the bond is dominated' so that a fundamental feature of Eurobonds is an incongruency between nationality of placement and currency of denomination (Clark 2002: 441).

4. See also: Aquanno (2008).

5. The IET was imposed on 18 July 1963.

6. In part, the build-up of dollars in Europe was driven by the transfer of aid from the US to war-torn European countries to facilitate European reconstruction. Orlin Grabbe (1996: 10) notes that 'while the total amount of Marshall Plan aid constituted only about 4 percent of European gross national product, it made up about 40 percent of European receipts of hard currency.' Further, the growth of the Eurodollar market can be attributed to a set of Cold War policies, as the Soviet government required a supply of hard currency to meet domestic and international objectives (Evans 1992: 42). Initially, these deposits were held inside the US state since financial convention linked domestic banks with domestic currency reserves (Grabbe 1996: 16). Following Cold War hostilities, fears that the US government would 'seize soviet-owned bank deposits in the United States' expanded, leading the Soviet government to transfer its hard currency deposits to banks in London and Paris (Evans 1992: 42). While Evans and Grabbe have made it apparent that Soviet banks were not front and centre in the development of the Eurodollar money market, the transfer of American dollars to Soviet-owned Eurobanks certainly enhanced the US dollar supply within the region, facilitating the liquidity that underwrote the development and continued growth of Eurobonds.

7. To the extent that the accessible pool of dollar reserves was insufficient to facilitate a robust international dollar financing circuit, the solution was to further exploit US banking regulations to expand dollar inflows.

8. In 1963, the Bank of International Settlements estimated the Eurodollar money market totalled $12.4 billion, of which $9.3 billion was in dollars (Hayes and Hubbard 1990: 29).

9. One of the results is that the interest income generated through Eurobonds has historically been tax free (Grabbe 1996: 268). In turn, Eurobonds have proven to be a cheaper source of credit when compared to similarly structured foreign and domestic issues. The relative absence of national regulations on Eurobond securities also allows issuers to avoid strict disclosure practices: in most nations, Eurobonds can be traded without meeting public disclosure or pre-offering registration requirements (ibid.: 268). Investors wishing to access Euromarket debt must rely on reputations and vague rating systems.

10. At least two other variables acted to restrict the Eurobond market's expansion in this period. First, US-based restrictions on the distribution of Eurobonds effectively closed the market to a large pool of capital. While the US government did not prevent Eurobonds from being sold to buyers outside the US, it prohibited US residents from participating in initial offers. US securities regulations allowed the sale of Eurobonds in secondary markets to US nationals after 90 days from the date of issue (Evans 1992: 44). The impact of this would have been more significant had the SEC not exempted US investment banking firms from underwriting and distributing Eurobonds (ibid.: 44–5). As it turns out, many of these firms, including Morgan Stanley, Goldman Sachs and First Boston, were instrumental in laying the institutional framework for the Euromarket. Second, the development of the Eurobond market was blocked by the growth of alternative financing sources in the European offshore market. Beginning in the late 1960s, syndicated Eurocurrency loan operations began to appear as a major source of large-scale

financing. Defined as a network of major banking institutions organized around a lead manager that finances longer-term debt by borrowing capital short-term, the syndicated Eurocredit market brought together large pools of capital, traditionally between $200 and $500 million, and 'provided it to borrowers in a single transaction, allowing them to lower costs and individually construct borrowing arrangements' (Clark 2002: 463–4). Critically the market helped banks finance developing-country balance of payments deficits, which emerged as a result of developmental projects and oil politics, throughout the 1970s. As a result, it grew exponentially during this period, systematically drawing financing opportunities from the Eurobond market. By the early 1980s syndicated Eurocurrency facilities amounted to about $100 billion while Eurobond issues totalled $46.44 billion (ibid.: 453).

11. It follows that the flow of dollars resulting from US balance of payments deficits was a key source of liquidity for Eurobonds (Hayes and Hubbard 1990: 28). Even if issues were not always denominated in dollars, markets relied heavily on them to make offsetting trades and balance portfolio risks. This nurtured the development of new forms of connectivity between American and European financial firms and markets and opened new channels for US risk power (Grabbe 1996: 25). At the same time, concerns relating to the growing spread between US gold reserves and US Treasury debt created opportunity for speculative attacks on the dollar and allowed political leaders such as De Gaulle, who 'opposed Bretton Woods because the international monetary system was organized with the US dollar as the reserve asset', to challenge the existing financial order (Grabbe 1996: 19). Between 1959 and 1969, US balance of payments deficits ranged from a low of $1.6 billion in to a high of $6.1 billion.

12. Despite restrictions imposed by the IET, the Yankee market easily remained the largest and more popular foreign bond market from 1963 to 1974. The international status of the Yankee market was only solidified with the removal of IET restrictions in 1974.

13. From 1974 to 1978 Canadian entities and international organizations represented between 60 and 80 per cent of the overall market (Fisher 1979).

5.   Volcker and the dollar standard

In the previous chapter we saw how the Bretton Woods system influenced demand for Tier 1 and Tier 2 debt. This foremost integrated US and European markets, as the relaxation of currency restrictions after 1958 acted with the build-up of an unregulated pool of Eurodollars, themselves a product of US investment and defence spending abroad, to create new dollar-based funding opportunities. The period following the late 1970s similarly reveals how abstract risk influenced the evolution of the IBM, promoting transatlantic interconnectivities anchored around dollar denominated debt. This developed and reinforced patterns established in the immediate postwar period, further integrating US and European markets. Yet this period also fostered new connectivities, as previously existing markets were dramatically expanded and others formed. This meant that the significant changes which occurred in offshore dollar markets during the 1960s were drawn forward and interacted with new patterns of dependency that in one way or another linked global investors to US debt. Most important were changes in the US domestic-international market, where the foreign purchase of Treasury debt increased significantly, from about 1.7 per cent of GDP in the 1960s to 4.2 per cent in the 1970s; by the end of the 1990s foreign purchases exceeded $1 trillion annually, accounting for nearly 15 per cent of US GDP. That this occurred alongside the internationalization of US corporate and agency bonds, and the rapid development of both these markets, meant that foreign ownership of onshore US dollar bonds now extended well beyond the Treasury market. As the US domestic-international market expanded in this way, reinforcing its prominence, Asian markets and investors were increasingly drawn into the orbit of US risk power, albeit in ways that were very different from what occurred in Europe. Another major development occurred in the Yankee market, as European banks increasingly turned to this market to hedge their dollar holdings. This allowed the Yankee market to fend off foreign competition and underwrote its historic expansion following 1993.

Here again, US risk power appeared through political negotiation and compromise, even while class relations slightly altered its institutional articulation. As we will see, Nixon's decision to de-link from gold was not ultimately a matter of fundamental transformation. This led in fact to a gradual re-institutionalization of abstract risk based on the same construction of credibility. And, as was previously the case, this took form through new state managerial capacities, only this time the main focus was the class contradictions embroiled in the Keynesian compromise.

THE POLITICAL ECONOMY OF RISK REPRODUCTION

The breakdown of Bretton Woods in 1971, while it allowed new markets to quickly acquire importance, did not completely overturn existing structures or empower new logics, as Nixon's actions were seen to entail an adjustment of par values (Panitch and Gindin 2012). From 1971 to 1973, attention focused on how the currency values previously established could be updated to reflect shifts in the global economy. Even after the Smithsonian Accord failed in 1973, few predicted a radical shift in international monetary relations, though the collapse of Bretton Woods institutions sparked no shortage of scholarly debate about the decline of US hegemony.

Still, the de-institutionalization of risk impacted debt markets, especially as it came to be seen more clearly as reflecting deep contradictions in the US accumulation strategy. Following the Second World War, US economic strength depended on the combination of rapid domestic consumption and the extension of corporate power abroad. This in turn required a class settlement at home ensuring manageable wage costs, labour peace, as well as the expansion of welfare programmes (to predominately white, male workers) that deepened commodification through the provision of limited economic supports and helped legitimate exploitative practices. In this context, Keynesian demand policies, coupled with the union strategy of productivism that emerged from the Treaty of Detroit, whereby labour organizations adopted non-militant, 'responsible' strategies for a share of productivity growth, were critical in sustaining the US growth model (Panitch and Gindin 2012; Roberts 2002; Yates 1993). Therefore, as Japan and Europe recovered through the 1950s and 1960s, US corporate profitability was squeezed by intensified global competition on the one hand and high wage settlements and corporate taxes on the other. That the combination of stagnation and inflation this produced occurred amidst growing demands for labour control over the managerial process meant that the limits of national Keynesianism had been reached.

These symptoms of crisis deepened with the decade's progress, exacerbating US domestic inflation and shaking confidence in the future value of the dollar (Eichengreen 1996; Obstfeld 1985). Yet while foreign exchange markets showed increasing signs of strain, including a 30 per cent decline in the dollar against the Deutschmark, the eroding credibility of US debt can be easily overstated. In fact, the abandonment of financial controls in the 1970s reflected the growth of dollar centred global financial markets – inasmuch as international demand outstripped the limits imposed by the dollar–gold link – and was thus something apart from the erosion of US financial hegemony

(Gowan 1999). What is clear is that as much as Western governments sought to adjust parity standards to maintain economic competitiveness, they had little interest upsetting US financial leadership, or rolling back the financial channels developed alongside international demand for US debt. This was especially true in Europe, where financial markets had already by this time internalized dollar-based investment strategies and were themselves increasingly beholden to US debt markets, leaving 'little room for maneuver' (Hudson 2003: 353).

The narrowing of options imposed by the Bretton Woods system and the web of transnational linkages it established thus structured a certain set of outcomes for policy makers. This gave a very different texture to the negotiations that started in the early 1970s, which were less about reimaging a new monetary landscape and more about how previous rationalities could be extended. As a result, the dollar standard evolved much more haphazardly than its predecessor, and without the benefit of entirely new international institutions, let alone a single international conference through which specific directives were elucidated. Rather, key policies were developed over time and evolved through the reconstruction of existing institutions, namely the IMF. This above all meant that the new rules unfolded in the context of US financial power. And unless this power was explicitly drawn down through new international constraints, or the material basis of US hegemony itself came unhinged, any movement in the direction of liberalization would only deepen US debt markets and fortify the dollar's international position. As we will see, the new monetary order bore remarkable resemblance to the old, precisely because US officials took measures to address these two potential threats.

The first step towards a new monetary system occurred in 1973 when the 'US prevailed on the Japanese and European states to embrace a system of floating exchange rates' (Panitch and Gindin 2012: 145). This was important because it set up subsequent reforms through the G7 and IMF Committee of 20, which eventually established a new institutional framework for floating currency rates. The 1975 Rambouillet Summit 'ratified' a system of exchange rates based on market forces and called on the IMF to shift its mandate from supporting central bank par values to surveilling 'the commitment of individual states to policies designed to ensure market discipline' (Shafer et al. 1983: 1; Panitch and Gindin 2012: 155). This set the framework for the 1976 Jamaica Conference where the C-20 revised the IMF articles of confederation to 'formalize' a new system of floating exchange rates based around US financial control (Obstfeld 1985: 369). While the dollar was not explicitly mentioned in the new IMF articles, the clear intention was to 'give the American state distinct seigniorage advantages as the reward for being responsible for securing and validating confidence in the dollar' (Panitch and Gindin 2012: 145). Thus as the new dollar standard set the framework for monetary relations after the collapse of Bretton Woods, it re-institutionalized the special credibility of the

US dollar around a new set of financial rules aimed at maintaining and enhancing the dollar's reserve currency status (Gowan 1999). As McKinnon (1993: 29) describes, the new dollar standard prescribed three basic monetary rules for the global system, calling on countries to maintain 'smooth, short-term fluctuations on [the] dollar exchange rate without committing to a par value', remove capital and current account restrictions, and 'use the dollar as the intervention currency' and US Treasury bonds as 'official exchange reserves'.

However, such international standards in no way addressed the profit crisis in the US economy. Whatever room now existed to impose market discipline, the state had to find a way to confront working class power and suppress inflation expectations. The appointment of Paul Volcker as chair of the Federal Reserve Board in 1979 was an attempt to respond to these concerns. Opposing capital control programmes, Volcker targeted limits on the annual growth of money supply by aggressively pursuing a passive interest rate policy. Under Volcker's early reign, the Fed ignored interest levels and set stable inflation as the sole requisite for domestic rates.

This 'stabilization program' effectively 'overtightened domestic monetary policy', offsetting 'for inflows from the offshore', which had grown in size to about 10 per cent of the M-3 money supply, and led to skyrocketing short-term interest rates (Helleiner 1994: 136).[1] The effect was predictable: as the US economy entered a severe recession in 1981, unemployment rapidly expanded, eventually exceeding 10 per cent. Volcker's policies also created dramatic short-term interest rate differentials in public debt markets and increased the real return on Treasury issues. As they did so, global investors flocked to US markets and stockpiled US public and private debt. Yet the important point to see is that this was itself underpinned by shifting class and institutional relations. The Volcker shock amounted to a ruthless and historic attack on American workers (Aquanno 2008; Harvey 2005). This, along with the punitive, market-enhancing reforms pushed by the Reagan administration, and the ongoing globalization of production, which financial markets were key in facilitating, directly undermined workplace militancy, union rights, and working class power. In turn it strengthened the material basis of the US economy, and stabilized the dollar against inflationary depreciation (Harvey 2005; Streeck 2014).

At the same time, such policy innovations expressed and reinforced shifts in the Fed's institutional capacity. Volcker's strategy in fact developed through a long process of institutional learning that started as early as the 1970 Penn Central crisis, in which the Fed initially imposed monetary restraint but later capitulated as market conditions deteriorated (Panitch and Gindin 2012; Aquanno 2015; 2014; Krippner 2007). Moreover, his commitment to disciplining inflation expectations and eventual victory greatly enhanced the Fed's political autonomy, giving rise to a new era of central bank independence. This marked a significant reversal from the 1970s, where the tendency had been to limit the Fed's political insulation – Nixon's close relationship to Arthur Burns as well as the 1977 Federal Reserve Reform Act, which enhanced congressional oversight, must be situated in this context.

If international negotiation was a key prerequisite, it was these material and state institutional transformations that ultimately underpinned the new monetary system: under conditions of heightened unemployment and monetary policy control over wage demands, economic gains could float to the top of the income scale, restoring wage differentials and corporate probability, and solidifying the material base of US financial power (Harvey 2005). This is the sense in which Panitch and Gindin (2012: 134) conclude: 'the continuing predominance of the dollar in the new era of flexible exchange rates could not have been realized without the increased role played by the American state, and its restructuring to accommodate this role.'

INTERNATIONAL BONDS IN THE POST-VOLCKER PERIOD: GENERAL TRENDS

If the 1970s crisis did not undermine US risk power, it severely impacted bond markets, and shaped international conditions. For starters, as the constraints imposed by the Bretton Woods system were removed, the US became a persistent net borrower to the rest of the world, a trend which began in the early 1980s and, with the exception of two quarters during the 1991 recession, has continued ever since (Figure 5.1). Above all, this supported the development of the US domestic-international market, as foreign borrowing primarily occurred through the issuance of US Treasury bonds, agency debt, and corporate debt. With the Yankee market continuing to stagnate through the 1980s, and US net borrowing expanding, shifts within the US domestic-international market – themselves influenced by the investment strategies pursued by European and Asian investors and central banks – greatly shaped future trends.

Inflation was another key force. As rates reached over 20 per cent after Carter's 1978 stimulus package, issuers lined up to offer new debt, attracted by low or negative real rates of interest, even as the same conditions depressed demand for debt securities.[2] This changed in the 1980s as rates of inflation in industrial countries dramatically declined (White 2008). If the Volcker shock was a key part of this, so too was the shift to inflation targeting, in which central banks assumed responsibility for wage inflation through pre-emptive interest rate adjustments targeting the so-called non-accelerating inflation rate of unemployment. Inflation targeting, in fact, greatly extended the insecurity imposed by the Volcker shock, ensuring a degree of permanent class discipline. With inflation anchored in this way, conditions in international debt markets began to stabilize, but not before the break-down of key funding channels propelled far-reaching transformations.[3]

Prior to the Volcker shock, the syndicate bank loan market diverted capital from the Eurobond market – it provided an alternative source of funding whereby borrowers raised capital through loans provided by a syndicate of banking institutions. Banks financed these loans by borrowing short term, offsetting interest rate risk by linking payments to prevailing rates (Clark 2002: 463). That this market played a key role financing important substitution industrialization through the 1960s and 1970s, meant it was particularly vulnerable when Volcker sent short-term rates skyrocketing. In response, banks exercised the floating rate option and adjusted interest rates on syndicated loans to meet the new costs of borrowing, massively increasing loan obligations for developing countries in the Global South, who were also contending with a slump in global commodity prices. By 1982 'approximately 40 nations were in arrears in their interest payments and a year later 27 nations – including the four major Latin American countries of Mexico, Brazil, Venezuela and Argentina – were in negotiations to restructure their existing loans' (FDIC 1997: 206).

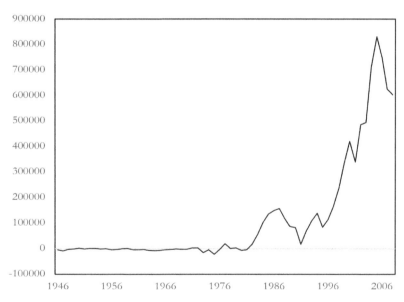

Source: Federal Reserve, FRED.

Figure 5.1   ROW net lending to the US market, 1948–2008 (USD billion)

The third world (or LDC: lesser developed country) debt crisis thus threat-ened the solvency of major US and European banks and provoked a long process debt rescheduling, which itself led to punishing structural adjustment programmes. But this was by no means the extent of its impact on financial markets. One additional effect was that it severely depressed the syndicated Eurocurrency loan market.[4] After expanding rapidly in the 1970s, this market slowed considerably in the 1980s, increasing by only $37 billion – and much of this growth 'was due to refinancing arrangements associated with the rescheduling of outstanding loans' (Clark 2002: 453, 463). The Eurocurrency loan market recovered in the 1990s, but not before credit financing became increasingly disintermediated, leading to what O'Brien has called 'the secu-ritization decade' (O'Brien 1992: 40). These dynamics facilitated a wave of expansion in the Eurobond market, with issues increasing from approximately $18.8 billion in 1980 to over $210 billion by the end of the decade. In fact, from 1982 to 1990, this market grew from less than half to more than double the size of the Eurocurrency loan market.[5] As we will see, this was part of a wider shift from bank credit to bond credit that is still taking place, which has itself enormously altered financial dynamics, not least by shaping the nature of state financial management and opening new opportunities for the internation-alization of US dollar debt.

With the decline of the syndicate market and continued build-up of offshore dollars, due to US current account deficits, Eurodollar bonds exploded, to the extent that this segment actually maintained much of the market share it gained in the 1960s. By 1986, for example, dollar denominated bonds as a total of international placements stood at 55 per cent (Das 1993: 9). In 1987, following the managed decline of the dollar orchestrated by the Plaza Accord, dollar denominated bonds fell to 37 per cent, while international bonds denom-inated in yen climbed from 10 per cent in 1986 to 15 per cent in 1987 (ibid.: 9).[6] However, as the dollar gained strength near the end of the decade, dollar denominated bonds regained their 50 per cent share and growth in the Euro and foreign bond market 'recovered to their former peak level activity' (ibid.: 11). These same trends continued following the 1980s, even as Eurobond place-ments grew rapidly, from $180 billion in 1990 to $735 billion in 1997 (OECD 1992; 1994; 1998a). By the end of the decade, new issuance reached $1.4 tril-lion.[7] Moreover, it was the dollar segment of this market, which accounted for 46 per cent of all placements, that continued to lead the way (O'Malley 2015: 168). This reflected how the growth of the market spun outward from its base in US dollar bonds, and how financial liberalization and innovation served to deepen rather than dilute US risk power, providing new opportunities for investors to access dollar bonds.

Such tendencies were also particularly evident with the development of so-called global bonds in 1989.[8] Though typically subject to more regulations than Eurobonds, global bonds thrived through the 1990s, growing in lock step with other segments of the international market (Figure 5.2). Already by the end of the decade the global bond market had become a major financing hub, with outstanding placements topping $1.6 trillion (Amira and Handorf 2004: 80–81). One reason for this growth is that global bonds reduced the financing costs associated with multiple placements, allowing firms and international organizations access to large pools of capital (Bedell 2001: 39). From 1989 to 1998 the average issue size was $670 million, and between 1999 and 2000 it jumped to nearly $1 billion (Amira and Handorf 2004: 80–81). Issuers were also attracted because non-standard placements, those supported by lower credit ratings and with longer maturities or additional embedded options, were frequently accepted (ibid.: 80).

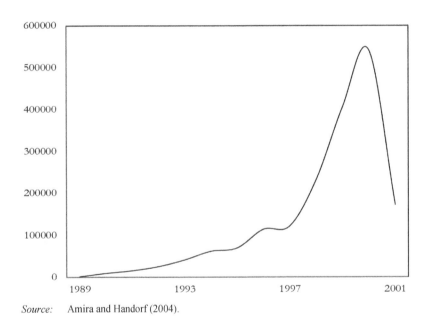

Source: Amira and Handorf (2004).

Figure 5.2   Global bonds issue volume, 1989–2001 (USD million)

Yet for all these benefits, the market operated as an extension of the Eurodollar bond market, its dynamics regulated by enhanced access to dollar denominated debt. As much as the offshore regulatory system liberalized markets and supported US risk power, it contained in-built tensions, namely since Eurodollar bonds could not be sold in the US market. This forced investors to trade lower levels of liquidity in European markets for access to offshore dollar placements. The global market overcame these challenges, albeit by simultaneously restricting access to large issuers. From the beginning, it principally served as an outlet for US dollar debt: from 1989 to 2001, 86 per cent of global bonds were denominated in dollars, accounting for nearly 90 per cent of the total capital raised (ibid.).[9] Thus if Eurodollar bonds had lost some of their market share by the early 2000s, this was only because investors had migrated to the global market. This reflected a new institutional intermeshing of US risk power and meant that the offshore market continued to be overwhelmingly dollar based.

If the offshore market remained a key component of the IBM, buoyed by the opening of new markets and provision of new issues, its development was in many respects overshadowed by the domestic-international market. This owed in small part to the rapid internationalization of German government securities, namely Bunds and Schatzes. German capital markets were an important source of internationalization in the 1960s and grew even more significantly in the 1980s.[10] As the most stable currency within the European Monetary System (EMS), the Deutschmark served as the anchor of the parity grid system, becoming the benchmark against which other currencies were measured. This asymmetry, as McKinnon (1993: 37) explains, meant that EMS countries intervened in foreign exchange markets to stabilize their rates against the Deutschmark, and were required to keep active exchange reserves in liquid interest-bearing German bonds. Subsequently, as the German government issued debt, global investors – particularly European central banks – paid whatever the cost (Goodhart 1995: 15). In 1987 debt obligations of the German government as a share of global reserve assets grew to 13.4 per cent, and by the late 1990s this figure had reached 16.4 per cent (New York University 2005).

More important were the changes occurring in the US market. Following 1971, with the risk of currency fluctuation now essentially privatized, foreign investors stockpiled US Treasury bonds: central banks used these as protection against currency devaluation, selling dollars in foreign exchange markets to support their domestic currency, and private investors increasingly used dollars for trade and investment purchases, given their perceived stability. At the same time, with the dollar no longer linked to gold, a major fiscal constraint was removed (Figure 5.1). Nixon's decision to abandon postwar par values in fact had immediate ramifications, as foreign purchases of Treasury securities as a percentage of US GDP more than doubled between 1970 and 1971, from 1.8 per cent to 4 per cent. Before this, growth was comparatively static, doubling only once from 1947 to 1970. Using the same metric, three additional expansions occurred after 1971: foreign ownership roughly doubled from 1972 to 1990; again from 1991 to 2007; and again from 2008 to 2019, reaching as high as 35 per cent of US GDP in 2014 (Table 5.1). While German placements became increasingly popular within the European community, this

Table 5.1   *Foreign holdings of US Treasury securities*

Period	Period increase in foreign holdings of US Treasury securities (as a percentage of US GDP)
1947–1970	72
1970–1971	114
1971–1990	108
1990–2007	99
2007–2019	92

Source: US Treasury, Treasury Bulletin; Federal Reserve, FRED.

had more to do with regional balance of payments disequilibrium – by contrast foreign demand for US domestic issues continued to have a much broader basis of support. Whether the expanded issuance of Treasury bonds came from military spending or massive tax cuts to upper class Americans, the dynamics of the federal deficit were not important for international investors, so long as the labour discipline imposed by the Volcker shock continued to guarantee the material, institutional and cultural basis of US financial power.

A second major change in the US domestic-international market occurred in 1984 when restrictions on the foreign sale of US corporate bonds were removed (Craven 1990: 34). These imposed a 30 per cent withholding tax on the payment of interest to foreigners, and effectively required that US corporations utilize foreign financing subsidiaries to access international capital (Grabbe 1996: 275). While this stimulated offshore investment banking and laid down crucial transatlantic financial linkages, connecting US and European markets, it also suppressed a key branch of the IBM. To be sure, the foreign purchase of US corporate bonds barely registered in 1980. Yet already by 1985 it had grown to $40 billion (Figure 5.3). After a temporary decline in the late 1980s, issue volume expanded every year through the 1990s and reached $704 billion in 2000. By 2002, foreign holdings passed $1 trillion, exceeding total foreign ownership of US Treasury debt. Though it later relinquished its top position, as the US states' crisis interventions again shifted the balance in favour of Treasury bonds, the historic growth of this market heralded a major change in the US onshore market towards private issues, serving as a clear demonstration that US risk power extended far beyond Tier 1 Treasury obligations, and in fact structured outcomes in private borrowing.

Crucially, the growth of this market was driven primarily by European investors. This reflected a number of factors: deep linkages between US and European capital, the earlier development of Eurodollar and Eurodollar bond markets, and the offshore placement of Yankee issues. In countries such as Germany, the UK, and Switzerland, liberalization deepened and extended the

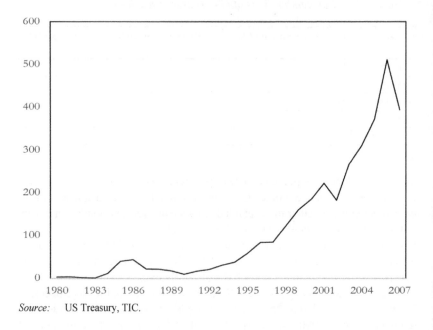

Source: US Treasury, TIC.

*Figure 5.3   Net foreign purchases of US corporate bonds, 1980–2007
(USD billion)*

transatlantic system and enriched portfolio diversification *inside* the dollar
market. By 1994 these three countries accounted for 22 per cent of foreign
holdings of long-term Treasury debt, but 89 per cent of US corporate debt,
with the UK alone accounting for nearly 60 per cent of foreign corporate
holdings. Moreover, while total holdings of Treasury bonds either increased
modestly or decreased from 1994 to 2007, foreign ownership of US corporate
debt skyrocketed, growing 1230 per cent in Switzerland, 1700 per cent in the
UK, and 2076 per cent in Germany. As we will see, strong European demand
for private issue dollar bonds, which contrasted with investment patterns in
Asia, whereby integration occurred principally through public investment,
underlay the expansion of US subprime debt and powerfully stretched the
market to its breaking point in 2008.

   About the time corporate markets were opening to foreign investment, US
agency debt was starting to have a great impact. This third major change in
the domestic-international market took shape after Fannie Mae 'essentially
invented the modern MBS market in 1981' (Schwartz 2009b: 95; see Table
5.2). This allowed Freddie Mac and Fannie Mae, which were chartered to

purchase mortgage debt from banks and thrifts to support lending and boost the market, to 'move mortgage loans off their books by selling those mortgages to the capital market'. At the same time, it accelerated demand for US home loans and provided a new way for investors to acquire US dollar debt (ibid.: 95). Moreover, because Freddie and Fannie were government sponsored entities (GSEs), chartered by Congress and closely linked to the US Treasury Department, their bonds, while neither entirely public nor private, were effectively backstopped by the US state. If not technically the case, regulators did not try hard to change such perceptions (Bernanke 2015: 231).

Yet even by these standards the popularity of agency debt was difficult to predict and could not have been completely foreseen: indeed while net annual foreign purchases more than quadrupled from 1981 to 1988, the major growth actually occurred between 1991 and 2006 when net foreign purchases increased from about $10 billion to nearly $300 billion, in no small part due to growing Chinese demand. Even though the agency market remained not insignificantly smaller than the corporate and Treasury bond markets in terms of foreign ownership (and in absolute terms), its growth was equally robust. In fact, from 2000 to 2007, the net foreign purchase of US agency and Treasury bonds were nearly identical. This all changed following 2008, as the US domestic-international market again converged around Treasury bonds, but not before agency bonds and the securitization of US mortgage debt dramatically altered financial conditions.

With these historic shifts in the US domestic-international market, and their impact on the IBM, expansion in the other international branch of the US onshore market, the Yankee market, was comparatively modest. This reflected how the Yankee market helped set the conditions for the internationalization of US debt in the early postwar period, but was itself often the victim of US risk power, given how liberalization and the growth of offshore dollars stimulated offshore borrowing. To be sure, gross issuance of US foreign bonds grew from $5.8 billion in 1978 to only $9.9 billion in 1990. The Swiss foreign bond market (CHF) – propped up by Swiss Bank Corporation, Union Bank and Credit Suisse – was well positioned to take advantage of this slowdown and challenge the Yankee market's international preeminence (University of Houston 2005).[11] In 1991 the CHF market temporarily eclipsed the Yankee market in terms of total issue volume, raising the equivalent of $20.2 billion in Swiss francs for foreign lenders (Table 5.3).

Still, these trends require broader framing, for they connect to specific organizational formations and market mechanisms. Whereas Swiss officials generally supported the CHF market, they took a very different track with offshore bonds. This was consolidated in 1963 through a 'Gentleman's Agreement' with major domestic banking interests that blocked the sale of Swiss franc Eurobonds and allowed regulators to control the offshore market

Table 5.2   Foreign holdings of bonds, domestic-international market
               (USD billion)

Year	Long-term Agency Debt	Long-term Corporate Debt	Long-term Treasury Debt
1994	107.2	275.5	463.5
2000	261.2	703.5	884
2005	790.6	1729	1598.7
2007	1304	2728	1964.9

Source: US Treasury, TIC.

Table 5.3   Foreign issues by market, 1991–1997 (USD billion)

	United States	Japan	Switzerland	Luxembourg	Other
1991	14.4	5.2	20.2	5.5	5.6
1992	23.2	7.4	18.1	5.5	3.4
1993	35.4	15.2	27.0	3.5	5.3
1994	15.0	11.2	20.0	11.0	3.0
1995	32.4	17.9	27.1	13.8	4.7
1996	40.5	35.5	25.9	8.4	9.6
1997	45.5	17.4	21.0	2.9	9.7

Source: OECD.

(Grabbe 1996: 281). The upshot was that international borrowers had to access
the Swiss foreign bond market to issue or acquire franc denominated bonds.
Moreover, when these bonds were issued in Switzerland, 'it [was] not necessarily the savings of Swiss citizens that are being borrowed ... but foreign
savers lending to foreign borrowers' (ibid.: 281). These regulatory patterns
were reinforced in the 1980s when Swiss authorities relaxed restrictions on
issue placements in the Swiss foreign bond market, but continued to restrict
Eurobond placements (ibid.: 281). For all intents and purposes, this meant that
the Swiss foreign bond functioned as an extension of the offshore Eurobond
market.

   Yet, if Swiss bonds played a much greater role in the foreign market,
whether as an extension of offshore issues or not, Yankee bonds attained a new
degree of popularity in the mid-1990s, and easily re-secured their hegemony.
Indeed, one of the most striking developments during this period was the
explosion in issuance volume by foreign corporations in the US market (Table
5.3; Figure 5.4). Even after dropping to $8.4 billion in 1994, net issuance of
foreign corporate bonds increased to $60 billion in 1995 and $67 billion in
1996. After dropping again in 1997, the market took off from 2003 to 2006,

hitting $258 billion in 2005.[12] This occurred as restrictions on the placement of Yankee bonds were further relaxed – particularly with the SEC's Rule 144A, which 'reduced the cost of meeting US disclosure standards' for large international firms – and as European banks increasingly turned to the market as a source of US dollars (Chaplinsky and Ramchand 2004: 1073). As these banks increasingly relied on the Yankee market to raise dollars, eventually using it for 20 per cent of their total bond issuance, they further linked the US offshore and onshore markets, creating a web of debt funding that stretched across the Atlantic (Montoriol-Garriga 2016). Despite higher regulatory standards in the US market, European banks used Yankee bonds to reduce their dollar funding costs, and perhaps also to hedge their dollar assets (Azahara and Gonzalez 2016). Thus while the Yankee market remained smaller in size than either the US-domestic international market or the Eurodollar bond market, it increasingly played an outsized role underwriting demand for US dollar debt.

Relating to this was a new priority given to substandard issues. One of the great ironies of liberalization was that as non-traditional countries began to solicit foreign capital, often with promises of higher return, investors turned to medium and lower grade sectors in the US foreign market, eager to gain higher spreads but not willing to entirely abandon risk standards. Whereas in 1988, 74 per cent of Yankee bond issues consisted of borrowers with an AA rating or better, in 1994, 60 per cent of total placement volume was comprised of issuers with an A rating or below (Merrill Lynch 1994). Geographically, metrics also changed, with volume as a percentage of total placements moving away from Canadian provinces and corporations and towards Asian, Latin American, and Eastern European borrowers (Merrill Lynch 1994). These shifts were supported by a new focus on foreign placements, which saw major investment banks preach the virtues of international diversification (Peagam 1992: 51). They also came about because investors were willing to forfeit higher rates of return in secondary markets for low grade placements in the US in order to gain the advantage of holding US dollar claims (Merrill Lynch 1994). As we will see, the international build-up of subprime mortgage bonds precisely reflected this bias for Tier 2 US debt.

ASIAN MARKETS: SAVINGS POOLS AND DOLLAR DEBT

As the dollar standard structured outcomes and centralized demand, the issue of financial integration once again came to the fore, only this time Asia took a large share of the attention. A key problem was that the surplus being produced here was bottled up by strict financial controls preventing the outward flow of capital. This limited the expansion of the IBM and greatly concerned US officials (Helleiner 1994: 152, 167). With Japan now a leading surplus

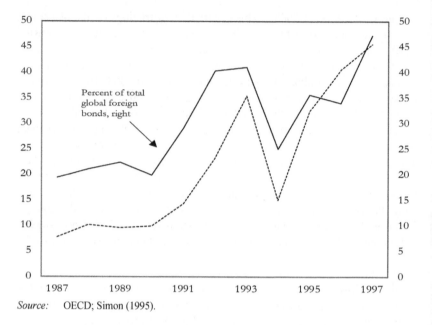

Source: OECD; Simon (1995).

Figure 5.4   *Gross issue and placement of foreign bonds in the US*
                 domestic market, 1987–1997 (USD billion)

country, its intricate web of restrictions were the main obstacle and most important target. Following the 1980 Foreign Exchange and Trade Control Law, which was viewed as a 'tentative' step towards liberalization, US regulators therefore pressured for more direct and far-reaching reform (Pigeoon 2000: 5). This led to the Yen–Dollar Agreement of 1983–1984, under which Japan expanded the Euroyen market (through the internationalization of the yen), and deregulated financial markets to treat foreign institutions more equitably (ibid.: 7). Not surprisingly, the crux of the agreement concerned the outward flow of domestic capital, rather than the inward flow of foreign capital. By contrast, as we have seen, the liberalization of European markets occurred along both fronts, and initially involved the latter, as Eurodollars, Yankee bonds, and Eurodollar bonds penetrated European financial markets in the early postwar period, even in some respects before currency restrictions were loosened in 1958. Though distinctions can be taken too far, this meant that *US risk power had very different institutional consequences in Japan than it did in Europe,* where firms issued, sold, and purchased US foreign and offshore debt (often through short-term dollar markets) and thereby deeply integrated their business practices around dollar bonds (Country Studies Series 2005).

As such opportunities remained limited, Japanese investors primarily participated in the IBM as savers. The annual net outflow of long-term Japanese capital increased from $10 billion in 1981 to $137 billion in 1987 (ibid.). Japan's accumulated holdings of foreign assets therefore grew from a net asset position of $11.5 billion in 1980 to $383 billion by 1991 (ibid.). In total, Japanese purchases of foreign securities (including stocks) grew from $4.2 billion in 1976 to $21 billion in 1980, and to $632 billion by 1991 (ibid.).

The impact of liberalization on yen denominated international bonds in the Samurai[13] and Euroyen market was thus less significant. Prior to the 1970s, Japan's financial system was 'designed ... to channel the ... savings of households through the banking system to the corporate sector for investment in expanding productive capacity' (Okuda and James 1990: 55). Cracks in this system appeared as early as 1970 when the Asian Development Bank issued the first Samurai bond. Yet this hardly consolidated new market-based tendencies, or dealt the *coup de grâce* to the old regime. The Ministry of Finance rather blocked any such changes by imposing strict eligibility requirements for issuing Samurai bonds, ensuring the market was fully captured and controlled by international institutions and foreign governments (Hoschka 2005: 13, 17). In fact, international firms were prevented from issuing bonds in the Japanese domestic market until 1979 (Grabbe 1996: 279). As a result, the Samurai market grew slowly from 1970 to 1980, raising a total of $7.2 billion.

When eligibility standards were relaxed in 1979 and again in 1984 and 1985, the market became a more efficient transmission belt for global capital. By 1987 total bond issues by non-Japanese residents in the Japanese domestic market reached Y631 billion ($4.7 billion), about 12 per cent of total foreign bond placements (Figure 5.5). By the end of the decade, the Samurai market was nearly as large as the Yankee market, raising Y1.2 trillion ($8.3 billion) for foreign issuers, approximately 20 per cent of all foreign bond capital globally. While the Samurai market would lose momentum in the 1990s, it remained an important source of internationalization, deepening convergence by diversifying market opportunities and opening financing channels.

The Euroyen market followed a similar trajectory, showing signs of life in the mid-1980s (Grabbe 1996: 279). By 1989 Eurobond issues denominated in yen climbed to a record $14.7 billion, making the Euroyen market one of the leading segments of the offshore market (Figure 5.6). Many issuers preferred the Euroyen to the Samurai market, since onshore issues faced burdensome procedural requirements and capital restrictions (Asami 2003: 4). However, while the Euroyen market continued to expand during the 1990s, temporarily becoming the second most important currency in the Eurobond market, with total issue volume at $65 billion in 1995, it remained subordinate to the off-

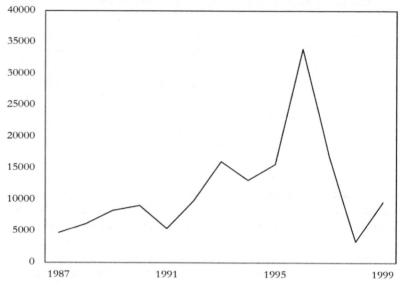

Note: Figure converted from 100 million Yen based on the average annual conversion rate
as published between the dollar and the Yen for the corresponding year.
Source: Japanese Ministry of Finance (2005).

Figure 5.5   *Bond issues by non-Japanese residents in the Japanese
                  domestic market, 1987–1999 (USD million)*

shore dollar market – like the Samurai market, it therefore attracted foreign
investment as part of a wider system that above all privileged US dollar debt
(OECD 1998a; 1998b).

   In fact, this restructuring and partial liberalization was deeply interconnected with changes in the US domestic-international market, and drove
forward investment processes that bolstered US risk power. Again, however,
Japanese investors turned more towards long-term US Treasury and agency
debt, unlike their European counterparts. Moreover, Japan's integration into
the US domestic-international market occurred mainly through central bank
asset holdings, as the Bank of Japan cycled massive current account surpluses,
accumulated in large part through persistent trade surpluses with the US,
back through the US market. Already by 1978 Japan was a major holder of
US long-term debt securities, and quite possibly the largest in the world. By
1984 it held about $26 billion in long-term debt securities, more than any
other reporting country, though considerably less that the $35 billion held
by the Middle Eastern oil exporting countries, including Saudi Arabia, Qatar
and the United Arab Emirates. Ten years later, Japan held more long-term

US Treasury bonds ($127 billion) than the next three countries combined, as well as about 35 per cent of US foreign agency debt, and was far and away the most important net lender in the IBM. Japan was also at this time the largest foreign holder of US corporate bonds, but its strategic focus on US agency and Treasury debt meant that European investors would easily take control of this market by the end of the decade.

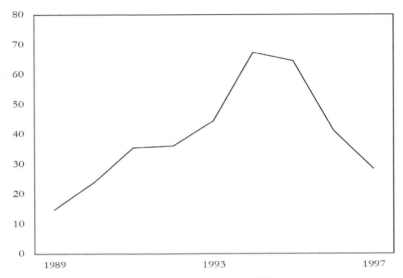

Note: Figures from 1989 to 1992 are converted from Ybillion using the average annual conversion rate as published between the dollar and the Yen for the corresponding year.
Source: OECD.

Figure 5.6   *Yen dominated Eurobond issues, 1989–1997 (USD billion)*

These patterns persisted in the lead up to the financial crisis. By 2007 Japanese investors, led by the Bank of Japan, owned 18 per cent of foreign agency bonds and 28 per cent of foreign Treasury bonds. Holdings of US corporate bonds were much smaller, only 4 per cent of total foreign placements, but nevertheless significant: such diversification was a key factor distinguishing Japanese and Chinese investment, as the latter held a miniscule portion of its overall US dollar portfolio in corporate bonds.

China's integration into the IBM nonetheless followed a similar trajectory, though it started much later and remained more burdened by restrictions limiting foreign ownership of onshore bonds (see Table 5.4). This meant that neither China's domestic-international market, nor its foreign market, played much of a role in the IBM prior to the subprime crisis. Indeed, China only removed restrictions on the placement of foreign bonds in 2005, allowing for the growth of the so-called Panda market. But if this was heralded as a key development, Chinese foreign bonds barely registered on international accounts. From 2005 to 2008 only three bonds were issued in the Panda market (Aglietta and Maarek 2007). This reflected how formal and informal rules, including stipulations that capital raised by Panda bonds be used in China, both limited liquidity and raised the cost of borrowing. The larger problem was that the entire onshore market remained inward looking and designed to serve public borrowing. While China's bond market developed rapidly following the Asian financial crisis, albeit from a relatively small base, most issues were placed by either governments or quasi-public policy banks, such as the China Development Bank and the Export-Import Bank of China, and government bonds were mostly held to maturity by domestic commercial banks (ibid.). This suppressed liquidity, pushed private borrowers to bank credit, and closed opportunities for foreign buyers. Even if the movement from bank credit has continued, many of these trends also characterized the post-crisis period (see Conclusion).

Similarly, restrictions stalled the development of offshore renminbi-denominated bonds. The Dim Sum market developed in 2007 to circumvent Chinese capital controls, as Hong Kong banks accumulated offshore RMB deposits to take advantage of the appreciation of the renminbi (against the dollar). While the post-crisis development of this market has been more successful, as Chinese officials have used this market as a part of a broader strategy to increase the reserve currency position of the renminbi, it too remains small by international comparison. In fact, though Dim Sum bonds are now issued in Europe and have extended beyond Hong Kong, the liberalization of Chinese capital markets since 2011 has above all spurred the growth of an offshore dollar bond market in China and Hong Kong.

With the Dim Sum and Panda markets effectively non-existent before 2008, and its domestic bond market 'basically closed to foreigners', China's participation in the IBM was distinctly one-sided: like Japan it integrated as a net lender and emphasized US domestic-international bonds, though this occurred almost exclusively through foreign official purchases and was targeted at US public and agency debt, in no small part because Chinese officials attempted to maintain the dollar peg established in 1994 (Fung et al. 2014: xii). Indeed, while China revalued the RMB in July 2005 and allowed a 'slow rate of upward crawl', current account surpluses created constant pressure for upward appreciation, particularly following 2000, requiring 'aggressive intervention in the foreign exchange market' (Roubini 2007: 71; McKinnon 2007). Subsequently by 2008 US corporate bonds accounted for only 2 per cent of the China US portfolio, and less than 1 per cent of total outstanding issues.

Table 5.4 *Foreign holdings of US Treasury and agency bonds, China and Japan, 2000–2008 (US billion)*

	Chinese Holdings of US Treasury Bonds	Chinese Holdings of US Agency Bonds	Japanese Holdings of US Treasury Bonds	Japanese Holdings of US Agency Bonds
2000	71.1	19.6	221.3	42.6
2004	189.2	114.9	552.1	99.9
2008	521.9	527.1	568.2	269.6

Source: US Treasury, TIC.

By contrast, China emerged as a major holder of US Treasury bonds in the 1990s. By 2000, it was already the second largest holder, behind Japan; and from 2000 to 2008, while this ranking remained unchanged, the gap between Chinese and Japanese foreign holdings, which was still massive in 2004, had almost entirely disappeared (Table 5.4). China's impact on the US agency market was even more significant: it overtook Japan as the largest holder of US agency debt in 2004, and in the four years leading up to the collapse of Lehman Brothers, absorbed nearly 50 per cent of all foreign placements. By 2008 China owned 24 per cent of foreign Treasury bonds, and 36 per cent of foreign agency bonds, and had overtaken Japan as the most important net lender in the IBM.

SUMMARY REMARKS

Following the collapse of par values in 1971 and the gradual liberalization of markets, the IBM expanded rapidly, propelled by new onshore and off-shore markets. This transformation of international placements, which took shape as the US financial position with the ROW turned decisively negative, marked one very significant change in the IBM. The diversification of the US onshore market and the growing reach of private issued US debt, especially in Europe, was another. Indeed, whereas the US Treasury market was the largest segment of the US domestic-international market at the end of the Bretton Woods period, and continued to expand rapidly in the post-Volcker period, it was increasingly displaced by foreign holdings of US corporate bonds. This occurred alongside the rapid expansion of US foreign bonds following the mid-1990s, as European banks came to use this market to raise dollars. A third shift occurred with the accumulation of large capital account surpluses in Japan and China and the partial opening of these markets. Again, this occurred on the foundations established in the postwar period, which above all tightly linked US and European markets. As Japan and China were pulled into the IBM, they quickly emerged as net lenders to the US economy, but remained strategically focused on public and agency debt. Whether or not this further pushed European countries towards corporate markets, it led to a different process of integration in Asia and Europe, whereby the former predominantly held public and quasi-public debt and the latter private US dollar debt. Crucially, both sides played a major role in the IBM. At the end of 2006, foreigners held an estimated $4.7 trillion in US bonds, about double foreign holdings of US equity: 32 per cent was held by Japanese and Chinese investors, primarily in foreign official accounts, another 30 per cent was held by a core group of countries in Europe, mainly as claims on US corporations. A good portion of the rest was held in offshore tax havens, and owned by US and European investors.

None of these changes marked the decline of US risk power. The Volcker shock in fact stabilized US financial hegemony by disciplining labour through a new low inflation regime. Although not the key argument this book makes, such changes appear to have reasserted the strength of American capitalism, rather than hiding unresolvable underlying conditions. Indeed, even as net US external debt increased $3.9 trillion between 2000 and 2006, the 'overall US net international investment position – the difference between all US assets and all US liabilities to the world – [didn't] deteriorate at the same pace' (Setser 2007: 66–7). This is because the rate of return on US investment abroad increased 'far more rapidly' than the rate of foreign investment in the US, due partly to demand for US dollar debt driving down interest payments (ibid.: 66–7). Most important is that while policy decisions helped inform the particular development of the IBM, this was itself shot through an underlying pattern of financial risk, expressive of the unique credibility of Tier 1 *and* Tier 2 debt, and grounded in shifts in US state capacity. Far from undermining US hegemony, this greatly added to it, creating new opportunities for investment and a comparative advantage in lending rates, which bolstered profitability. Paradoxically, the surge in mortgage lending and internationalization of sub-prime debt, from which the 2008 crisis appeared, was not separate from this, but a further important reflection of US financial power.

NOTES

1. Due to the Volcker shock the US prime rate reached a high of 21.5 per cent in 1980 (Tames 2019).
2. Inflation was, as Jane D'Arista (1994: 93) notes, 'the dominant influence on financial markets and the [US] economy in the 1970's': rising rates led to negative real rates of interest and discouraged long-term investment by banks, capital formation and subsequently new issues placement in stocks and bonds.
3. The growth of international bonds during this period occurred as major European and Asian economies, led by the French, Japanese and Italian governments, took steps to loosen issuance restrictions on international placements. In France and Italy, attempts were made to grow Euro-lira, Euro-franc, and foreign issu-

ance activity by overhauling tax restrictions and limits on placement activity (Mailander 1997: 362). Japan expanded previous initiatives by extending foreign access to yen-denominated bonds (ibid.: 362). While the impact of these measures on the Samurai and Euroyen markets is difficult to measure, given the deflationary impacts of the Asian financial crisis in the late 1990s, these policies further removed important limitations on the growth of yen-denominated bonds in both markets.

4. Syndicated Eurocurrency loans are underwritten by large international banks and are typically provided in Eurodollars.

5. According to Clark (2002: 453), the 'real development of the Eurobond market came after 1982 when the debt crisis shut down the growth of the syndicated Euro loan'.

6. In the same period, owing in part to currency instability, the Euro and foreign bond market contracted subtly and net annual foreign purchases of US corporate and public Treasury securities declined from highs in the mid-1980s.

7. Comparing the US domestic-international and Eurobond markets in this way is problematic, as the latter is a truly global funding source, attracting borrowers and lenders from around the world, including US firms. By contrast, the former excludes US domestic borrowers by definition, and issues are isolated to one market. The problem of comparison became even more pronounced with the development of the euro in 1999, since this effectively merged certain European foreign bond markets into the offshore market. That the US domestic-international market remained competitive in this context, and a major source of financial globalization, speaks to its historic growth and how the internationalization of the US domestic market underpinned global financial connectivity.

8. Global bonds are offshore securities simultaneously issued in different international markets by a broad syndicate of investment banks and sold both inside and outside the country of denomination (Amira and Handorf 2004: 80).

9. Euro-denominated debt accounted for the second highest total with only 3.5 per cent of the market share (Amira and Handorf 2004).

10. In the face of US resistance, and to revitalize interest in European (economic) unification, the membership of the EEC shifted attention to a regional grouping and choreographed the European Monetary System in 1979 (Grabbe 1996: 37). The EMS was designed to create a broader and more coordinated system of capital stability than the European currency snake (which the EEC implemented following the Smithsonian Agreement). The EMS required countries to stabilize currency values within a 2.25 per cent band (6 per cent for Italy and later the United Kingdom) of a declared central parity, the European Currency Unit (comprised of a basket of EMS currencies), and to practise coordinated intervention when currency values threatened to escape their bilateral threshold (McKinnon 1993: 36). For some countries more than others, stability requirements were achieved with the aid of capital controls programmes: the French and Italian states took steps to protect the franc and lira by keeping residents from selling their own currencies (Kenen 1995: 183). These controls co-existed with a myriad of financial regulations which extended beyond and pre-existed the EMS, making for a relatively controlled European financial climate in the 1970s and through most of the 1980s.

11. These drew foreign issuers to the Swiss market and were involved in all major transactions, as foreign international banks could 'not lead-manage, co-manage or underwrite issues by foreign borrowers except through subsidiaries in Switzerland' (University of Houston 2005).

12. This information is drawn from the Federal Reserve Z.1 financial accounts, which, among other things, measures net issuance of US corporate bonds by ROW issuers. The information in this account is different from that provided by either the Treasury Department or the OECD and includes US 144A issues. Calculations of the size of the Yankee market use this accounting.
13. The Samurai market is Japan's foreign bond market.

6. Bonding global markets

US risk power did not merely entail deeper markets and the internationalization of dollar denominated bonds. It entailed the restructuring and reorientation of global financial markets and the empowerment of new state logics and capacities, all of which entrenched a certain form of US economic hegemony. Two points are especially important. First, US risk power altered institutional trajectories: the credibility of US debt acted not just through but *on* institutional settlements, forging in the process a nexus of financial control linking global investors to US denominated bonds. This took place as international demand configured and reinforced financial circuits binding US and European markets. These same circuits were at the very centre of the subprime crisis. Second, state institutional formations shaped the international monetary system itself, influencing the contours of its specific reproduction. This can be seen especially with regard to the political management of US risk power as regulators continuously opened new possibilities by containing financial distress and utilizing crisis conditions to extend internationalization.

This chapter and the next (Chapter 7) turn to these points, with specific focus on the institutional mutations relevant to the subprime crisis. This chapter shows that US risk power set down the conditions for a transatlantic hub-and-spoke financial system based around Wall Street. The next chapter looks at the mechanisms of financial management sustaining the credibility of US debt and the growth of dollar bond markets.

BOND MARKETS AND PATH DEPENDENCY

While it receives much less attention, the bond market, including outstanding financial and non-financial bonds and public debt securities, is approximately 35 per cent larger than the global equity market (sifma 2019).[1] Given the remarkable expansion of financial derivatives following the 1980s, the global over-the-counter (OTC) derivatives market is now much larger – the BIS estimates the notional amount of OTC derivatives at approximately $540 trillion. Yet it is important that this market hardly existed in the 1960s and 1970s when the institutional foundations of the contemporary financial system were being established and set forth. During this period of foundational development, bond markets were far and away the most important segment of the financial system, eclipsing all other markets in both size and depth. It is in this respect that we can place special emphasis on the growth of international bonds in shaping the strategic direction of Wall Street and European firms as well as the priorities of financial regulators.

We also need to consider the stability and durability of institutional formations. The concept of path dependency argues that 'small contingent changes at the beginning of a path can have large and long-term consequences' and that 'increasing returns to political and social institutions explain actors' reticence about changing those institutions' (Schwartz n.d.: 4). Even relatively minor events occurring at critical junctures can 'have a profound influence on subsequent events and patterns of change' because increasing returns 'crowd out all alternatives to the status quo ... and provide a durable mechanism locking actors into a particular, contingently derived path' (Pierson 2000: 251; Schwartz n.d.: 5).[2]

It goes without saying that this concept is severely flawed – institutional rationalities and forms of organization are in fact always relatively open and contingent. This is the result not only of capitalist contradictions, but the subjectivity and creativity of human agents. Institutions are sticky in this sense because underlying logics and pressures do not immediately transform them. Yet as institutional change occurs due to struggle between human agents commanding different institutional resources, and as this resource mix is itself laced together with deeper nodes of power, organizational formations are not easily altered and therefore often sediment and routinize certain actions.[3] It is important that this permits us some flexibility to focus on the critical junctures which lay down new trajectories, and the institutional learning processes that occur within periods of incremental development.

MARKETS AND FIRMS

The institutional consequences of US risk power are obviously varied and impossible to fully quantify. However, a few stand out and deserve special consideration, for the simple reason that they helped alter financial practices and were at the heart of structural changes that fortified key dependencies. Most importantly, US leadership in the IBM nurtured the development of a transatlantic system of financial intermediation centred on Wall Street. This is because the international issuance of debt securities in the foreign, domestic-international, and offshore markets often privileged US merchant banks, as well as the investment divisions of US commercial banks, and encouraged the cross-penetration of US and European firms and markets.

For instance, the Yankee market dramatically boosted underwriting opportunities inside the US, and accelerated the growth of key Wall Street firms.[4] This occurred due to SEC regulations requiring that domestic bonds be issued by investment banks or lead managers operating and registered in the US market. As foreign investment banks were excluded in this way, and could only access the market by distributing Yankee placements internationally for US lead managers or by setting up foreign offices in the US domestic market, US investment firms initially 'earned most of the new issue fees' on Yankee issues. Subsequently, firms such as Kuhn Loeb, First Boston, Lazard Freres and Morgan Stanley were the major beneficiaries of the direction taken by this market (O'Malley 2015: 14).

Yankee bonds also played a critical role integrating US and European firms through the early postwar period, since many issues could not be fully absorbed by the US market, due partly to restrictions preventing institutional investors from buying foreign bonds (ibid.: 14). As a result, US underwriters regularly turned to European firms to distribute their foreign bonds in the European market. As noted in Chapter 4, Yankee issues were attractive in Europe because they were frequently issued by well-known European borrowers. One consequence was that European financial institutions came to serve as intermediaries for the sale of US denominated debt in Europe. This helped set the institutional basis for Europe's entry into the US subprime market in 2003. Another consequence was the migration of financial firms across the Atlantic. As European firms toiled under their American counterparts in the investment syndicates responsible for the origination and distribution of Yankee bonds, they searched for ways to increase their fees. Gradually, this led them into the US market to handle the 'entire new issue process themselves' (ibid.: 15). It also stimulated the development of secondary trading markets in Yankee placements inside Europe. Again, this was critical in binding European investors to dollar bonds and in teaching European firms how to manage and profit from US originated debt obligations. Moreover, the development of the Yankee market inside Europe encouraged US firms to 're-establish an overseas presence' in Europe (ibid.: 15). This came to organize the path of US financial expansion, setting the European market as a critical distribution channel for US denominated debt.

The Eurodollar bond market reinforced these institutional patterns. Recall that Eurobonds are issued in US dollars but underwritten in multiple non-US markets to non-US residents. Despite this, US banks were at the centre of the market's evolution, especially its early evolution. This is because New Deal restrictions permitted commercial banks to underwrite foreign securities by setting up offshore syndicates, and at the same time created a 'restrictive ... regulatory regime inside the US market' (Green 2016: 432; Burn 1999; 2006). To grow their operations and maintain a foothold in the underwriting business, and also to take advantage of the growing Eurodollar market, large US banks established subsidiaries inside Europe, particularly in the City of London, to issue and trade in the Eurodollar bond market.

Consequently, the growth of the offshore bond and dollar market occurred alongside the internationalization of American finance. As Burn (2006: 138–9) shows, the expansion of Eurodollar activity, which took place with the development of the Eurodollar bond market in 1963, 'encouraged the belated arrival in London of American banks eager to conduct Eurobusiness'. As US banks proceeded to London 'en masse' through the 1960s, they easily 'captured the Eurodollar market' from British overseas and Commonwealth banks (Green 2016: 434). By the mid-1970s '58 US bank branches has been established in the City' and by the early 1980s four of the top five lead managers in the Eurobond market were American domiciled international banks (Rattner 1982). Apart from their size and sophistication, US syndicates captured such a large share of the market because issuing organizations tended to select lead underwriters based on the underlying currency of the bond (Balder et al. 1991).

This migration of US financial institutions proved very important to European firms as well, given how they were also actively involved in the investment syndicates bringing these issues to market, and benefited from the subsequent deepening of the Eurodollar market. European investment banks were often turned to in order to distribute offshore issues, given their social basis inside Europe. This had the impact of linking the European issuers of Eurodollar bonds to the European banks responsible for this distribution, under the direction of US lead managers. More broadly, this intermeshed US and European funding markets in a way that encouraged financial innovation and the far greater diffusion of transatlantic capital flows: indeed 'as more American banks decamped to London, their role in funnelling funds to their US head offices led to an increasing interactivity of interest rates on each side of the Atlantic' (Green 2016: 436). This relationship between the Eurodollar Rate and the Federal Funds Rate 'integrated the US Eurodollar and European markets much more tightly' and 'created a form of *hub and spokes* relationship' whereby European capital markets were exposed to movements in US interest rates (ibid.: 438, my emphasis). From this point on, European firms were ever more pulled into US financial markets, even if they only practised in Europe. At the same time, the open space afforded by the offshore market and lack of regulation stimulated wide ranging experimentation, accelerating and altering the growth of US and European firms (Burn 1999; 2006; Green 2016).

The 'novel institutional forms of hybrid Anglo-America financial development' established through the offshore market following the 1960s were then accelerated by the US Treasury bond market (ibid.: 425). The development of this market occurred in part through the US primary dealer system, which was established in 1960 to assist in the implementation of US monetary policy. Primary dealers are banks and broker dealers that have been approved by the Federal Reserve to deal directly in US government bonds. These firms are required to bid competitively on every Treasury auction and to assist in monetary policy implementation through the secondary market by acting as counterparties to the New York Federal Reserve, as either buyers or sellers of US government debt. From the 1960s to the mid-1980s the Federal Reserve restricted the primary dealer market to US domiciled firms. This meant that US financial firms were initially at the very centre of the domestic-international market and that the foreign sale of US Treasury bonds occurred mostly through US institutions.

After 1985, the New York Federal Reserve Bank increasingly accepted foreign primary dealer applications, first by allowing US banks acquired by non-US holding companies to maintain their primary dealer status, and then by allowing foreign parent companies with US subsidiaries to act directly as primary dealers. In the 50 years between 1960 and 2010 the percentage of US domiciled primary dealers therefore fell from 100 to 35 (Figure 6.1). What this entailed above all was the expanded entry of European firms into the US Treasury market: of the 49 internationally domiciled primary dealer applications approved by the New York Federal Reserve between 1990 and 2017, 62 per cent were from European banks, 25 per cent were from Canadian firms and just 14 per cent were from Asian (primarily Japanese) firms (see Figure 6.2). These new connections supported a slightly different hub-and-spoke relationship, with US Treasury bonds operating at the centre and non-US firms increasingly serving as the main nodes of distribution. Critically, this meant that foreign firms were increasingly responsible not only for the international sale of US Treasury bonds but their placement in the US domestic market as well. Moreover, it meant that European firms had regular access to US Treasury bonds and a steady volume of dollar liquidity. With expanding availability of offshore Eurodollars, which was not altogether separate, this cleared the way for deeper involvement in dollar bond markets, and increased the magnitude and pace of activity. In fact, as these firms raised capital in dollar money markets to fund their purchase of Treasury debt, and sold Treasury bonds to foreign buyers, they were utilizing the exact channels that destabilized the US MBS market in 2008.

Therefore as US risk power shaped market outcomes through a common sense approach to investment, at a deeper level it set up new institutional tendencies and orders of operation. This ignited a self-reinforcing cycle of market integration, fostering a transatlantic financial system based around dollar denominated debt. Within this system US and European firms migrated across the Atlantic and established funding channels that enabled further access to US dollar markets, and increasingly synchronized the European financial system around US markets, in a hub-and-spoke relationship. This helped turn Wall Street into a global financial entrepôt, and influenced the process of US financialization. If we consider the political ramifications of these shifting relations

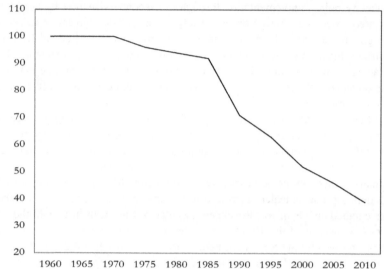

Note: Firms are domiciled in accordance with the domestic origin of their holding company
or operating organization.
Source: Federal Reserve.

*Figure 6.1   US domiciled primary dealer banks as a percentage of total
US primary dealers, 1960–2010*

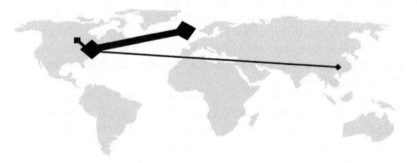

Note: The line width reflects successful primary dealer bids, as a percentage of total
successful foreign bids.
Source: Federal Reserve.

*Figure 6.2   Market integration and US Treasury bonds: foreign
domiciled US primary dealers, 1990–2017*

and their impact on key branches of the US state, the point can be stretched even further.

European Interbank Funding Markets

There is also a nodal relationship between the IBM and the international money market, particularly the Eurodollar market. The money market is a combination of different short-term funding markets, namely the commercial paper market, the repo market, the Eurodollar market, and short-term public debt markets. It links cash pools from insurance firms, pension funds and commercial banks with borrowers, such as governments, hedge funds, corporations, and broker-dealers.[5] As a result, the money market serves as a key funding centre, providing access to the short-term capital required for long-term investments. The size and depth of the market is influenced on the supply side by the pool of cash held by institutional investors looking for safe, liquid return, and on the demand side by the availability of attractive long-term assets. The latter is often overlooked, but the relationship is critical and straightforward: without a long-position opportunity satisfactory to risk adverse investors, firms lack the incentive to raise short-term funds and expand leverage.

It is primarily in this regard that the capital pumped into dollar bonds, through offshore markets, shaped the Eurodollar market and its connection to European financial firms. Recall that Eurodollars are the largest component of the broader Eurocurrency market which consists of 'bank deposits located in jurisdictions outside that of the currency of denomination' (Savona and Sutija 1985: 1). The vast majority of Eurodollars are time deposits or certificates of deposit; for receiving banks they represent cash holdings exchanged for fixed maturity interest-bearing assets that can either be used to fund dollar obligations or further lent out to financial or non-financial institutions (Goodfriend 1981; 1998). Because the 'most common Eurodollar transactions are loans between and among different banks', the Eurodollar market functions as an interbank market that collects and distributes short-term dollar deposits outside the US domestic market (Fowler 2014: 835; Goodfriend 1998).

As we saw in Chapter 4, the Eurodollar bond market developed from wholesale currency markets where banks could raise dollars, cover dollar shortfalls, and trade dollar surpluses. However, the relation was not altogether one-sided. The Eurodollar bond market also fed into offshore currency holdings, and stimulated issuance in the Eurodollar market. In this respect, the position of Eurodollar bonds in the offshore market registered in the dollar composition of the Eurocurrency market, where Eurodollars have consistently represented about 60 to 70 per cent of the total market (Goodfriend 1981: 13; 1998: 49).

It is important not to overstate this connection. As 'an integral segment of the total market for dollar credit', the Eurodollar market served a much broader purpose than Eurodollar bond funding (Savona and Sutija 1985: 6). Yet as the Eurobond market emerged as one of the most important capital markets globally, it brought European financial institutions deeper inside the European interbank market, while at the same time expanding the depth of the market and making it even more attractive as a funding source. This synergy was captured very early on by the Bank of International Settlements: 'That the Eurodollar market and the Eurobond market should grow together is no coincidence ... The ... banks that underwrite these bond issues need to maintain a supply of dollars' (as quoted in Walmsley 1991: 196).

As the European money market developed in this way, pushed forward by the Eurobond market and underlying patterns of risk, it both encouraged and enabled the purchase of dollar assets outside the US. Indeed, wholesale access to dollars made it easier and less risky to trade dollar obligations, and the demand for dollars created short-term funding opportunities for those firms with surplus holdings. Moreover, the connection between Eurodollars and Eurodollar bonds meant that European firms were always drawn into the international money market as they participated in the IBM. Lacking an onshore deposit base of dollars, European firms – looking to hold, distribute, or underwrite US dollar bonds in their domestic market – had to develop the capacity to fund their positions through the wholesale channels operating as short-term dollar markets. From this base of institutional familiarity and learning, built up through the development of the offshore market, European firms utilized international money markets to stockpile US subprime mortgages, as new investment opportunities opened through the 1990s and early 2000s. The flipside was that the European financial system became increasingly vulnerable to a seizure of dollar liquidity. As such forms of interconnectivity deepened, dollar funding channels became ever more vital, not just to the firms trading US debt, but to the major players in the wholesale funding system.

DERIVATIVES AND INTERNATIONAL BONDS

US risk power also opened new space for financial engineering and shaped the internality of derivatives markets, though the connection here is less straightforward. It is crucial to recognize that Nixon's decision to abandon the gold link reflected a certain degree of confidence that balance of payments deficits could be funded through the IBM (Casey 1973; Gowan 1999; Hudson 2003). To some degree, US officials believed that a freer international currency model allowed the US to 'maintain and strengthen [its] ability to raise capital throughout the world' and that a growth model highly dependent on the 'export of securities' could achieve some form of non-contradictory payment equilibrium (Casey 1973). In this sense, the movement away from gold, which began in August 1971 and ended in March 1973 with the collapse of the Smithsonian

Agreement, reflected underlying trends in the IBM and the circulation of capital to US markets.

This is important because the disintegration of par values opened space for a 'new financial order' based on futures markets in foreign exchange, in which 'speculators were a necessary component' (Melamed 2003: 59). As firms broadened their horizons, and production and consumption networks globalized, new forms of volatility emerged. These 'risks produced by connectivity', themselves rooted in the complex interplay between markets, jeopardized the broader system of accumulation and thus created strong pressure for new forms of risk management (Lipuma and Lee 2004: 45). But this is only part of the story. The Bretton Woods system not only linked the dollar to gold, it structured global currency relations – the decision to delink from gold not only privatized currency risk, it undermined the very basic reference points used to construct and contest currency values. In the new environment market actors were forced to think in relational terms, and to bear the risk of currency fluctuations independently (Nesvetailova 2007; Eatwell and Taylor 2000; Strange 1997). The European monetary snake helped to re-calibrate national currencies, but a truly international understanding of the relationship between national currencies remained. It was only in this context that traders from the Chicago Mercantile Exchange formed the International Money Market and started exploring distinct and untapped areas in financial engineering (Melamed 2003).

At the same time, the credibility of dollar bonds influenced the decision to ease capital controls, and expanded the range of freedoms firms had to explore innovative change. Very soon after par values collapsed, officials acknowledged that the growth curve in bond markets was indissociable from liberalization, and that reform was a precondition for the deployment of financial power. This was at least the key message coming from the Department of State. In 1973, Undersecretary for Economic Affairs William Casey (1973) concluded that the magnitude of capital in international financial markets 'is at least largely attributable to US measures' and that any attempt to reverse financial imbalances requires removing the protective controls originally put in place in the 1960s and '[strengthening] America's role in world capital markets.' Not soon after, Ford scrapped the Commodity Exchange Act and passed the Commodities Futures Trading Commission Act, authorizing the continuation of advanced forms of derivatives trading and transferring jurisdiction over the trading of commodity futures from the Department of Agriculture to the CFTC, a newly created independent five-member supervisory committee. Most importantly, in creating a relatively strong system of federal oversight, the bill legitimated US derivatives markets and created space for the development of forward and futures markets in short- and long-term US government debt. The establishment of open futures contracts on Treasury bills (1975) and bonds (1977), as Melamed (2003: 108) argues, would have been 'impossible to implement' without a 'federal stamp of approval'.

If the CFTC promoted risk management in this way, it also established critical market efficiencies, and pushed US firms deeper into the practice of financial engineering. Despite worries from within the Treasury Department that financial futures could 'prove harmful', these fuelled public issues and became a powerful mechanism of market development (ibid.: 127). Such concerns about the impact of derivative flows were addressed by a 1982 report commissioned by the Federal Reserve titled *A Study of the Effects on the Economy of Trading in Futures and Options*. The report concludes: 'it appears that financial futures and options markets have, if anything, generally increased cash market liquidity, perhaps most particularly, liquidity in markets for Treasury securities' (as quoted in: Melamed 2003: 127). According to the Fed, financial derivatives supported debt management operations and reduced the auction rate on short- and long-term obligations, namely because they gave investors a conduit to manage US financial risk, as meagre as it was (ibid.: 128).

This synergy between derivatives and bonds fuelled additional financial innovation in the 1980s and 1990s, especially in the swaps market. Swaps allowed investors to trade interest rate and currency risk, as well as other quantifiable or concrete risks, and allowed investors to take large positions in the IBM without shouldering much of the liability.[6] Thus as financial firms increasingly participated in the IBM, both as dealers and traders, they did so with one eye on how swap contracts could protect and expand placement activity. As Evans (1992: 446) concludes: the financial gains associated with the emergence of interest rate and currency swaps 'have been important enough that most Eurobond issues since around 1986 have been swap-driven'. In fact, the connection between the Eurobond market and the derivatives market was already so significant that by the start of the 1990s the Bank of England viewed the IBM as 'a leading channel of financial market innovation' (BOE 1991: 525).[7]

Moreover, such forms of interaction intensified pressure for more liquid markets and in turn further pressured financial restructuring. From their experience in the IBM and other financial markets, Wall Street firms 'recognized that for derivatives to function effectively, the markets needed to be liquid, the principles able to purchase and sell securities as their needs demanded' (Lipuma and Lee 2004: 21). This concern with liquidity encouraged financial speculation, in part as firms sought new investments to secure their own positions or strategic orientations (ibid.).

Thus US risk power was deeply connected with the reorientation of financial markets in the early 1970s, forming part of a complex evolutionary process that culminated in vast changes and new forms of power. Moreover, it set in motion a number of market synergies, not least by dramatically expanding the commodity derivatives infrastructure. This all fostered a culture of engineering inside Wall Street firms, of which the high priority given to financial innovation was a key trait, and provided US firms with a 'first-mover advantage' that 'spectacularly changed the course and history of futures markets' (Melamed 2009: xiii, xiv; Chappe et al. 2015: 128; Jessop and Scherrer 2015). By 1982 this 'revolutionary fervor' had already engulfed the membership of the CME and the Chicago Board of Trade, and by the 1990s it had shaped swap and credit default markets, while ensuring that US institutions remained key drivers of the global over-the-counter derivatives market (Melamed 2003: 43; Lipuma and Lee 2004).

Crucially, these institutional transformations and processes reflected a deeper set of linkages and were not merely set in motion by the collapse of Bretton Woods par values. As we saw, derivatives are themselves constituted by a 'culture of circulation' – their 'formal and quantifiable' appearance erected from socio-historical forms of representative power (Lipuma and Lee 2004: 60, 64). Such abstract constructions both simplify the 'variegated character of the social phenomena that require national and global interconnectivity' and enframe social narratives about different cultures and communities representative of a particular structure of historical domination (ibid.: 64). The upshot is that these markets are subject to the same diffuse patterns of risk and credibility organizing international bond markets. As derivative products priced connectivity on this basis, they presented unique opportunities for US and European firms, given their special access to US Treasury markets and hub-and-spoke relationship. This spurred new innovations and strategic shifts within firms, and above all entrenched transatlantic connectivities (Millman 1995: 3; Lipuma and Lee 2004: 73).

SUMMARY REMARKS

This chapter argued that the IBM imprinted on, though by no means fully determined, the institutional evolution of US and global financial markets. It showed that US dollars and bonds functioned as a mechanism of reproduction across Europe. This meant that key European financial circuits operated through dollar funding channels and that firms in London and across the continent stockpiled US debt obligations, both for their own portfolio and to sell to their clients. In the US, the postwar risk imaginary meant stronger, larger and more innovative financial firms that took leadership in the creation and sale of derivative obligations and nurtured a complex web of foreign financial linkages. All in all, this crystallized in a dollar based transatlantic financial apparatus oriented around derivative contracts and short-term funding channels, and based on the accumulation and underwriting of US denominated debt by European firms and the distribution of this debt to European investors.

NOTES

1. At the start of 2019 total outstanding bonds reached about $103 trillion (sifma 2019).
2. This should not be interpreted to mean that institutional priorities crystallize from previously constituted human interactions; as noted, this point violates the IM view of institutional formation that emphasizes the combination of human agents and the transfactual pressures of capitalist organization. But it does call attention to the institutional embeddedness of human action and how agential subjectivity is always passed through an institutional logic that is itself formed from the uneven distribution of social authority, as institutional formations always pre-exist the agents responsible for their reproduction. The difference then is between erasing human subjectivity and ignoring the emergence of institutional processes within the crisis-prone nature of capitalism, and recognizing the internal processes that shape, activate and reproduce institutional formations and the human experiences contained within them.
3. This is the same as saying that 'man makes his own history, but he does not make it out of the whole cloth; he does not make it out of conditions chosen by himself but out of such that he finds close at hand' (Marx 1852: 17). Marx (1852: 17) continues by adding: 'the tradition of all dead generations weights like a nightmare on the brains of the living.'
4. The characteristics of private debt issuance, domestic or international, are such that each security is brought to market by an investment bank which underwrites the entire issue by essentially buying it from the issuing organization. The investment bank then sells the issue to the public or to other dealers, acting as an intermediary between the end buyer and issuer. Underwriting organizations may also choose to absorb a portion of the total issue for their own books, although there are usually restrictions on this process. In those instances where the bond issue is especially large, as is typically the case with Yankee issues, investment banks often group together, forming a syndicate, and act collectively to absorb and sell the issue.
5. While the money market is also used by non-financial corporations to meet payroll and other short-term needs, financial institutions are key players as both direct issuers and dealer issuers.
6. As Mailander (1997: 358) explains, for example, currency swaps permit investors 'to hedge the principle and interest payments in the currency of issue against a currency preferred.'
7. Moreover, as Bryan (2008: 496) notes, foreign exchange derivative markets have developed alongside an unofficial dollar 'anchor', with investors holding and trading US Treasury claims mainly to hedge and speculate against alternative currencies. The most important expression of this trend has been in the swaps market where US dollar claims have traditionally been a partner in about 80 or 90 per cent of all currency trades.

7. Regulating risk

We have already established the special perceptions of risk attached to US bonds in the IBM, and the institutional impacts of this on European and US firms and markets. This chapter precedes the discussion on subprime management and post-crisis regulation in Chapter 9 by examining the relationship between US risk power and the US state. It develops and affirms earlier conclusions regarding the Bretton Woods system and dollar standard, which saw the challenge of extending financial confidence largely as one of developing state institutional capacities. The goal is to clarify the interconnectivity between state and financial power by looking at the different ways the state supported the IBM and created the conditions for its remarkable development, as well as the wider structural conditions underpinning, though not always clearly directing, its actions.

The chapter moves from a theoretical to a historical analysis and makes a number of related points. It shows that financial crises have been used to extend US risk power and how the gradual development of market-based credit, which underpinned the explosive growth of US bonds seen in Chapter 5, itself occurred through a sequence of adaptive responses to economic contradictions, shaped and enabled by the patterns of risk established by the Bretton Woods system. It also shows that regulators took a number of direct actions to support the internationalization of US debt and that such actions, as well as those not directly aimed at international bond markets, advanced US risk power.

STATE THEORY AND RISK POWER

It is important first to understand that while state institutions are not instruments of economic power, blindly serving the interests of the economic elite, neither are they completely autonomous. The concept of *emergence* from critical realism and IM posits that more concrete organizational systems, while possessing distinct proprieties and causal mechanisms, are ultimately shaped by wider structural pressures and bound by their directional logic (Creaven 2000: 34, 59, 41; Maher and Aquanno 2018). In this account, state institutions support the conditions for capitalist economic development but also possess a degree of autonomy.

This way of thinking about state power echoes tenets of Marxist state theory. In the custom of Miliband (1969; 1970), Poulantzas (1976; 1978), O'Connor (1973) and Panitch (1981, 1999),[1] the concept of relative autonomy teaches us that capitalist states promote accumulation 'within the framework of containing and mediating relationships among the various fractions of capital and between subordinate and dominant classes' (Panitch 1981: 26–7). The state therefore is neither a thing, merely expressing the interests of a dominant economic class, nor a subject, completely independent from class relations and power. Rather, like capital, it is a social relation: dominant classes and fractions do not confront the state as an external force; these relations are internalized within the state itself – they traverse its different branches and networks, giving rise to various contradictions and struggles. As the state does not represent the interests of the dominant class mechanistically, it has its own political relevance, an 'opacity and resistance of its own': states are fragmented, but nevertheless organize and unify the power bloc, representing the 'long term political interests of the whole bourgeoisie' under the leadership of the dominant fraction (Poulantzas 1978: 364, 356).

It follows that states are neither static and monolithic organizations nor 'an assembly of detachable parts' (ibid.: 380). Policy is established through a process of intra-state conflict, struggle, and mutual adaptation in which different branches each positioned differently in the 'relationship of forces', collide to produce decisions (ibid.: 374). Such decisions do not follow an abstract logic or precise linearity, but are themselves dynamic, 'characterized by about-turns, hesitation and changes' (ibid.: 378–9). Yet policy ultimately has a 'certain coherence', reflecting that states have an 'apparatus unity' written into their 'hierarchic-bureaucratized framework', through which 'certain dominant mechanisms, modes and decision-making centers are made impermeable to all but [hegemonic] interests'; these are centres 'for switching the rails of state policy or for bottling up measures taken elsewhere in the state that favour other fractions of capital' or class interests (ibid.: 382).

Arising from this theorization are three key points, all of which clarify the relationship between the US state and the IBM, and provide a basis for the ensuing historical analysis. These have been taken up more fully elsewhere and for our purposes require only passing acknowledgement. First, while state institutions exert a certain autonomy as emergent social organizations, they ultimately function 'under the hegemony of a class or fraction located within it' (ibid.: 381). This means that policies tend to prioritize objectives that reinforce the long-term interests of the dominant class, and especially those supporting the general interests of the entire bourgeoisie. It is very important in this sense that the IBM greatly enhanced US financial and economic power. This has especially been the case in the US domestic-international market where government spending and the liquidity of credit markets have long depended on foreign capital inflows. From the early 1960s, with the dollar glut having been entirely reversed, the credibility of the dollar created a 'vortex', funnelling international capital to the US market to sustain private and state expenditures, such as the Vietnam War and Johnson's Great Society programs, and all the while expanding key financing channels – making them more robust and resilient and spurring innovation (Konings and Panitch 2009: 234; Konings 2011). Seen in this way, US risk power benefited not only the financial bloc through deeper and more dynamic markets, but industrial interests as well, providing access to cheap sources of capital and international pools of dollar credit. In fact, part of what allowed US firms to expand their global footprint, and impact on the class relations in other countries, was the ability to fund production in US offshore bond and dollar markets. The Eurobond market gave US financial and manufacturing corporations an important advantage because it offset the currency risk normally associated with international activity and production.

At the same time, such a view draws attention to changes within the hierarchy of state institutions and how certain branches function as policy making nodes. Clearly, with the turn to neoliberalism and financialization of accumulation, authority has been diverted from what Poulantzas termed the ideological and coercive apparatuses of the US state. It has instead come to rest above all in the economic apparatus, especially those branches that are insulated from Congressional pressure. This has led to the growing influence of the Treasury Department, and within the Office of the Comptroller of the Currency, and the Federal Reserve. Indeed, if these institutions have always played a key role supporting and superintending financial firms, over the last four decades they have become ever more important centres of state power.

Finally, we can see that state institutions play a key role managing accumulation, but that the capacity to do so does not fall from the heavens; it rather occurs through different struggles and learning processes. As accumulation strategies never occur through 'straightforward manipulation of the bourgeoisie' and do not represent one single set of interests, they are themselves contradictory and fluid (Poulantzas 1978: 386). State activities in this sense are conjunctural – they develop out of processes of accommodation, trial and error experimentation, and mutual adjustment within and among different networks and often between different goals.[2] As such, the management of US risk power sometimes reflected direct intent, but it was most often the product of struggle and the way in which strategies ran up against structural boundaries. Even if regulators were not often aware of how their actions would impact the long-term flow of funds, their mandate and agenda became rather tightly attached to the IBM and to preserving key markets. This was the basis upon which occurred the long process of management and institutional learning underpinning US risk power and the subprime financial crisis.

STATE MANAGEMENT AND INSTITUTIONAL
LEARNING: 1940–1970

Turning to the historical analysis, we must first understand that it took US regulators some time to understand the emerging financial system as it developed
in the early postwar period through new forms of transatlantic connectivity.
It is clear, for example, that US officials initially failed to grasp the strategic
significance of the Eurodollar market, and at any rate were too preoccupied
with how it threatened US control over the money supply (Burn 2006). As
a result, many of their actions involved supporting one fragment of the IBM
at the expense of others and, on the whole, the primary aim was seldom to
advance US risk power.

Indirect support was a different matter. As we have seen, the fiscal deficits
appearing after 1960, occurring as they did in the context of the Bretton Woods
dollar system, gradually reshaped the contour of debt markets: as countries
increasingly held reserve balances in US Treasury bonds, supplementing these
for gold, they greatly 'boosted the size and turnover in the Anglo-American
financial system', further incentivizing investors to raise capital in US debt
markets, within the transatlantic financial system (Gowan 1999: 18). The
so-called Triffin dilemma – based on a growing imbalance between the global
supply of dollars and the US gold stockpile – reflected this internationalization, and the cross-penetration of US and European markets it engendered. All
this supported the foreign position of US Treasury bonds, as much as it did
the development of Eurodollar and Eurodollar bond markets, and increasingly
subjugated global markets to the rhythms of US Treasury bond and dollar
markets.

The 'structural power' the US gained by removing Bretton Woods constraints, far from occurring spontaneously, emerged from these financial
relations, in so far as they foretold what liberalization and market competition
would entail (Helleiner 1994: 13, 114). Such relations showed US officials that
open markets 'would preserve the privileged global financial position of the
US and the dollar's central international role' (Gowan 1999: 17). Moreover,
the growth of Euromarkets always required US regulatory approval. Though
these markets were offshore, US officials had the power to shut them down,
given the outsized role that US banks and corporations played in their operation and development. The choice not to, along with the British state's 'strong
support' for their physical location in London, were therefore necessary
prerequisites for their development from the very beginning (Helleiner 1994).
This support for Euromarkets only intensified through the 1960s as officials
'actively encouraged American banks and corporations to move their operations to the offshore London markets', through policies such as the voluntary

restraint programme (Helleiner 1994: 82). This support for Euromarkets 'did not derive simply from a concern for the interests of the country's banks and corporations', it equally reflected an attempt to increase 'the attractiveness of dollar holdings to foreigners' (ibid.: 90).

Above all, the back and forth in policy indicates that state management was contingent on institutional learning, and reflective of the material structure of reproduction and class domination characteristic of the so-called managerial or Keynesian era. Though the financial sector was hardly suppressed during this period, as opportunities for expansion increasingly emerged, it clearly played a more limited role. By contrast, the neoliberal period has been 'underpinned by financialization', albeit *due to the maturation of the financial relations developed during the postwar period*, and therefore characterized by the increasing influence of financial firms, markets, and actors in the economy (Fine and Saad-Filho 2017: 685).

All this has to be further understood in terms of the conditions imposed by the Bretton Woods system, which, as Gowan (1999: 24) notes, 'constrained' what the US state could do. The postwar settlement limited global financial flows and tied regulators to managing the dollar's relationship to gold. At the same time, it limited the type of financial volatility that was to become a constitutive part of US risk power. In large part, the management of abstract risk was about expanding the liquidity of the dollar in international markets and preserving the credibility of US debt by managing the dollar–gold link. The upshot was that the US state managed risk power and bond internationalization very differently in the early postwar period, and took less direct measures to support the IBM than following the 1970s.

The Korean War was probably most significant in the eventual creation of a dollar glut in Europe and is therefore often discussed as an important factor in the development of the Eurobond market and other such dollar allocation channels.[3] Even while capital was still flowing into US markets, the build-up of dollars in the form of offshore transactions and reserve holdings stalled through the 1940s, as the world experienced a serious dollar shortage. The Marshall Plan also played a critical role. Although the State Department and the Economic Cooperation Administration (ECA) were certainly concerned with providing aid to accommodate expansionary economic policies, one objective of Marshall Plan aid was to balance disequilibrating European capital exports to the US to compensate for the absence of strong joint controls on the cross-border movement of funds (Helleiner 1994: 58–61). This is partly why, in determining the precise allocation of aid, US Treasury officials divided funds on the basis of 'consensus forecasts of [European balance of payments] deficits' (Eichengreen 1996: 102). Drawing on John Snyder's testimony to Congress, Helleiner (1994: 61) describes the provision of offsetting financing under the European Recovery Program as a conscious attempt to 'prevent the disruptive impact of capital flight in a way that was compatible with an open trading order, stable exchange rates and the liberal inclinations of the American financial community'. This created a broader role for US Treasury debt inside European financial markets.

Yet as regulators realized they could influence markets without impeding the flow of capital, they were forced to confront new contradictions, relating to the success of Marshall Plan intervention.[4] While the dollar glut laid the foundation for a return to convertibility, it impacted the gold peg, as investors questioned first the appropriate gold price for dollars and then the market relationship between major international currencies (Triffin 1978: 272; Eichengreen 1996: 127). Because industrial countries were reluctant to re-price their currencies within the bands allotted by the IMF, and US officials were still very much 'unwilling to contemplate' changing the international system, this created new problems to address and oversee. As regulators focused on the Triffin dilemma, they fixed on protecting the dollar–gold link without disrupting the interpenetration of US and European markets.

Initially, this involved stemming speculative currency shifts through coordinated intervention. In 1961 the member countries of the BIS, led by the Federal Reserve and Treasury, secretly created the London Gold Pool to reduce the incentive to demand gold from the Treasury and recalibrate the ratio of dollars to gold outside of the US. Under the arrangement, industrial countries 'pledged to refrain from converting their dollar exchange' and agreed to 'sell gold out of their reserves' to create demand and supply balances which could justify $35 per ounce (ibid.:122). The Bank of England played the role of market coordinator, buying and selling gold on the London market when conditions warranted, and collecting from each member according to their percentage ownership of the pool (the US was the single most important contributor controlling 50 per cent of the pool). Yet neither the United States nor Europe was willing to 'subordinate other economic and political objectives to defending the dollar price of gold' (ibid.: 122). As a result, the Gold Pool was only partly successful, and was closed in 1968. According to the Federal Reserve: the Gold Pool 'worked quite well' in moderating swings in dollar and gold prices but was no more than 'a stop gap until some fundamental change was agreed upon' (US Federal Reserve 1967: 4).

With the Gold Pool limited in this way, and the ramifications of the Triffin dilemma more conspicuous, regulators invented other ways to exert influence and discipline. One approach involved utilizing the evolving Eurodollar market. The IET can be seen in these terms, to the degree that regulators only approved the tax after realizing that offshore dollars could be used to sustain dollar financing outside the New York market (Walmsley 1991). Another approach involved establishing reciprocal swap facilities with industrial countries to balance the international flow of dollars. By the beginning of 1968 the

Federal Reserve was counterparty to swap networks with 14 central banks as well as the Bank of International Settlements (BIS). Under the arrangements, the Fed acquired foreign currency from central banks that 'held too many US dollars and then used the newly acquired currency to buy excess dollars from the same foreign central bank[s]' (Humpage and Shenk 2008). The transactions did not change foreign public exposure to Treasury bonds, but rather limited foreign exposure to US currency risk, as surplus foreign dollars were mainly held under swap contracts 'with an established single rate for both the forward and spot legs of the transactions ... that protected foreign central bank[s] ... against any dollar depreciation' (ibid.). In swapping for short-term foreign capital, the Fed absorbed 'forward sales of dollars', manipulated currency markets, and once again drove up demand for US Treasury bonds, essentially creating a dollar-based 'portfolio substitute to gold' (US Treasury 2009; Makin 1971: 355). This more closely tied recipient countries to the US segment of the domestic-international bond market as well as the dollar segment of the offshore market (ibid.: 355).

Because the Federal Open Market Committee (FOMC) set a one-year limit on transactions, the swap program led to new problems, as expired contracts created foreign currency liabilities on the Fed's balance sheet. Though swaps could be renegotiated on an annual basis, this created long-term vulnerabilities for the Fed in terms of currency risk, and was not desirable from an administrative perspective. As a solution, the Treasury issued so-called Roosa bonds – 'non-marketable foreign currency-denominated medium-term securities' – and transferred the revenue to the Federal Reserve (US Treasury 2009). These created a portfolio substitute for gold which buttressed US placements, both in the IBM and more broadly. To be sure, the Treasury used only part of the proceeds to cover swap balances – the remaining sales were designed to 'relieve potential future strain' on foreign dollar claims by channelling short-term currency holdings into long-term currency protected Treasury claims (Kindleberger 1968: 452; as quoted in Makin 1971: 350). As Makin (1971: 350) and Kindleberger (1968: 452) both show, Roosa bonds were configured as 'a means for the US to substitute future liabilities against current liabilities and for foreign central banks to exchange their dollars for an asset, other than gold, that [was] free of exchange risk.' In the end, Roosa bonds acted much like swap lines, only instead of increasing net international dollar claims, they intensified interdependence by directly expanding foreign central bank exposure to US Treasury default risk.

Therefore, the postwar credibility of the dollar was not just a product of US economic power. Neither can it be reduced to the cultural and institutional expression of this power at the international level. It embodied all of these forces. But it was also the sum of a dense web of supportive state policies, some of which curtailed formal regulations on US offshore dollar holdings, others which provided dollar liquidity to international markets to stem concerns that holding US debt would backfire in the future.

MARKET-BASED FINANCE AND LIBERALIZATION: STATE MANAGEMENT AFTER 1970

The period following 1971 expressed a different organization of financial relations and thereby threw up different challenges for US officials. With the dollar–gold link no longer relevant, capital controls increasingly limited, and financial markets playing an increasingly important role in the economy, the Federal Reserve and Treasury Department occupied a privileged position in the economic policy apparatus, crystallizing the interests of a nascent financial ruling bloc. These agencies supported transatlantic financial networks, protected major markets, and developed new tools and rationalities to serve US risk power. This involved supporting too-big-to-fail firms, extending key markets through liberalization and political negotiation and, perhaps above all, gently promoting a more market-based system of credit. Even so, regulators never framed their action in terms of protecting the IBM, nor was it ever clear that this was their main objective – such interventions were contradictory and reflective of underlying divisions within the financial system itself, as well as broader patterns of class struggle. In what remains, the chapter sifts through these different actions and tries to make sense of them. As above, the discussion focuses on the policies and strategies adopted during this period, rather than underlying patterns of class struggle, and therefore only provides a surface level accounting.

Too-Big-to-Fail and Euromarkets

As we have seen, the development of offshore Eurocurrency and bond markets required the support of US and European governments. This involved the decision to leave these markets unregulated, as well as more active policies to facilitate their development. Yet though such policies proved successful, the growth of these markets was nevertheless constrained by Bretton Woods era regulations. As such, the gradual liberalization of US financial markets, which was substantially initiated in 1974 with the removal of certain capital controls, was both a regulatory touchstone, and key moment in the reproduction of US risk power. If this allowed US investors and corporations freer access to Euromarkets, it also reinforced the intermeshing of US domestic and offshore markets, which often involved investors using the latter to hedge dollar holdings, including holdings of US domestic-international bonds. At the same time, liberalization put increasing pressure on European governments to follow suit, especially since their financial markets had already been integrated into the

US system in a hub-and-spoke relationship. The removal of European capital account restrictions over the next 10 years thus only further extended US risk power.

But even with the increasing mobility of capital, Euromarkets still faced a major problem, ironically owing to the very feature which made them attractive to global investors: their offshore status. Because these markets operated outside the reach of regulators, they technically fell beyond the US state's lender-of-last-resort responsibilities. This was not a serious concern when Eurodollar markets were small and financial volatility was limited by tight international regulations. But as these markets grew, investors faced a sudden seizure of dollar liquidity, outside the US market. Unlike onshore markets, which were backstopped by the Fed's discount window (and other supports), offshore markets enjoyed no equivalent safety valve.

While a permanent solution to this problem only emerged in 2008 when unlimited SWAP lines of credit were established between key central banks, the Fed's decision to provide emergency assistance to Franklin National Bank in 1974, the same year capital controls were liberalized, was a major step forward. Franklin's failure sent shockwaves through offshore dollar markets, due to its close connectivity to the European banking system and Eurocurrency and bond markets. US regulators could not ignore Franklin's impact on domestic firms and markets, but they were more concerned with its effect on the transatlantic funding system, and the functionality of key offshore markets: from the beginning, the major issue was whether the US state's 'lender-of-last-resort functions would be extended to the new offshore Eurodollar market' (Helleiner 1994: 171; Kapstein 1992; 1994). Thus when the Federal Reserve quickly contained the crisis, both by 'purchas[ing] securities on Franklin's behalf' and 'assur[ing] foreign creditors that they would be paid', it greatly 'bolstered the confidence of private international financial operators', reassuring them that despite the offshore nature of Eurodollars, the Federal Reserve would backstop liquidity in this market (Panitch and Gindin 2012: 153; Spero 1988–1989; Helleiner 1994: 12). This was a key condition for the further development of offshore bond markets. It also signalled a core aspect of US financial management in the post-Bretton Woods period: *that crises would be instrumentalized to extend US risk power and the development of US debt markets.*

As it turned out, the Franklin bailout formed part of an emerging strategy of protecting systemically important financial firms. According to the Federal Reserve, regulators began supporting too-big-to-fail banks in 1972, when the Federal Deposit Insurance Corporation (FDIC) used its essentiality powers (which allow it to protect banks that play an essential financial function) to bail out Bank of the Commonwealth (Nurisso and Prescott 2017). After Franklin National, the same uncertainty about systemic financial instability drove regulators to support First Pennsylvania Bank in 1980. This 'policy of too-big-to-fail bailouts' was then further entrenched when the FDIC and Federal Reserve teamed up to prevent the failure of Seafirst Bank in 1983, and Continental Illinois in 1984 (ibid.). Crucially, as this policy extended to banks of different sizes, including those such as Commonwealth that were only too-big-to-fail in the widest sense, it demonstrated deep concern about the stability of the banking system and a broad interpretation of lender-of-last-resort responsibilities. One effect was to reinforce the US state's perceived commitment to critical markets, including offshore funding channels in Europe.

At about the same time, US officials began working towards common international banking standards through the Bank of International Settlements. The liberalization of financial markets encouraged action, but so did the dense linkages between financial firms that had been established through the development of the IBM in the 1960s and early 1970s. As these forms of risk connectivity matured, alongside new forms of financial intermediation, it became more important to coordinate supervision across national borders. The Committee on Banking Regulations and Supervisory Practices, established through the G10 in 1974, attempted to do exactly this.

The Committee's 1975 Concordat addressed key underlying problems in international debt and dollar markets. By clarifying responsibility for cross-border liquidity flows, it reduced informational barriers and fashioned a new sense of optimism about offshore markets. Moreover, once the Federal Reserve and other major central banks coordinated lender-of-last-resort provisions and increased information sharing, international debt markets were less exposed to counterparty default risk; now while cross-border transactions were still susceptible to institutional collapse, there was additional assurance that governments would intervene to limit contagion and, at the very least, prevent the complete seizure of important funding channels. This bolstered the protection provided by the Franklin bailout, providing a new set of institutional supports for the Eurodollar bond market. The Federal Reserve went so far as to declare that its mandate included taking 'into account the safety and soundness of banks abroad' (Wallich 1979: 187).

The Concordat was less far-reaching than the measures proposed by US officials a few years later. These took shape in the late 1970s and led to the proposed Euro-currency Control Act (1979), which would have imposed reserve requirements on banks' international currency activities, effectively regulating the Eurodollar and Eurodollar bond markets. Recognizing that such restrictions would have to be coordinated with other central banks, regulators spearheaded negotiations through the BIS, establishing a secret working group to consider tighter controls in April 1979 (Kaminska 2016; Helleiner 1994: 137). The initiative was eventually defeated on both fronts, as it met with 'strong opposition from the US banking community' as well as the Bank of England

and the Swiss National Bank (Helleiner 1994: 137). This ensured the explosive development of offshore bond markets following the Volcker shock and ratified the basic asymmetry the Federal Reserve had tried to correct: between its increasing willingness to protect offshore markets, and its inability to control their size. Yet though the Fed pushed the issue at the BIS and saw the value of regulating Euromarkets, its support for the initiative was always lukewarm. Indeed, it stopped far short of publicly embracing regulation, committing only to study its impacts, and even this came with the demand that such restrictions provide 'competitive equality between the home section of the dollar market and the foreign sectors' (Wallich 1979: 187).

In proposing regulation, the Fed was not trying to close offshore markets, it clearly recognized their vital contribution – as Governor Wallich's testimony to Congress on behalf of the Federal Reserve Board made clear. Rather, it saw reserve requirements as a way to limit domestic inflation and bolster confidence in the dollar; it also recognized that any retreat from offshore dollar markets would benefit the US domestic-international and Yankee markets (ibid.). In this way, the failure to regulate Euromarkets shaped the specific composition of the IBM, more than it did the extension of US risk power, and hardly represented a renewed push for financial constraint inside the Federal Reserve, as some have suggested.

The 1973 oil shock also affected regulatory orientations and gave officials leeway to manipulate capital flows on a more powerful scale. This redistributed foreign trade flows and produced large surpluses for oil producers and deficits for non-oil-producing countries, creating a competitive problem resembling the 'beggar-thy-neighbour [paradox] of the 1930s', so far as any attempt by one country to offset current account liabilities by seeking to attract an offsetting volume of petrodollars would generate equally sharp deficits in another (Spiro 1999: 29). One solution was to bypass the market by creating a system of 'intergovernmental coordination [designed to] consign oil monies to nations with oil related trade deficits' (ibid.: 42). This involved recycling petrodollars through the IMF from surplus to deficit countries to ease the burden of the oil price increase and produce financing options for deficit countries. According to the House Committee on Banking and Currency: governments 'must recognize that the more OPEC money [they] can attract in [their] own coffers, the greater [their] responsibility to ensure adequate recycling to countries with legitimate balance of payments deficits' (ibid.: 43).

This cooperative endeavour got nowhere, as did other similar attempts. US officials saw these as dead-ends, and never took them too seriously.[5] From their standpoint, OPEC surpluses should be recycled through the transatlantic financial system and held inside the US segment of the international bond market. Meetings held through the Joint Commission on Economic Cooperation provided the forum for this agenda, and allowed US officials to

'persuade Saudi Arabia to invest a sizeable portion of its surplus in US government obligations and to keep oil priced in dollars' (ibid.: 91). This is what
originally prompted the sizeable differences in foreign asset holdings between
the Saudi Arabian Monetary Agency (SAMA) and other OPEC monetary
authorities. At the end of the 1970s, 83 per cent of Saudi Arabia's portfolio was
denominated in foreign dollar bonds and 30 per cent was held in an account
at the Federal Reserve Bank of New York (ibid.: 59, 125). Kuwait's foreign
portfolio, by contrast, held 50 per cent of total claims in US dollars and only 5
per cent in US government obligations (ibid.: 113).

The 1974 add-on agreement extended the scope of this relationship. Secretly
negotiated by Treasury Secretary William Simon and Undersecretary Jack
Bennett, this allowed SAMA to purchase Treasury obligations outside competitive auction, and gave Saudi officials access to Treasury bonds at a cheaper
price (ibid.: 107–109). It also artificially increased competition for US Treasury
bonds by taking a portion of debt out of each auction. No less important, the
add-on guaranteed SAMA a specified amount of Treasury bonds, and allowed
public financing operations to be conducted 'on a central bank to central bank
basis' (ibid.: 109). The upshot was dense new forms of financial interconnectivity, linking Saudi Arabian oil surpluses to US domestic-international bonds:
from the time the add-on was introduced to the end of 1977, Saudi Arabia's
share of Treasury bonds held by Middle Eastern oil exporters grew to 90 per
cent and the region's exposure to Treasury obligations (as a percentage of total
US investments) expanded from 43 per cent to 65 per cent (ibid.: 113). Though
Japan and China would later overtake Middle Eastern oil producers as the
major holders of US government debt, this set the tracks for the growth of US
markets following the Volcker shock by adding to their depth and liquidity.[6]

Debt recycling had another long-term effect on the IBM. As current account
surpluses were funnelled through the transatlantic banking system and into
Latin America, both to support development and to offset oil-related trade
deficits, US commercial banks established vast new financing webs with
developing-country governments, often through syndicated loans organized
through the same European banks purchasing dollar bonds in the IBM. By
1982, 'the nine-largest US money-centered banks held Latin American debt
amounting to 176 percent of their capital; their total LDC debt was nearly 290
percent of capital' (Sims and Romero 2013; Sachs 1988). This was in fact
encouraged by US officials and part of the liberalization and financial bailout
policies adopted in the early 1970s: US banks, as Gowan (1999: 17) notes,
'were initially far from happy about recycling the petrodollar to countries in
the south'. As a result the 'US government had to lean on them to do so', both
by committing to remove US capital controls and to bail them out if they 'got
into difficulties' (ibid.: 17). If this boosted offshore markets, it also shifted the
course of financial intermediation, as the Latin American debt crisis provoked

a wide-ranging shift in US credit markets, away from bank financing and towards securitization and market-based finance.

Market-based Finance

Though the offshore dollar bond market continued its ascent through the post-Volcker period, it was probably never the most important segment of the IBM, given how the US domestic-international market set interest rates, served as a key source of dollars, and remained more liquid and safe. Yet this way of analysing the IBM, as a competition between markets, misses the key point: that these segments were in fact mutually constitutive and interconnected and that US risk power was lodged at the very heart of the international debt system and increasingly brought to bear on its expanded reproduction. In this sense, the development of Euromarkets opened new opportunities for the Yankee and US domestic-international markets, even as it created funding opportunities outside the US market. The reverse was also the case, as European banks often issued offshore dollar bonds to either hedge their exposure to US domestic-international bonds or obtain long-term dollar funding to expand their holdings in this market. As we saw earlier, Yankee bonds deepened global connectivity in much the same way, especially following the 1990s recession (Azahara and Gonzalez 2016).

This interconnectivity meant that changes in the US banking and credit system impacted the entire IBM, creating new opportunities in the US domestic-international market and in turn driving dollar issuance in Europe and drawing firms to the Yankee market. These changes in US financial intermediation, which saw bank credit gradually replaced by market credit, were critical to the development of international debt markets. Though securities markets always played an important role in the US financial system, given its decentralized structure and absence of large universal banks, banks remained a leading source of funding into the 1970s, accounting for 62 per cent of total US lending in 1974 (Fritzdixon 2019; Konings 2011; Culpepper 2005; Zysman 1983). As much as this permitted US banks to expand operations and seek new opportunities in offshore markets, deepening transatlantic connectivity, it meant that bond markets played a reduced role. In the following 30 years, this changed entirely. The bank share of total loans fell to about 30 per cent by 2007, as 'corporations shifted towards market-based financing and issued debt securities like bonds and commercial paper': corporate bonds as a percentage of non-financial borrowing increased from 42 per cent in 1974 to about 50 per cent on the eve of the subprime crisis, after reaching nearly 60 per cent in the early 2000s (ibid.: 32). That the decline of bank credit coincided with the securitization of US mortgages was also no coincidence. While securitized bonds were virtually non-existent in the mid-1970s, by 2007 they accounted for over 30 per cent of all US loans (ibid.).

The explosion in bond financing discussed in Chapter 5, particularly in the US domestic-international market, therefore reflected a wider transformation of the US financial system that offered vast new opportunities for bond financing. This involved not so much the decline of large commercial banks, but their reorientation, away from providing loans, especially to corporations, and towards facilitating a wider process of financial intermediation. These banks also moved into different sections of the financial system, namely derivatives markets, aided by the gradual erosion of Glass–Steagall regulations and the privatization of currency and interest rate risk (Lapavitsas 2014: 57).

But US regulators did not simply open the door to this restructuring. By gradually implementing rules and policies that limited bank credit and expanding opportunities for market-based financing, they facilitated and even encouraged it. The state's motivations in this respect are not easy to decipher, but regulators were no doubt keen to limit volatility and ensure the growth of complementary markets that diversified risk, while providing maximum opportunity for innovation and accumulation. This is precisely what Greenspan was referring to in 1999 when he praised the resiliency of the US financial system, and the ability of credit markets to 'substitute for the loss of bank financial intermediation' during moments of distress (Greenspan 1999a). If regulators were not keen to prevent crises, as this meant capital controls or other restrictive policies, they were clearly concerned to build a 'robust' financial infrastructure and increasingly came to see credit markets as a core part of this (Greenspan 1999a; Panitch and Gindin 2012). That these markets helped turn banks into trading firms (reducing their portfolio risk), spurred financial innovation, and lowered borrowing costs, also proved important (Greenspan 1999a).

The Fed's new low inflation regime seriously impacted its priorities as well. To be sure, as the Fed started steering short-term interest rates with 'more precision and consistency', it effectively reduced 'uncertainty over future access to liquidity', reinsuring 'fragile liquidity structures' and enabling 'arbitrage along the yield curve' (Walter and Wansleben 2019: 4–5; Adrian and Shin 2008; Mehrling 2011). This 'more strongly entangled' the Fed in market-based financial processes, and gradually shifted its preference towards these structures, making it a 'key architect of a market-based transnational liquidity regime' (Walter and Wansleben 2019: 5; Gabor 2016). Meanwhile, the initial volatility created by shifting interest rates led to new profit opportunities, which banks increasingly took advantage of by investing in bonds and other securities (Panitch and Gindin 2012: 175).

While the Volcker shock drew the Fed deeper into market-based practices, the financial turbulence it provoked simultaneously let to further restructuring in this direction. The high interest rates necessary to stabilize inflation and dis-cipline the US working class set off a broad-based banking crisis, though the deep roots of this turmoil certainly lay elsewhere. The international banks who had traded capital account liberalization for petrodollar financing in the early 1970s and built up large exposure to LDC debt were one casualty: the spike in US interests increased the carrying cost of this debt, bringing many Latin American countries to the brink of default, and leaving large international banks with a massive portfolio of underperforming loans. In many respects, the regulatory response compounded the problem. Instead of immediately absorbing the bad debt, regulators shifted accounting policies, 'applying lax prudential standards to banks with large LDC exposures', and pressured Latin American countries to continue interest payments (Sachs and Huizinga 1987: 557). This allowed the US Treasury and IMF to impose structural adjustment policies in the Global South; it also protected balance sheets and maintained profit rates, but did so artificially, by masking bad loans. In response, banks pulled away from overseas lending and increasingly pushed towards secu-ritization, as this offered better returns and an opportunity to increase capital (Sachs and Huizinga 1987; McNally 2010: 98). After Mexico announced it would default on loan payments in 1982, the portion of bank lending in new credit fell by half, even as corporate bond financing remained steady and soon exploded (Jefferis 1990). Regulators eventually wrote-down the value of Latin America debt through the so-called Brady plan, which 'swapped illiquid, opaque syndicated loans for a standardized marketable bond', but the impact had already been registered (Gambau-Brisa and Mann 2009: 10).

The crisis was a driving force behind a slate of new financial regulations. The 1986 Tax Reform Act significantly impacted bank balance sheets, as it eliminated a number of key tax preferences, namely the deductibility of consumer interest payments, municipal bonds, and loan loss reserves. This impacted banks directly and indirectly and was at least partly a response to the favourable treatment banks received during the crisis. By allowing banks to realize loan losses without charging off non-performing loans, deduction for bad debt reserves enabled banks to 'spread out the losses from bad debts' (Neuberger 1988). Eliminating this effectively made bad loans more burden-some, and increased the volatility of reported incomes, pressuring banks to find new stable sources of revenue and shift assets off balance sheet. New rules preventing banks from deducting the interest on debt used to buy munic-ipal bonds, and consumers from deducting the interest on consumer loans, similarly impacted bank asset portfolios and investment strategies, and made mortgage loans, which remained tax deductible, significantly more attractive. In fact, such a 'decline in the share of banks portfolios taken up by tax-exempt bonds and consumer loans and … rise in the share held by real estate loans' was, according to one Federal Reserve report, the objective, or expected outcome, of the new tax policies (Neuberger 1988).

Another regulatory outcome was the Basel I Accord. While US regulators long deemed reserve requirements insufficient and problematic, the LDC debt crisis stiffened the resolve for tighter rules and heightened frustration with the pace of international change. This first led to the International Lending Supervision Act (1983), which required 'higher capital standards and greater supervision of US bank foreign lending' and provided federal supervisors 'clear enforcement authority for capital requirements' (Kobrak and Troege 2015: 144; Walter and Wansleben 2019: 9). Next, US supervisors within the Basel Committee spearheaded a new capital adequacy framework 'that enabled central bankers to compare their national methodologies and statistics with those of their colleagues' (Kapstein 1992: 276–8). Alongside this, the Fed encouraged the Office of the Comptroller of the Currency (OCC) and FDIC to adopt risk weighted standards similar to the ones used in Britain. Once FDIC chair William Seidman fell into line with this agenda, effectively submitting all institutions that carried federal deposit insurance to the new capital adequacy proposals, Volcker initiated bilateral negotiations with the Bank of England to create an Anglo-American regime. With other central bankers faced with 'the need to consider the implications of any regulatory standard taking effect in New York and London', and US and UK officials still very much focused on creating standards for all international banks, the Basel Committee convened intense negotiations in the spring of 1987 and announced an agreement 'on the international convergence of capital measurements and capital standards' on 10 December (Gowan 1999: 15).

The provisions of the final agreement were therefore 'skewed towards serving US interests' (Gowan 1999: 15). As government bonds were given a zero risk-weight, banks could subtract sovereign debt from their net assets in measuring capital at risk, and were incentivized to hold the safest and most liquid sovereign debt: US Treasury bonds. Basel I also levelled the playing field for US and UK banks – who had lost market share to Japanese banks offering competitive rates due to low equity ratios – and thereby bolstered the transatlantic funding system (Kobrak and Troege 2015: 144). Yet while the effect can be overdrawn, US banks, like other internationally active G-10 banks, were also constrained by the agreement, forced as they were to maintain higher capital ratios. This impacted lending as many banks increased their capital ratios by both raising capital and reducing lending, especially in the three years following the agreement (Jackson et al. 1999). Even if banks did not strengthen their capital ratios by reducing risk weighted assets, fixed capital requirements imposed limits on total lending. In fact, because of these limits banks increasingly migrated towards asset securitization. Indeed, this emerged as a key tool for 'increasing bank risk relative to minimum capital ratios' and was 'an important driver behind securitization', as it effectively allowed banks to escape the burden of capital ratios (Jackson et al. 1999: 3).

The Savings and Loans (S&L) (or thrift) industry was another casualty of the Volcker shock. These specialized banks offered attractive interest rates on deposit accounts to provide fixed rate home mortgages, thereby transforming short-term savings into long-term loans and profiting from the interest rate spread. From the mid-1960s, the business model was underwritten by Regulation Q restrictions on the amount of interest deposit-taking institutions could pay out; this limited competition for funds and ensured that mortgage rates were affordable. Subsequently, these banks were not well positioned for financial deregulation and were particularly susceptible to a sudden prolonged spike in interest rates. As Volcker's tight money policy increased the market cost of borrowing above the return on mortgages held by S&L institutions, producing negative spreads, it led to a widespread crisis, in which the 'vast majority of the almost 4000 Savings and Loans banks still in operation were insolvent' (Tooze 2018: 91).

Regulators confronted this instability in two ways. First, they provided temporary support by shifting accounting policies and removing regulatory restraints. This occurred, above all, through the 1980 Depository Institutions Deregulation and Monetary Control Act, and the 1982 Garn–St Germain Act. While these policies 'widened the state's regulatory remit over the whole banking system', demonstrating, as Panitch and Gindin (2012: 170) note, 'the futility of seeing things in terms of a dichotomy between regulation and deregulation', they created a certain amount of flexibility for thrifts, as they set a schedule for phasing out Regulation Q ratios and allowed them to make commercial and consumer loans. This strategy of 'forbearance', which echoed the response to the LDC crisis, only delayed problems, creating so-called zombie firms propped up by unsustainable deposit rates and risky, high yield loans (Robinson 2013). In fact, as thrifts struggled to stay solvent they took on a key role in the junk bond market, working closely with investment banks and corporate raiders to finance new issues, raise money, and fund corporate takeovers (Knight 1990). This all made their gradual failure functional to the corporate bond market, especially as junk bonds came to play a prominent role in this market and its internationalization. The eventual solution to the S&L crisis, which emerged with the establishment of the Resolution Trust Corporation (RTC) in 1989, also extended market-based finance. In an attempt to resolve insolvent thrifts and reallocate their assets, the RTC turned to securitization, developing its 'own model for mortgage-backed securities, known as Ritzy Maes' (Kim 1998: 359). This involved the standard sale of single-family home mortgages, but it also included so-called multi-family mortgages, securities backed by non-residential commercial loans, in which the RTC was 'something of a trailblazer' (Kim 1998: 359).

Second, regulators took direct steps to expand mortgage securitization, though such measures again reflected wider changes in the financial system and were not simply about resolving the S&L crisis. Securitization developed in 1970 when Ginnie Mae pioneered the first mortgage 'pass-through', whereby the revenue from a pool of mortgages was transferred to investors, and was given a great boost in the early 1980s when Freddie Mac, another Government Sponsored Entity (GSE), issued the first Collateralized Mortgage Obligation (CMO). This divided and repackaged pools of mortgages according to the risk of the underlying debt, creating tranches or asset tiers that allowed investors to select investments based on their risk profile. A key impetus for the development of CMOs was the interest rate volatility created by the Volcker shock: this encouraged GSEs to look for new ways to sell their stockpile of underperforming loans, even at a discount. Yet the development of this market remained hampered by federal and state laws limiting the secondary purchase, private issuance, and marketability of mortgage bonds. The Secondary Mortgage Market Enhancement Act of 1984 changed this, radically altering the market for securitized debt by allowing national banks to purchase mortgage-backed securities and overriding statutory limitations effecting state-chartered financial institutions. This enabled international banks, in trouble with LDC loans, to adjust their investment strategies, and transferred increasing control of the market to GSEs and other non-traditional mortgage bankers interested in transforming home loans into securitized bonds.

At the start of the 1990s, after nearly 20 years of turmoil in the banking industry, the US financial system was thus very different. Encouraged by the Federal Reserve and Treasury Department, the remaining banks and thrifts consolidated their operations, and Wall Street investment firms now played a more prominent role, in no small part due to the expansion of bond, equity, and derivatives markets (Panitch and Gindin 2012). For regulators, securitization was a cornerstone piece of this restructuring since it provided 'greater institutional diversity', bolstered the 'resiliency' of the financial system, and allowed for the 'uninterrupted flow of mortgage credit' (Greenspan 1999b; Panitch and Gindin 2012). But this merely reflected a wider trend towards a market-based system of credit provision, enabled and reinforced by key state policies and regulatory decisions that dramatically increased the size of the IBM and the internationalization of US bonds.

The Asian Financial Crisis and Liberalization

With the long crisis in the US banking system resolved and securities markets now playing an outsized role in the US credit system, attention turned to further liberalizing international markets. This principally involved managing related financial crises in South Korea, Taiwan, and Malaysia, which were triggered by the rapid flow of short-term foreign portfolio capital – '[f]rom 1990 to 1997 foreign capital inflows quadrupled into the region' – and poor lending practices (Rubin 1998a). Inasmuch as these countries required international assistance, such conditions were utilized to further open Asian markets and bolster engagements that supported US risk power. This especially occurred because financial restrictions and regulations limited demand for US dollar debt and inhibited development of the two-way, in-and-out flows that integrated and synchronized US and European markets.

Resolving the crisis therefore meant extending some variant of the Yen–Dollar Accord to other Asian centres, and further opening Japanese financial markets. As Treasury Secretary Rubin declared in announcing the US-driven IMF rescue package: 'The fundamental objectives of these reforms are to restore financial stability and confidence, attract new flows of capital, restore economic growth and promote stronger and more stable exchange rates' (Rubin 1998b). This movement towards 'appropriate' monetary policy rules was necessary to protect the system of 'vastly increased capital flows that have benefited the American people' because it simultaneously opened up key sources of financial demand and pushed against the type of financial isolation that closed key economies to US markets (Rubin 1998a). Not surprisingly, as conditions worsened in Japan and the deflationary spiral became more entrenched, US officials quickly stabilized foreign outflows and pushed regulators there to 'take the steps necessary to deal with the issues in its financial system to generate solid growth in domestic demand and to open its markets' (ibid.).

This intervention secured and bolstered Asian investment in US onshore markets and underpinned the internationalization of US Treasury and agency bonds in the 10 years leading up to the subprime crisis. Moreover, that it reinforced previous regulatory lessons inside the Fed and Treasury only points to the central role of the US economic apparatus in superintending debt markets, as well as the futility of viewing the development of bond markets – during the neoliberal period or before – as a purely market driven dynamic. Indeed, as much as ideas of market efficiency had crept into the Federal Reserve and Treasury Department by the 1990s, these were never taken too far. Rubin emphasized this at the peak of the Asian crisis: 'let me say as someone who spent 26 years in Wall Street and who has an enormous belief in markets, there are problems that markets alone simply cannot solve' (ibid.).

SUMMARY REMARKS

We have seen that key regulatory branches of the US state form part of the institutional ensemble comprising the post-Second World War risk imaginary. They laid the basis for the development of the Bretton Woods system in the

1930s and the dollar standard in the 1970s, and mediated its global extension through different policy manoeuvres. This chapter showed that US financial regulators also played a key role managing and extending US risk power, directly and indirectly. This involved supporting too-big-to-fail firms and dollar liquidity in European markets, building a supervisory network to stabilize the transatlantic financial system, and dismantling barriers to foreign demand. Moreover, it involved supporting the development of market-based financial practices that were themselves a constitutive part of the post-Bretton Woods financial order: if the impact of the Volcker shock – the particular way it opened new investment opportunities and destabilized commercial and S&L banks – shifted financial possibilities, the gradual extension of market-based lending only occurred as US officials supported different actions. This all took shape as regulatory strategies evolved alongside changing objective conditions, through a process of institutional learning.

At the root of the discussion is another key point: that financial crises have been instrumental for the expansion of US risk power and a key aspect of its development. In one way or another they have been utilized to further the internationalization of dollar denominated bonds, drawing countries deeper into the hub-and-spoke financial system created after the Second World War. And this has not just been about Treasury bonds – US private bonds, whether in offshore or onshore markets, have equally benefited. Crucially, regulators have not always acted consciously in this regard, nor has their behaviour always been straightforward. Rather, such instrumentalization has taken shape against the conditions set by US risk power, which established a certain underlying force within financial markets. Acting within this framework, and focused on organizing financial hegemony, US officials managed financial crises by extending US risk power, leading over time to the growing internationalization of US bonds. As we will see in the next part of the book, the subprime crisis emerged from these historical processes and provoked a similar regulatory response, setting up the further expansion of US risk power.

NOTES

1. See also Panitch and Gindin (2004), Panitch and Konings (2009), Panitch et al. (2009).
2. See also: Lipietz (1986); Clarke (1987); Bonefeld (1987); Jessop (1988).
3. See, for example, Block (1977: 140–44), Borden (1984: 176–80), and Helleiner (1994: 74).
4. By 1958, excess US dollar credit to the ROW exceeded $2.25 billion.
5. It was recognized that European deficit economies would need proper access to capital financing, but this problem was not viewed as critical, given their easy access to Eurobond and dollar markets (Spiro 1999).
6. Here again, the roots of the crisis run much deeper than the Volcker shock.

PART III

The subprime crisis as the crisis of risk

The previous parts of the book offered an interpretation of financial demand and traced the development of the international bond market, examining different trends and sub-markets where possible. We saw how US risk power engulfed Tier 1 and Tier 2 bonds and, in the process, impacted the development of US and global financial markets, even while the credibility of dollar denominated debt was itself shaped by the institutional channels through which it evolved. This part sees the same trends at play in the subprime collapse. It suggests that the crisis expressed and carried forward the institutional and intersubjective conditions outlined above.

However, assessing the development of the IBM during this period is slightly more complicated, owing to the rise of the euro and changes in accounting practice. As market distinctions continued to blur, the BIS and OECD merged euro, global, and foreign bonds into a single category, and no longer tracked developments in each market. Further, the trends indicated by this new categorization were not always clear. Following the introduction of the euro, dollar placements initially increased, reaching 51 per cent of total issues in 2001. From 2003 to 2009 the euro was the preferred currency for new issues (Figure III.1). Ostensibly, this portrays a temporary shift from dollar denominated debt in offshore and foreign markets, along the lines seen in the Yankee market during the late 1980s.

Yet we must be careful of combining foreign and offshore markets in this way. Indeed, by including the entire euro area foreign bond market, without adjusting for euro denominated government issues, and taking no account of the dollar denominated foreign government funding market, such figures exaggerate demand for euro international bonds. Because the ECB did not issue debt to accommodate participant country fiscal imbalances, eurozone members, including their local and regional governments, often issued euro denominated debt in the offshore market to raise capital. By contrast, US federal, state, and local debt is issued in the domestic market, or the foreign

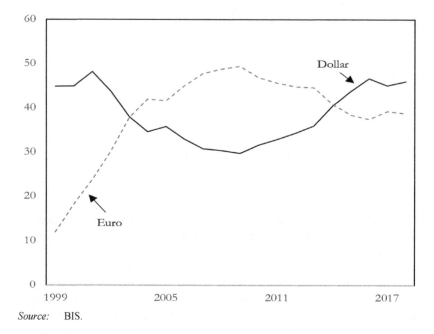

Source: BIS.

Figure III.1   Dollar and euro denominated international bonds, as percentage of total outstanding

branch of the US Treasury market, and is not reflected in BIS measures. When government issued notes and bonds are removed, the size of the euro denominated market decreases by approximately 15 per cent, whereas the dollar market remains basically unchanged (BIS 2009). This means the percentage of euro and dollar denominated international bonds was in fact roughly equal from 2003 to 2007.

This adjustment of figures is confirmed by foreign currency holdings of international banks, assuming such deposits indicate foreign demand for international securities (Grabbe 1996). To be sure, dollar holdings of international banks as a percentage of total offshore currency claims remained strong during this period, even following the introduction of the euro. Using December 1995 as a baseline, the total portion of dollar assets held by depository and commercial banks increased by 25 percentage points by 1999, and on average remained 25 points higher from 2000 to 2005 (Figure III.2). From 2006 to 2007, the spread dropped to plus 17, yet with the baseline itself reflecting half of all offshore currency assets, this remained extraordinary (Figure III.2).

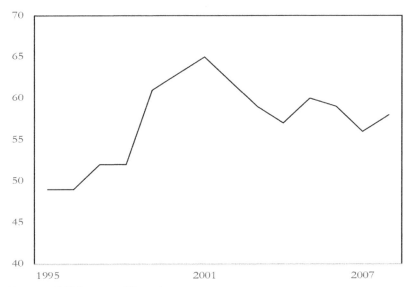

Note: 2009 figures as of September.
Source: BIS.

Figure III.2 *USD as a percentage of foreign currency assets held by reporting banks, 1995–2009*

But even if the dollar component of the foreign and offshore market slipped after 2002, this was only because European and global investors were flocking to the foreign branch of the US domestic market, searching for US Treasury bonds but also, increasingly, US public and private issue mortgage bonds. It is hardly surprising that as foreign demand for US MBS fell following 2008, US dollar denominated international bonds increasingly captured the offshore market, easily outstripping euro denominated debt, despite the accounting biases discussed above.

Therefore, the most important new trend in the IBM was not, as many had been projecting, that the euro replaced the dollar as an international store of value, or even that Asian investors moved out of their dollar positions. Rather, it was that US private and agency-issued mortgage debt became an increasingly important component of the IBM, alongside the ever-growing significance of the US Treasury market (Figure III.3). Euro denominated debt still played an important role – by all accounts many countries were holding euros as reserve assets, and a very large portion of international bond placements were euro denominated – but US risk power remained closely in line with postwar trends.

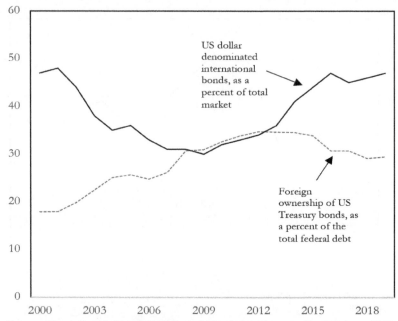

Note: Foreign ownership of US Treasury debt, calculated by comparing TIC data and US
historical debt outstanding (available through TreasuryDirect). Foreign ownership of US publicly
held debt is much higher, as it excludes debt held in Federal Reserve and US government
accounts. For example, foreign holdings as a percentage of total publicly held debt averaged 44
per cent from 2014 to 2018 (Congressional Research Service 2019).
Source: BIS; US Treasury, TIC, TreasuryDirect.

Figure III.3   *Foreign demand for US debt: international bonds vs*
                   domestic-international, 2000–2018

8. The risk crisis

The study of the subprime crisis began with underlying problems in the US economy and the contradictions of finance-based accumulation (Blackburn 2008; Kliman 2008; Foster and Magdoff 2009; Harman 2009; Lapavitsas 2009). Some authors emphasized the defeat of working class organizations in the early neoliberal period, others the rising power of financial firms and the normalization of fraudulent business practices, part of which reflected modulations in state power and capacity. The central notion was that the crisis reflected distinctly US economic and social conditions, and disseminated through its anchorage in the US mortgage market (Dymski 2010; Posner 2009; Cohen 2009; Zandi 2009; Schwartz 2009a). The international aspects of the crisis have more recently taken centre-stage, namely with Tooze's work connecting the accumulation of US private MBS to the European sovereign debt crisis (Tooze 2018). This newer literature has been instrumental in contesting narrow views of the crisis as 'made in America'.

Yet it can be very misleading to look back at the crisis without considering how and why US mortgage bonds gained such credibility and global prominence. It is insufficient to claim that traders and bankers acted capriciously without reason, or that firms took excessive risks to maximize profitability. Such examinations are far too simple and unconvincingly avoid key underlying practices and mechanisms. Instead we must approach the crisis through a recall of events spanning 60 years, and even slightly more, understanding at the outset that the US mortgage bonds proliferated as part of a wider process of internationalization.

MORTGAGE DEBT, CONSUMER DEMAND

The relationship between the subprime crisis and the US housing market is straightforward and widely understood. Between 1965 and 1994 US home-ownership rates were stable, oscillating between 63 and 66 per cent. The period following 1995 was very different, with rates dramatically increasing, first exceeding 66 per cent in 1996 and then reaching nearly 70 per cent in 2005. This was itself linked to the Volcker shock and rollback of labour rights underpinning the dollar standard. In the face of 30 years of stagnant real wages and the rejection of public housing programmes in favour of market-based solutions, the real estate market offered a glimmer of economic hope, especially for racialized minorities who, due to overlapping forms of exploitation, faced huge obstacles.

With these conditions, and the Clinton administration ushering in a 'third way' agenda to consolidate neoliberal domination, albeit through liberal forms of identity-based inclusion, new buyers entered the market and house prices slowly increased. Even as inflation initially kept the real pace of growth flat, the nominal medium price of residential homes increased. As the pricing cycle continued, demand swelled even more, and asset inflation became a key aspect of economic prosperity. Between 1997 and 1999 the real House Price Index (HPI) increased 14 per cent, causing home prices to increase from $145 682 to $167 142. But the real growth occurred between 2000 and 2006 when the HPI appreciated 51 per cent – more than in any other period in recent history – and medium real home prices grew from $169 428 to $276 324.

Supporting this was a wider political shift aimed at drawing workers ever more deeply into financial markets.[1] The 1986 Tax Reform Act allowed homeowners to continue deducting mortgage interest payments from taxable income. This incentivized large mortgage loans and reinforced regulatory changes occurring at the state and federal level that made it easier for banks to offer home equity lines of credit. After Clinton strengthened the Community Reinvestment Act to limit redlining, whereby banks deny mortgage loans to radicalized communities, Bush further targeted the housing gap between white and minority populations. This involved passing the American Dream Down Payment Act, financing the Single Family Affordable Housing Tax Credit, and reforming the Real Estate Settlement Procedures Act (Weicher 2006). These policies, which represented the core of Bush's 'Home Ownership Challenge', reduced closing costs and minimum down payments, and increased tax subsidies for first-time buyers (Becker et al. 2008). They also led to $1.1 trillion in loans to low income and minority buyers, creating what Karger (2007) called a new 'American Bill of Goods' (Global Marketing Network 2009).

As demand grew and property values exploded, mortgage payments stressed household balance sheets. In 1995 the ratio between median house price and median household income (Median Multiple) measured 2.6 in metropolitan areas and 2.4 in areas outside primary markets (DIHS 2008).[2] By 2005 the national Median Multiple reached 3.5 (ibid.). In the 65 largest metropolitan areas, where the majority of US residents lived and most structured mortgages were originated, it topped 4.5, with a handful of major cities showing ratios above 9.0. This put downward pressure on the US savings rate and helped drive a 40 per cent increase in the ratio between household disposable income and debt. In part, homeowners were able to manage this burden by drawing from the equity in their homes and (re)financing at attractive interest rates: in 2004 borrowing against home mortgages accounted for 7 per cent of personal disposable income, compared to 3 per cent in 2000 and 1 per cent in 1994 (Ip

2005). But the 10-year real inflation in mortgages was not offset by an equal appreciation of wages, as the class victory ushered in by the Volcker shock continued to discipline working class demands. Indeed, after a small increase in the late 1990s real wage growth was 'sluggish' between 2000 and 2005, and the 'bottom 95 percent of income recipients experienced decreasing real average household income between 2003 and 2004' (Foster 2006: 2).

As these class contradictions weighed on the market, lenders shifted to speciality mortgages offering flexible payment options and tiered interest rates. The majority of these loans were adjustable rate mortgages (ARMs) with two year, fixed-rate periods at lower interest rates. This adjustability allowed issuers to manage interest rate risk and also build higher interest payments into the loan structure to account for higher expected default rates, temporarily offsetting the problems created by stagnant wages and price appreciation. In 2005 when the 'teaser period' ended for the first significant pool of subprime borrowers, the average national variable mortgage rate increased from 5.3 per cent to 6.2 per cent (US Census Bureau 2007). In some cases, rates on subprime mortgages increased 6 per cent annually (Kirchhoff and Keen 2007). The Federal Reserve compounded this problem by tightening interest rates, in part further to discipline workers and protect the Fed's inflationary commitment under the dollar standard. The increasing cost of credit drastically raised the carrying cost of ARMs and the interest premium on subprime issues. Borrowers trapped by these events still had the luxury of raising house prices and could access the equity in their homes to offset additional mortgage costs, but with interest rates climbing as high as 15.5 per cent, this only postponed the crisis (Kirchhoff and Keen 2007). Starting in 2006, interest rate pressures showed up in the number of subprime loans overdue, with delinquent issues (defined as being in foreclosure, entering the foreclosure process or more than 30 days past due) rising by 4.4 per cent in 2006 and 16.7 per cent in 2007 (US Census Bureau 2006; 2007; 2008).

The increasing rate of delinquency on subprime loans was not by itself exceptional; total overdue loans exceeded 30 per cent between 2000 and 2002 (US Census Bureau 2004). The difference was that non-conventional loans had grown significantly as a portion of the total US market, not only in terms of mortgage issues, but in terms of MBS. By 2006 subprime loans represented 28 per cent of total mortgages and subprime residential mortgage-backed securities were the largest component of the US ABS market, accounting for nearly half of all issues (Weaver 2008). In 2002, by contrast, subprime loans represented only 10 per cent of the residential mortgage market. With the majority of these loans directed at precariously employed and historically marginalized populations – those most jeopardized by neoliberalism's exploitative practices – and even standard mortgage holders increasingly drawing into the value of their inflated property to sustain living conditions, the mortgage debt held by the financial system became increasingly toxic.

ABSTRACT RISK AND THE IBM

Yet we must be careful not to explain the crisis simply through the expansion of US consumer demand, neoliberal wage repression, and financial reregulation. If the crisis first appeared in the US housing market, it did so only through a deeper process of financial engineering and intermediation, which had strong roots in the IBM and US risk power. For all intents and purposes, the growth of toxic US mortgage debt was sustained and underpinned by three interrelated processes: (1) the securitization of US home loans, especially through off-balance sheet investment vehicles in the shadow banking system; (2) the use of derivative contracts by Wall Street firms; and (3) *the global demand for US MBS.*

1.   Securitization and Mortgage Bonds

We must first acknowledge that the US housing bubble was part of a more complex process of financial engineering and innovation. As we saw, such practices were given shape by the LDC and S&L banking crisis, and reregulation of the financial system fostering market-based credit. They were also tied to developments in the US onshore and offshore markets, which stimulated trial and error experimentation and pioneered strategic shifts within firms. Stoked by these practices and lessons and caught in the same funding vice that trapped thrifts in the early 1980s, commercial banks increasingly transformed their asset base by bundling liabilities, such as home loans and mortgages, into asset-backed securities (mortgage-backed securities have only mortgage debt as their underlying base) (Figure 8.1). But instead of serving as conveyer belts for whole loans, banks looked for ways to shift assets without completely losing them. The major problem was that mortgage pass-throughs diversified risk but limited profit: they exchanged a long-term fixed return for the combination of liquidity and small upfront administrative fees. The solution was off-balance sheet funding entities, namely structured investment vehicles (SIVs), and collateralized debt obligations (CDOs).[3]

In a typical structured transaction banks sell sets of loans to a special purpose vehicle. As virtual companies spun off from commercial banks, SIVs purchase bonds (usually asset backed securities) and fund the transaction by issuing money market securities (asset backed commercial paper) at low interest rates. SIVs achieve high ratings on their senior debt for three reasons: they issue money market funds; their capital notes are basically protected by high quality securitized debt; and they are affiliated with major banking institutions.

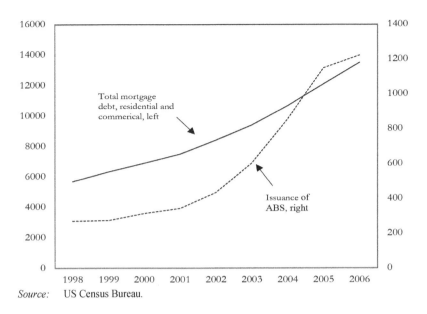

Figure 8.1   *US mortgage origination and securitization, 1998–2006 (USD billion)*

For their part, CDOs are independently organized and managed investment instruments used to distribute asset-backed debt instruments according to credit risk exposure. The structuring company acquires a portfolio of fixed income debt before dividing the securities into tranches according to counterparty default risk. Three tranche classes are usually created: senior (rated AAA), mezzanine (rated from AA to BB), and equity (unrated). Market losses incurred on the portfolio are applied in accordance to the seniority of debt, with junior or equity tranches absorbing first losses. As a result, credit risky junior tranches offer higher coupon rates. Collateralized debt obligations differ from structured investment vehicles in that they profit through administrative charges rather than the spread between different maturities of debt.

Increasingly, then, financial institutions sought flexibility by off-loading and packaging a portion of their mortgage portfolio, thereby diversifying debt and turning their existing pool of mortgages into a secondary market underwritten by parcels of consumer loans. In the process of cleaning their balance sheets, commercial banks created an army of financial entities which greatly boosted the stockpile of home mortgage loans. Slowly, these practices gave form to a new world of off-balance sheet funding which became a key branch of the so-called shadow banking system (Davies 2008). In the period between

1998 and 2006, while the amount of home mortgages held by commercial banks, credit unions, and savings institutions continued to decline, and the shadow banking system exploded, issuance volume in the US asset-backed securities market increased from $271 billion to $1.2 trillion, almost doubling the percentage increase in total US mortgage debt. As this suggests, financial regulation and engineering tied to the IBM greatly shaped asset securitization in the US mortgage market, leading to the rapid growth of subprime loans.

2.   Derivative Innovation and Mortgage Bonds

A similar connection can be made with derivative markets. Clearly, derivative contracts played a critical role in the crisis by turbocharging volatility. As Blyth (2013: 30) concludes, derivatives 'amplified the crisis because rather than lessening correlation [they] actually boosted it'. The extent of the connection is apparent in the collapse of Lehman Brothers which, at the time of its failure, had 'close to one million derivative contracts on its books with hundreds of financial firms' (Stulz 2010: 81). It is not, then, a question of how these contracts contributed to the crisis by creating perverse incentives or by multiplying risk, this issue has been dealt with elsewhere, but how financial firms built on their institutional knowledge and manipulated the relatively open space for financial experimentation afforded by the hub-and-spoke relationship between US and European financial markets, as well as the synergy between international bonds and financial derivatives, to expand the flow of MBS and accelerate global volatility.

Above all we can see an expression of this in the way US and European firms developed and manipulated credit default swaps (CDS) to support their participation in US mortgage bond markets.[4] While CDS directly written on MBS represented only about 13 per cent of total issuance in 2007, these markets were complementary and mutually reinforcing. This is because US and European firms, both banks and non-banks, used innovative approaches to deepen the pool of accessible mortgage bonds (Markose et al. 2015: 579–80). It is especially important that CDS markets functioned 'as alternative trading venues for both hedging and speculation' in the international bond market, and pivoted around large US firms, most of which were lead underwriters in the US MBS market (Oehmke and Zawadowski 2016: 33).

In fact, the vast majority of the market, both in the US and globally, was controlled by just a handful of US banks, namely JP Morgan, Bank of America, Citibank, Morgan Stanley, and Goldman Sachs. In 2008, after the failure of Bear Stearns and AIG further consolidated the market, these banks accounted for 92 per cent of the gross notional value of the global CDS issues (Markose et al. 2012: 629). This role of US firms, as central players in the market, took shape through the interaction between international bonds and financial derivatives discussed in Chapter 6, and on the basis of the dense connections between banks and broker dealers set by the transatlantic financial system: issuance volume in the CDS market was driven through a form of 'network connectivity' between different firms, whereby contracts were spun out through central hub banks into the broader CDS cluster in Europe (ibid.: 637). In this process, US dealers continually bought and sold CDS contracts in a practice known as spread trading. In a spread trade firms either act as intermediaries between buyers or sellers or sell from their portfolio to purchase an offsetting contract to profit from the spread between the two contracts. With no limit on the amount of short and long positions firms could take on a single contract, this created a chain of obligations through the financial system that fortified existing linkages between key US and European firms, creating a 'highly clustered' web of interconnectivity (ibid.: 632). The system drove issuance by allowing core dealers to 'manage liquidity requirements' and resulted in European firms becoming 'systemically important players in the US sector of the CDS market' (ibid.: 632, 643).

US and European firms used CDS contracts to support the extension of US mortgage bonds in three different ways.[5] First, they acted as protection sellers by issuing CDS as protection against the default of mortgage bonds sold to market. In practice this meant selling CDS insurance on different tranches of debt within collateralized debt obligations. By selling insurance on the default risk of pools of mortgages within CDOs, investment firms not only gained fees, but considerably expanded CDO placements. Firms buying CDOs could hedge their exposure by taking an offsetting obligation on the CDO. CDS contracts on MBS were particularly attractive because when 'one asset in the underlying asset pool default[ed] the CDS ... triggered to compensate for any reduction in payments' and continued to exist, 'protecting against further defaults in the pool's assets until maturity' (Mirochnik 2010: 4–5). This symmetry was by no means accidental, given that many of the same firms issuing CDS maintained a major presence in the CDO market, usually through off-balance sheet structured investment vehicles. As Young et al. (2010: 31) summarize: 'selling a CDO backed by pools of mortgages and credit default swaps which provided insurance against losses on the CDO generated [the] enormous fees [which allowed] ... the CDS market to balloon'. In fact, the use of CDS to limit CDO exposure among US investment firms became so widespread that in 2006 'derivatives based on indexes of CDS's on subprime securitizations were introduced' (Stulz 2009: 66). These so-called ABX indexes 'helped financial institutions and investors to assess the value of subprime securities' and provided 'a good hedge instrument' (ibid.: 66–7).

The flip side was that US banks and financial firms used credit derivatives to limit risk exposure to owned assets, thereby acting as protection buyers by purchasing CDS insurance. This became a mainstay of structured finance because

Basel II treated CDS and other credit derivatives 'as instruments of risk mitigation' and allowed banks to use them to 'reduce their capital' (Shan et al. 2014; Levine 2012: 47). In practice, CDS were used to hedge against non-core capital assets, and allowed banks to expand their portfolio of mortgage-backed securities. As subprime issuance grew, and CDO tranches become more volatile, demand for CDS placements exploded: as long as the total cost of the CDS contract was less than the gains from the additional stockpiling of assets minus interbank interest, banks had an incentive to inventory both securitized bonds and CDS. This makes it possible to understand why 72 per cent of the CDS sold by AIG Financial Products division in 2007 were 'used by banks for capital relief' (ibid.). The acquisition of MBS persisted despite the increasing penetration of subprime placements only by means of the opportunity afforded by CDS contracts.

Third, US firms took positions as both protection sellers and buyers, purchasing CDS to hedge against the CDS protection sold in the equivalent amount. Often this meant that dealers either bought CDS on the protection sellers issuing the CDS they purchased to protect against loss in the CDO market, or bought protection on the same CDO on which they sold protection. This so-called 'daisy-chain' meant that instead of actually holding any CDS risk, financial institutions often served merely as 'intermediates between the ultimate buyer and seller of protection' (Mirochnik 2010: 5). The notable exception was American Insurance Group Financial Productions division, which opted not to hedge its CDS exposure and thus ran an unmatched book. In the main, AIG simply sold CDS 'on super senior tranches of securitizations' (Stulz 2010: 83).

Again, this extension of the CDS market registered as the expansion of CDO placements. As more precarious bonds came to market and the probability of default expanded, protection sellers were reluctant to extend credit protection and endlessly accommodate demand. For most institutions there was a threshold level of unmatched CDS that they were not willing to exceed. In this context, CDS daisy-chains emerged as a critical sustaining feature of the MBS market because they liquidated the flow of CDS protection to end holders. By running matched books, large US investment and commercial banks, namely Lehman Brothers, Bear Stearns, and JP Morgan, were able to provide the type of market protection required for the expanded growth of the US MBS market.

Thus these characteristics of institutional innovation and connectivity – protection selling, buying, and daisy-chains – greatly extended the issuance of US mortgage bonds, leading at the same time to increased correlation risk and volatility. From this point of view, the CDS market failed to hedge default risk and acted instead as a carrier of systemic financial risk: it was a major cause of the subprime crisis. But this is only one side of the story. CDS evolved hand in hand with a wider process of innovation, and through the hub-and-spoke relationship between US and European financial firms. This institutional capacity and connectivity, which spurred new collateralized debt obligations, structured investment vehicles and other patterns of shadow banking, did not fall from the sky, but at least partly emerged from the postwar bond market and US risk power.

3.   The IBM and US Risk

Any analysis that stops at this point fails to read fully the onion-like layers of financial control underpinning the subprime crisis. Two qualitative shifts within the IBM fuelled these associated changes in structured credit and derivative markets, and altered conditions across the US mortgage market: foreign demand for US agency debt from Asia and foreign demand for US private MBS from Europe.

In short, foreign demand permitted the unsustainable expansion of US MBS, and eventually subprime bonds. Cross-border investment inflows created a 'massive surge in the domestic supply of credit' that both distorted market signals and allowed the US banking system to extend mortgage operations; these inflows essentially freed banks 'from the constraint of the domestic funding base' and thereby 'enable[d] [the] domestic credit boom' that supported new demand (McCauley 2018: 44). This was especially the case following the early part of 2004 when the Federal Reserve began aggressively tightening the money supply chain. Under these conditions, cross-border investment inflows drove new issuance (Aliber and Kindleberger 2015: 3). Crucially, this happened as the US MBS market became ever more saturated with subprime debt, especially the riskiest forms of subprime debt: 'from 2004, fully half of the subprime issues being fed into the system had incomplete or zero documentation and 30 percent were interest only loans to people who had no prospect of making basic repayment' (Tooze 2018: 125).

The surge in foreign credit from Asia and Europe had two related effects. First, it supported the initial wave of expansion in the US MBS market from the late 1990s to the early 2000s that saw the extension of traditional mortgage loans and basically emptied the US market of qualified borrowers – this can be connected to Asian investment in US agency debt. Second, and more importantly, demand from Europe was at the root of the subsequent boom in non-conventional mortgage loans following 2002, which dramatically brought subprime borrowers into the market and eventually toxified the entire US MBS market. The expansion of subprime debt would have been unthinkable had the US mortgage market not 'reshaped its pricing around the needs of foreign banks in the 2000s' (McCauley 2018: 50). With subprime placements growing out of foreign investment inflows in this way, 'the dramatic surge in US real estate prices after 2002 followed an increase in foreign purchases of US dollar securities', rather than the 'wayward behaviour' of US financial firms (Aliber and Kindleberger 2015: 3).

As this shows, US mortgage bonds are indissociable from the IBM and postwar risk imaginary. This is critical for understanding investor demand for US mortgage bonds following the mid-1990s, which is typically seen apart from the credibility of US Treasury debt. Such narrow accounting also creates a dividing line between demand for US private MBS in Europe and demand for US agency MBS in Asia, even though both reflect US risk power. The important underlying point is that US mortgage bonds piggybacked on the very same patterns of financial risk that shaped the IBM following 1944, which privileged US public and private bonds. To be sure, 'by 2008 roughly a quarter of all securitized mortgages were held by foreign investors' and China alone held an estimated $500–600 billion in US agency bonds (Tooze 2018: 140). In the private MBS market, where Freddie and Fannie did not operate, European investors held a staggering 29 per cent of all US issues. This meant that by 2007 foreign banks held exposure to as much as 60 per cent of all US originated asset backed bonds (Kamin and DeMarco 2010). *The international market for US MBS was merely the newest segment of the US domestic-international market.*

Demand for US MBS was also conjunctural, the result of various intersecting patterns of risk in the IBM. In fact, firms stockpiled mortgage obligations due to intense competition for US denominated debt in the Yankee, euro, and domestic-international market, which itself reflected low rates of return on risk-free Treasury bonds. One result of the 2000 recession and tech bubble collapse was that the Federal Reserve aggressively discounted coupon rates, lowering the interest return from 650 basis points to 100 basis points. As the yield on Treasury debt dropped, demand slowed, and US mortgage bonds boomed – for pension funds and other institutional investors they were an especially attractive alternative (Cowan 2003). This involved a transfer of funds from the US public domestic-international market to the private section of the same market, and was no doubt assisted by the US Office of the Comptroller of Currency, which set regulatory guidelines in 1996 encouraging firms to invest in such bonds as a 'progressive and effective risk management tool' (Kothari 2006: 905).

This way of viewing foreign demand for US mortgage debt takes our understanding of Freddie Mac and Fannie Mae, and their role in the crisis, a significant step forward. As GSEs entered the secondary mortgage market as an extension of the Treasury Department, they more or less *tied together* sections of the agency US MBS market and the US Treasury bond market. As noted, mortgage focused GSEs were initially chartered as public organizations, but to support the dollar and stabilize thrift financing this changed in 1968, when Fannie Mae was converted to a private corporation. Under the terms of the arrangement, Fannie's close relationship to the US state was preserved, both implicitly and explicitly. Most importantly, its charter permitted the Treasury Department to purchase $2.25 billion of company debt (McLean 2005). This gave it a special line of credit with the government and effectively linked its debt to the credibility of the US state.[6] Paul Krugman (2008) has written of Freddie and Fannie that the most 'important privilege they enjoy is implicit: the belief of investors that [if either company] is threatened with failure, the federal government will come to their rescue.'[7]

Subsequently, the interest on Freddie and Fannie US mortgage debt more or less reflected the risk-free status of Tier 1 debt, and foreign accumulation was consistently strong (Liu 2008; Figure 8.2). On the eve of the subprime crisis, with Fannie and Freddie holding or guaranteeing $5.4 trillion of US mortgage debt – approximately 48 per cent of the overall US market – about 30 per cent of US GSE debt was owned by foreigners, especially emerging market investors (Nesvetailova and Palan 2008; Tooze 2018: 140). Further, because both firms constantly entered the secondary market, and were key drivers of liquidity, they influenced demand for private MBS as well, though this was far less important for Alt A and subprime loans, since federal regulations limited GSEs to traditional issues. According to the BIS: 'implicit Treasury support transform[ed] private assets and private equity into safe assets ... without any immediate counterpart in the Federal government's cash borrowing requirement' (McCauley 2019: 4). Not only this, the high demand for US agency debt coming from Asia and other emerging market economies opened financial engineering opportunities in dollar assets: locked out of the agency market by foreign demand, US institutional investors, such as pension funds and life insurance funds, frequently turned to AAA rated private MBS securities and increasingly acquired subprime and Alt A debt (Tooze 2018: 114). What's more, these same investors turned their pools of cash funds over to the money market and fed the accumulation of private mortgage bonds in Europe (ibid.: 114–16).

International demand for US MBS thus emerged from the semiotic construction of risk in the IBM,[8] and marked only an extension of historically normal patterns. This market derived special benefit from the supply of collateralized debt and low coupon rates on Treasury securities, as well as its unique connection to the US state. In the end, US mortgage bonds expressed a hybrid form of risk: the relation between GSEs and the Treasury Department, and the former's active role in the market, meant that even private US MBS (Tier 2 debt) carried some form of government guarantee, not only regarding the promise of forward dollar worth but *the actual credit risk on the bond.*

Still, we must be careful not to exaggerate the impact or importance of Freddie and Fannie. The accumulation of US agency debt cannot be separated from the foreign accumulation of private issue MBS, not least because the two

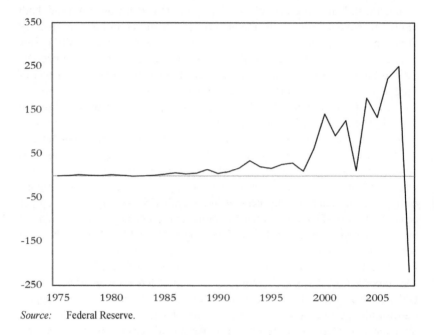

Source: Federal Reserve.

Figure 8.2   *Foreign held US agency and GSE backed securities, annual purchases 1971–2008 (USD billion)*

markets were informed by the same risk standards. But, as we saw above, the subprime loan market found its principal form of support in Europe – it had a separate basis in the IBM, tied to the hub-and-spoke relationship between US and European markets. With the historically strong demand for US debt from European banks and investors, this involved a portfolio shift from 'mostly safe Treasury and agency securities [and] … plain vanilla US corporate bonds' to variable rate asset backed securities with comparatively higher rates of return (McCauley 2018: 50). From 2003 to 2007 European investors expanded their portfolio holdings of US ABS from 9 per cent to 32 per cent, while dropping their portfolio share of Treasury and corporate debt from 91 per cent to 68 per cent. Again, this did not mean European investors stopped accumulating US public and corporate debt, in fact investment in these instrument nearly doubled. It meant that investment in adjustable rate mortgages, a large portion of which were subprime loans, exploded – growth actually exceeded 800 per cent, from $93 billion to $855 billion. As European banks rearranged their dollar portfolios in this way, they 'claimed a market share of a third or more in the production of highly leveraged MBS' and came 'to dominate the market' (ibid.: 51; Tooze 2018: 140). Thus while 'twice as much money flowed into US bonds from March 2000 to mid-2007 from Asian official holders as flowed into US private asset-backed securities from European banks and others between end-2002 and mid-2007', the nature of European investment placed it at the centre of the subprime storm (McCauley 2018: 41). In fact, European demand led US mortgage brokers to shift 'to using offshore Libor as the reference' for the floating rate attached to subprime loans. As the ABS market grew in this way, 'the Libor-linked share of subprime reached practically 100%' (ibid.: 50). Meanwhile, the volume of cross-border inflows from European banks 'drove US mortgage finance away from government guarantees to private credit risk', leading to a major decline in conventional fixed rate issues and the agency portion of the US MBS market (ibid.: 45). As a result, *the issuance of subprime loans to poor US consumers occurred on the foundation of the transatlantic system of demand inside the IBM.* It was, above all, European involvement that turned the MBS market into a mixed soup of consumer loans and tied it to the specific forms of racialized class subordination and dispossession brought by neoliberal accumulation.

From this perspective, it is not surprising that European banks were prone to fund subprime accumulation by participating in the securitization process inside the US market. From 2002 to 2007, three of the top seven underwriters of US subprime MBS deals were European banks: Greenwich RBS, Credit Suisse, Deutsche Bank, and RBS alone controlled over 9 per cent of the total market (ibid.: 47). This process of 'integrating down the supply chain so as to control mortgage origination itself', further involved European banks in the development of the subprime market and expressed a different consequence of European demand for non-agency mortgages (Tooze 2018: 143).

All told, European banks headlined the subprime market and served as 'critical nodes of contagion' (Chesnais 2016: 234). They 'bulked large' as ultimate holders and even distributors of subprime debt, and constantly 'signal[led] to mortgage bankers to extend more credit' (McCauley 2018: 47). None of this, however, marked more than an incremental adjustment of previous patterns. As European investors drove subprime issuance, they did so on the basis of a much longer and deeper process of financial demand. The very same logic, rooted in the post-Second World War risk imaginary, drew Asian investors to US agency debt.

It is important, finally, that this complex process of origination and distribution was also forged out of the institutional capacities previously developed through the IBM. As European banks underwrote US dollar issues in the US market, and either held a portion of these placements on their own books or sold them to European investors, they were technically participating in the US domestic-international market. But this also marked an extension of their long participation in the Yankee and Eurodollar market as underwriters and distributors of private US dollar bonds to European investors, meaning that neither the purchase nor sale of US private MBS was anything different. Moreover, it is not a coincidence that the major European underwriters of US MBS had a long history in the US Treasury bond market as primary dealers. Whereas Deutsche Bank became a US primary dealer bank in 1990, RBS's involvement can be traced to 1984 through Greenwich Capital (acquired by RBS in 2009). For its part, Credit Suisse was approved as a primary dealer in 1993 when it took over First Boston, which had been involved in the market since its inception in 1960.

A GLOBAL CRISIS IN THE MAKING

Clearly, the subsequent collapse of European financial markets was not due to public sector debt, let alone lavish welfare benefits. It rather reflected the historical roots of the subprime loan market and configuration of the transatlantic financial system, of which dollar denominated debt was a major component. As the crisis ripped through US markets, European firms were left with declining assets and ensnarled in a process of 'direct contagion involving co-movements in asset prices' (Kamin and DeMarco 2010). In short, European demand for US mortgage bonds created a direct transmission channel for sub-prime volatility that was felt through mark-to-market losses.

However, this was all part of a larger totality of events. As we saw, net European exposure to US ABS reached $855 billion in June 2007, and gross foreign exposure to issues backed by US home loans totalled about $2.5 trillion, or 60 per cent of the value of the US ABS market (ibid.). Even assuming a 'rather large loss factor of 30 per cent to the estimated gross exposure of foreigners to US ABS', total foreign losses only amounted to about $770 billion. This was 'less than 2 per cent of the foreign bond market capitalization outstanding ... and only about a fifth of the bank capital of the major non-US economies' (ibid.: 9). While exposure to toxic US debt was indeed massive, it insufficiently explains the crisis' impact across the Europe. According to the Federal Reserve, it 'is not clear that direct exposure to base US assets was, by itself, enough to turn the US subprime crisis into a global financial crisis' (ibid.: 9).

It is here where the reciprocal mediation between US international bond flows and offshore dollar funding markets discussed in Chapter 6 is especially significant. Recall that the growth of offshore dollar funding allowed European banks to purchase US international bonds: offshore dollar markets provided the liquidity to hold US dollar assets and allowed European investors to fund long-term dollar loans with short-term dollar denominated debt. The exact same pattern held with US MBS markets, only on a larger scale, as the

US dollar money market, including the Eurodollar market, stood behind the accumulation of private MBS issues in Europe. Simply put: European financial institutions accumulated short-term dollar liabilities in the money market to fund floating rate MBS. As the BIS explains: 'Large gross flows from Europe to the US were balanced by flow in the opposite direction: European banks funded portfolios of US assets by round-tripping dollar funds from the US and back again ... Dollars raised from US money market funds flowed back Stateside through purchase of private MBS' (McCauley 2018: 41).

By contrast, Asian investment in fixed rate US agency debt was funded by the savings glut from US current account deficits. The European funding model thus made non-conventional floating rate ABS particularly appealing to European banks, as these hedged against interest rate risk. This is why adjustable rate mortgages 'predominated in private label MBS', representing 62 per cent of private issues (ibid.: 45).

At the same time, this meant that European firms funded subprime debt through dollar liabilities that had to be continually rolled over. Incidentally, these loans were often sourced from the institutional investors driven to the money market by Asian control of the US agency market. Moreover, these short-term loans frequently took the form of asset-backed commercial paper, given they were collateralized by the same long-term US mortgage debt that drove European investors into the money market. The upshot was that US subprime loans were essentially supported by a massive pile of unfunded dollar liabilities held by European banks that were sensitive to downward movement in the US MBS market. Because many of these dollar liabilities were sourced from the Eurodollar market, through the process of 'round tripping' in the US money market, European banks' exposure to US subprime debt was fed through European interbank channels and rapidly inflated the London interbank offer rate.

Making matters worse, European banks used the dollar money market as a general funding source, including to support their positions in other dollar bond markets. As a result, when US subprime borrowers began defaulting on their home loans in 2006, European banks faced massive dollar funding shortfalls (Tooze 2018: 28). By the middle of 2007, 'the major European banks had a US dollar funding gap of at least $1.0–1.2 trillion and as possibly high as $6.5 trillion' (Fowler 2014: 838). Ultimately, this was a second vector of contagion between European and US financial markets. As the crisis spread in the US, offshore dollar funding markets seized and financial institutions, increasingly concerned with the health of their counterparties in interbank transactions and their own exposure to US subprime volatility, hoarded excess capital. This meant that European banks could no longer fund their dollar liabilities through currency swaps, Eurodollar interbank loans, or US-based money markets, and faced immediate insolvency (ibid.: 838).

As this suggests, the sudden interruption of dollar funding circuits severely impacted international mortgage markets, and US debt markets more generally. Without functional short-term dollar markets, banks had to sell assets into a declining market to roll over their debt obligations and maintain operations. It was only because the US Fed established swap lines of credit with central bank counterparties in Europe and globally, whereby foreign central banks traded domestic cash for US dollars and then used these dollars to ease funding restraints in domestic markets, that this dollar liquidity crisis spread without provoking a complete collapse of international markets. That the Fed made 'swap line loans of a total of 10 trillion to the ECB, the Bank of England and the National Bank of Switzerland and other banking centres' shows how much the crisis crippled European banks and interbank markets, and how it was ultimately steeped in international demand for US dollar bonds (Tooze 2017).

SUMMARY REMARKS

This chapter sketched the complex relationship between the subprime crisis and the IBM – the correlation between US risk power and subprime volatility. Rather than recounting the details of the crisis, it focused on key points of contact between the international bond market and the 2008 collapse, highlighting how the post-Second World War risk imaginary impacted events. Most importantly, we saw that European demand for non-conventional floating rate ABS stimulated subprime issuance, and thereby amplified all of the dangerous forms of financial engineering already playing out in the traditional mortgage market. Moreover, demand for private issue US mortgages brought European banks deeper inside the US dollar money market. As international demand for US denominated mortgage debt magnified existing contradictions, the collapse of this market drew in the global financial system like a vortex. Europe and Asia were not caught in a 'made in America' crisis; they were rather at the very centre of the storm from the beginning. In this respect, the subprime crisis actually developed from a series of portfolio transformations within the IBM – from offshore and foreign holdings to US domestic-international holdings, and from public holdings in the domestic-international market to private non-conventional holdings. We also saw that certain institutional legacies, linked to the IBM, impacted financial practices and the trajectory of subprime volatility. Such institutional level connections especially involved CDS markets and European offshore dollar markets. Of course, this does not mean that US risk power tracked an irremovable course. It suggests rather that transcendent patterns of risk in the IBM interacted with other generative mechanisms, mapping a financial pathway that resulted in the subprime crisis.

NOTES

1. This accompanied the wider shift to market-based credit discussed in Chapter 7.
2. This was consistent with historical trends.
3. This is not to say that off-balance sheet vehicles only became popular as banks sought to clean up their accounts. Following the debt crisis, supervisors at the BIS discovered that many commercial banks had 'a large number of potential assets ... off balance sheet' (Kapstein 1992: 275).
4. Credit default swaps are over-the-counter agreements to make fixed periodic payments for a specific term in exchange for the default risk of a third-party reference entity, paid upon a specified credit event such as failed payments, insolvency, or debt restructuring (Kolb and Overdahl 2003: 174). In a typical agreement the protection buyer purchases insurance against the default of a corporation or financial instrument in a specified notional amount in exchange for a series of regular payments to the protection seller. Unlike conventional insurance contracts, however, the protection buyer does not have to be directly exposed to the underlying entity or corporation to purchase default protection; naked CDS allowed buyers to place bets on assets they do not hold.
5. As Stulz (2010: 80) notes, financial institutions 'believed that it was advantageous to hold ... tranches of securitizations on their books if they insured them with credit default swaps.'
6. It was in this context that the Department of Commerce began actively marketing Federal National Mortgage Association securities to foreign central banks in 1976 (Spiro 1999: 113).
7. See also Bernanke (2015).
8. The BIS has acknowledged this point, noting that the credibility of US MBS issues was politically created and involved extending the credibility of the US state to the agency market. As McCauley (2019) notes: 'US government support for housing agencies Fannie Mae and Freddie Mac has made their debt into safe assets.'

9. Management renewed

As the US and global financial system stood on the brink of collapse in 2008, US officials organized the most sweeping intervention in the history of global capitalism, first arranging and providing loans to troubled firms, then backstopping key markets. In the process, the Fed turned from a lender-of-last-resort to a liquidity provider of last report, seemingly focused less on troubled institutions and more on the key markets underpinning the financial system. This served as the clearest possible indication of the connection between US risk power and the US state. As we saw, the Fed's willingness to extend liquidity to protect key markets underpinned the development of US risk power in the 1930s and 1940s. But this was even more important with the dollar standard. The liberalization of capital presented both a major opportunity and threat to US risk power: the former because global investors could more easily access dollar denominated debt, to fund US deficits, corporate expansion, and consumption; the latter because such freedom created enormous volatility. Moreover, the elimination of par values and the deregulation of interest rates created more uncertainty and more opportunity for financial collapse.

One solution was found with the development of financial derivatives, which allowed investors to hedge risks. But this only extended financialization. The major solution was found with the strategy of failure containment, whereby US regulators supported innovation and financial liberalization but also intervened in markets to manage volatility and protect key firms and credit channels. This took shape well before the subprime crisis: it occurred during the LDC crisis, the 1987 stock market crisis, the Asian financial crisis and the Long-Term Capital Management (LTCM) crisis, as well as other similar episodes of financial distress. According to one senior Fed official, these interventions involved the Fed and Treasury supporting 'all non-idiosyncratic bank risk' and served as major episodes of institutional learning (Sooklal 2012). The subprime crisis thus marked only the most significant form of this financial management, supporting the dollar standard and US risk power. As financial officials prepared a rescue package for monoline insurance firms, attempted to backstop structured investment vehicles, managed the collapse of Bear Stearns, Freddie and Fannie, AIG and even Lehman Brothers, they applied these lessons of financial containment, ensuring that key markets serving as custodians for US risk power and financial hegemony continued to function. The same was true as it backstopped key firms, like Citigroup and Bank of

America, and organized the conversion of Morgan Stanley into a bank holding company.

Yet this management also involved the further development of debt markets, and continued earlier trends of supporting market-based credit which served to extend US risk power through the IBM. It therefore sparked a wave of internationalization, which in fact made dollar dominated debt ever more central to the world financial system. This took shape through two key programmes of financial management: the Fed's quantitative easing programme and its swap lines of credit to G7 central banks; as well as two major pieces of financial regulation. Through these programmes and regulations the crisis was instrumentalized, much like the 1980s banking crisis, to extend US risk power across different segments of the IBM (Albo et al. 2010). This chapter turns to these issues, building on existing literature which carefully charts these interventions and the remarkable extension of state capacity they entailed.

SUBPRIME MANAGEMENT AND THE IBM

It is important first to understand that the crisis reinforced US risk power and led to the expansion of dollar denominated international bonds (Figures 9.1–9.5). This involved key changes in different market segments – the gradual decline of some and the increase of others – but overall dollar debt became an ever more significant component of the IBM. Not surprisingly, one of the markets to suffer most was the US agency market. As we saw, this had become a major segment of the IBM by the early 2000s, supported mainly by Asian investors. The crisis hit this market hard for a number of reasons: with the collapse of the US housing market new issuance declined, so did the market value of outstanding mortgage pools. Meanwhile, investors, including foreign central banks, pulled back and looked to other forms of dollar debt. The total outstanding volume of agency and GSE-backed mortgage pools subsequently plunged from 2008 to 2010. Gross foreign purchases of US agency bonds also collapsed, falling from $56 billion to $24 billion over the same period, and were slow to recover (Figure 9.1; Figure 8.2). By 2019 gross foreign purchases in fact remained well below pre-crisis levels, and total foreign ownership stood at just over $1.1 trillion, almost $300 billion less than in 2008 (McCauley 2019). Thus while the agency segment of the US domestic-international market remained significant, and gradually recovered after 2013, it was no longer a leading force.[1]

This was offset by changes in the US Treasury and corporate markets, where foreign ownership remained strong. The US corporate market slowly recovered from 2010 to 2012, and expanded rapidly from that point forward. By 2019 foreign ownership totalled nearly $4 trillion – a 35 per cent increase from its peak in 2008, and 62 per cent higher from where it stood in 2009. Even

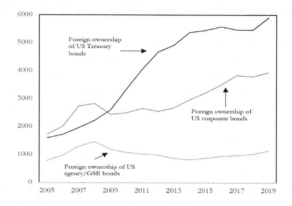

Source: US Treasury Department, TIC.

Figure 9.1   *US domestic-international market, major segments*
2005–2019

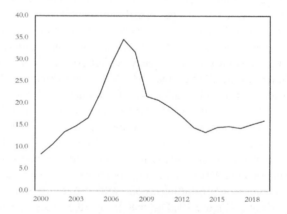

Notes: Foreign ownership calculated using TIC data on total short- and long-term foreign
held agency debt in comparison to Federal Reserve data on total outstanding GSE debt. This
slightly overstates the percentage of foreign ownership, as agency debt includes a wider portion
of securities than are captured in the Federal Reserve calculations. However, foreign ownership,
especially foreign official ownership, has always been very heavily focused on GSE debt,
particularly that offered by Freddie and Fannie.
Source: US Treasury Department, TIC; Federal Reserve, FRED.

Figure 9.2   *Foreign ownership of agency (GSE) backed securities, as*
a percentage of total market, 2000–2019

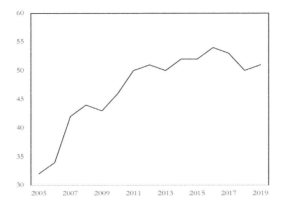

Note: Foreign ownership of US domestic bonds calculated by adding total foreign
ownership of US corporate, agency and Treasury bonds.
Source: US Treasury Department, TIC.

Figure 9.3   *Foreign ownership of US domestic bonds (US
domestic-international market), as a percentage of GDP,
2005–2019*

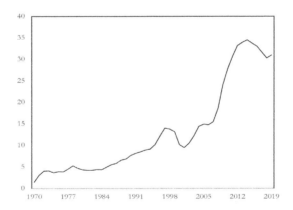

Source: US Treasury department, TIC; Federal Reserve, FRED.

Figure 9.4   *Foreign ownership of US federal debt, as a percentage of US
GDP, 1970–2019*

Source: BIS.

Figure 9.5   *Total international bonds (foreign and offshore), 1966–2020*

more impressive was the performance of the US Treasury market: leading up to the crisis it had been supplanted by the corporate market in terms of total foreign ownership, especially as investors turned to agency debt due to higher yields. By 2009, as foreigners stockpiled US federal debt and as corporate issues stalled, the Treasury market once again became the most significant component of the domestic-international market. What can be seen here is a shift within the US market, as the foreign demand for agency debt which drove issuance prior to the crisis shifted to the Treasury market. Coupled with the already strong demand for Treasury issues, especially from foreign central banks, and growing US deficits, foreign ownership of Treasury debt increased 166 per cent from 2008 to 2019, and total foreign holdings of US federal debt skyrocketed from 19 per cent to 31 per cent, making international demand ever more integral (Figure III.3; McCauley 2019).[2]

Similar trends took shape in the foreign and offshore markets. Yankee and Eurodollar bonds always led the development of these markets, consistently accounting for about half of total issuance. This changed in the early 2000s following the introduction of the euro. By 2009 the share of bonds denominated in euros reached 49 per cent, compared to only 30 per cent for the dollar (Figure III.3).[3] Yet this mainly involved the expansion of other dollar segments of the international market, including public and private agency markets and US corporate markets. As European investors turned to the US domestic-international market in this way, they increasingly turned their back on Eurodollar bonds. Further, as we saw, there is difficulty treating euro and dollar denominated international bonds in the same way, as the former are often issued inside the eurozone, to investors in different countries but within the same currency zone.

At any rate, dollar denominated offshore and foreign bonds slowly regained their top position as the crisis dragged on. By 2020 the dollar again accounted for nearly 50 per cent of total foreign and offshore bonds, while the euro share had declined to 38 per cent (Figure 9.5). This is even more remarkable since many US issuers were drawn to euro denominated debt due to low and negative interest rates. Indeed, one of the key trends during this period was the growth of the so-called reverse Yankee market, where US firms issued euro-denominated bonds in offshore markets, often to swap the proceeds into dollars. By 2019 about 20 per cent of the European corporate bond market was attributable to such arrangements.[4]

Therefore, while demand for dollar denominated debt soared in the pre-crisis period, in a way that created immense financial volatility, it has for all intents and purposes been even stronger since 2008, driven by both private and public demand. This was not a contingent historical process but rather a product of how regulators responded to the crisis and utilized conditions to further transform the financial system. In fact, the regulatory capacity to contain the crisis, by way of creating an abundance of liquidity, itself hinged on demand for US debt in the IBM – these processes were not separate but rather mutually interconnected. This found its most visible expression in the Troubled Asset Relief Program (TARP), passed by Congress in the aftermath of the Lehman's failure, which raised money to support key financial firms through the sale of new Treasury bonds, and thus took shape through strong foreign demand in the domestic-international market.[5] The TARP allowed the Treasury to purchase equity stakes in financial institutions and resulted in the government taking an ownership claim in Goldman Sachs Group, Morgan Stanley, JP Morgan Chase, Bank of America Corp. (including Merrill Lynch), Citigroup, Wells Fargo, Bank of New York Mellon, and State Street. At the same time, firms were forced to accept restrictions on executive compensation and dividend payments.

The expansion of the Fed's balance sheet also required global investors to buy and hold additional dollar debt. As the Fed transformed itself into a liquidity provider of last resort after the Lehman's collapse, it flooded the financial system with dollars and abandoned earlier sterilization programmes.[6] As a result, bank claims held at the Fed quickly ballooned, from less than $500 million to over $3 trillion. Yet this could only work if investors either held these dollars on reserve or invested them in dollar denominated bonds, otherwise such measures threatened the low inflation mandate sustaining the dollar standard. The Fed helped in this direction by establishing a new system of paying interest on reserve holdings, essentially incentivizing banks to hold excess dollars. This meant that the Fed bought debt from financial firms and then paid these same firms to hold the dollars received from these sales, essentially cleansing bank balance sheets. But this only went so far: investors also had to use this new liquidity to purchase debt securities – this further sterilized excess dollars, allowing the Fed to function as a liquidity provider of last resort. Not only institutional adaption, but strong demand for dollar debt, itself reflecting how investors everywhere flocked to safety, lay at the heart of US financial management.

Moreover, this provision of liquidity was reinforced by the Fed's explicit support for key debt markets, epitomized to some degree by its bailout of Freddie Mac and Fannie Mae. As custodians of Tier 1 risk, these firms were part of the central nervous system of the financial apparatus, critical to US consumer liquidity, interbank rates, and above all the credibility of US Treasury debt. Under these circumstances, certain options were immediately taken off the table, namely that market forces could be unleashed to manage conditions, and officials stressed the need to prevent any serious discussion of default. If there was ever any doubt intervention would involve public money, and the state backstopping outstanding debt, this was quickly put to rest as major foreign holders pressured the Fed and Treasury to guarantee agency bonds. According to Bernanke:

> As doubts grew about the GSEs, both Hank Paulson and I received calls from central bank governors, sovereign wealth fund managers and government officials in East Asia and the Middle East. Were the companies safe? Would the US government stand behind them? Several of my callers had not realized that the government did not already guarantee the GSEs. News coverage had alerted them to the risk. (Bernanke 2015: 231)

Making matters worse, financial markets were continuing to deteriorate and US officials were fully aware that future liquidity required the special credibility of Tier 1 debt.

It was these mechanisms, and the continuing deterioration of both companies through July and August, not some abstract functionalism, that forced US officials into action. However the bailout, which recapitalized both Freddie and Fannie and put them into a government conservatorship, stopped short of 'putting the full faith and credit of the federal government behind these entities' (McCauley 2019: 8). Instead, 'the government entered a keep-well arrangement to cover losses in order. This kept their debt off the Treasury's balance sheet and from counting towards the debt limit', and thereby preserved a separation between US Treasury debt on the one hand and agency securities on the other (ibid.: 8).

To some extent, the terms of this arrangement more firmly tied GSE obligations to US Treasury bonds, as the government's willingness to guarantee repayment was no longer implicit. It is no surprise in this context that the bailout package did not completely undermine, and to some degree sustained, the popularity of US GSE debt. From this, a critical distinction ensued: while private MBS were allowed to collapse in value, Tier 1 hybrid obligations were guaranteed. As a result, *the collapse played out as a crisis of mortgage bonds rather than US risk power, even though the conception of risk tied to US dollar assets was critical in stimulating foreign demand for US MBSs*. It was on the basis of this separation that the Fed and Treasury Department proceeded to rescue the global financial system. At the same time, by reinforcing the distinction between agency and Treasury debt, US officials made it ever more difficult for foreign buyers to conflate the two issues – the implicit guarantee used for this end had shown its limits. This in fact meant that 'US agency securities lost some of their safety *after* US government support became explicit in September 2008', even if the market remained a significant reflection of US risk power (ibid.: 8).

REMAKING MARKETS, REINFORCING RISK POWER

If the containment strategies rolled out by the Fed and Treasury Department rested on US financial credibility and reinforced pre-crisis patterns of risk, they also gave a great boost to dollar denominated international bonds. To assess the financial rescue merely in terms of supporting existing firms and markets is to pay insufficient attention to the generative forces and pressures created by emergency interventions, chief among them the Fed's programme of quantitative easing (QE). This aimed to 'foster improved conditions in financial markets' through the purchase of US denominated debt, and involved the Fed expanding its balance sheet and greatly increasing excess reserves in the banking system. Unlike the Bank of Japan, which initiated a similar programme in the early 2000s, aimed at supporting banks by injecting a targeted amount of liquidity, the Fed's initial experiment with QE was more about backstopping the US agency market. The centrepiece of QE1, the so-called Agency MBS Purchase Facility, involved the purchase of $1.25 trillion of GSE insured mortgage debt. Through this, the Fed became the single largest holder of US agency debt globally, effectively absorbing the securities offloaded by domestic and foreign investors (Figure 9.6). Further, as the Fed absorbed excess capacity in this way, it effectively put a floor under yields and liquidity, and drew investors back to the market.

QE3 marked a continuation of this trend, and a second major wave of asset purchases. From 2012 to 2014, the Fed nearly doubled its holdings of GSE debt, purchasing an additional $823 billion, and by the end of the period owned nearly 25 per cent of the entire market. Again, this bolstered foreign official demand, especially from Asia: even as China's official holdings continued to decline, this was offset by rapidly increasing demand from Japan and Taiwan.

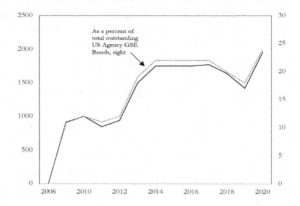

Source: Federal Reserve.

Figure 9.6   Federal Reserve holdings of US agency MBS, 2008–2020

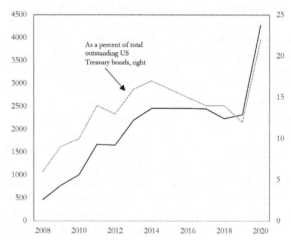

Source: Federal Reserve.

Figure 9.7   Federal Reserve holdings of US Treasury debt, 2008–2020

Moreover, by structuring QE around bond purchases rather than troubled institutions, the Fed acted as a custodian for European banking risk. This involved transferring liquidity to foreign banks in the US through large-scale asset purchases, and is registered in the explosion in cash assets held by foreign banks in the US, which by 2014 exceeded the cash held by domestically chartered US banks (Panitch et al. 2015). Even through these banks held small positions in the agency market, the liquidity provided by these operations allowed them to avoid unravelling their private MBS stockpiles to meet funding needs.

At the same time, QE put a floor under the US Treasury market and supported foreign demand for US corporate, foreign, and offshore bonds (Figure 9.7). This occurred as sellers of agency MBS initially used the proceeds to buy US Treasury bonds, reinforcing the demand created by the Fed's own purchases, which through QE1 totalled $300 billion. Both factors set the conditions for subsequent assets purchases: with US agency and Treasury debt guaranteed, not just by the implicit promise of the US state, but the active support of the US Federal Reserve, QE2 and QE3 had a much broader impact. From 2010 to 2014, as the Fed's purchases of Treasury bonds swelled, reaching nearly $1.4 trillion, investors were driven into private dollar markets. Such portfolio rebalancing, from low yield public dollar bonds to higher yield private dollar bonds, noticeably strengthened demand for Yankee, Eurodollar, and corporate issues and occurred in a way that accommodated growing US federal deficits. Moreover, it involved the Fed backstopping US denominated private markets, to the extent that its growing portfolio of US Treasury bonds pushed investors out along the yield curve. By explicitly acknowledging this substitution effect, the Fed sent a strong message to global investors that these private markets were not beyond its supervisory and managerial scope, and in fact were key to its overall mandate of ensuring financial stability.

As the Fed purchased agency and Treasury debt from foreign banks, it not only stabilized key markets, but added to the pool of available offshore dollars, which had rapidly depleted when short-term funding markets seized in 2008. This in turn helped drive new issuance of dollar denominated debt and enabled firms to fund unbalanced dollar exposures, thereby further preserving the attractiveness of private offshore markets. To be sure, Eurobond markets would have quickly collapsed had firms been unable to meet existing obligations due to a shortage of dollar liquidity. Further, as Gillian Tett (2020) notes, US financial officials were keenly aware that such instability in offshore markets would have reverberated to US onshore markets, potentially threatening the Treasury sector.

Yet with regard to offshore dollar liquidity, quantitative easing only played a complementary role. Adam Tooze (2018) has shown that central bank swaps lines were the primary means of addressing the dollar funding gap in offshore markets, itself rooted in European demand for private issue MBS. These allowed foreign central banks to provide dollar liquidity to domestic firms by swapping domestic currency for dollars at prevailing rates, essentially making European and Asian central banks custodians of US monetary policy. At the start of the crisis the Federal Reserve introduced two major swap lines to protect the Eurodollar market, one with the ECB totalling $20 billion and the other with the SNB for $4 billion (Shedlock 2007). The second action occurred early in the morning on 18 September 2008 in response to the turmoil created by the Lehman's collapse. After gradually extending its credit lines with the ECB and tripling its offerings to the Swiss National bank between March and August, the Fed introduced new swap arrangements totalling $180 billion with five central banks (Torres and Adam 2008). Under the terms of the agreements, the Fed increased its offering to the ECB and SNB, and created new arrangements with the Bank of Japan, the Bank of England, and the Bank of Canada. Unlike earlier swap arrangements, set up to compensate for balance of payments deficits, these aimed at providing international liquidity, with the additional effect of getting foreign central banks to act as conduits for the Fed's looser monetary policy. The Fed followed this by converting its patchwork of existing swap arrangements into permanent standing facilities in 2013, creating a 'coherent structure for managing liberalized financial flows centred around the US state that could especially penetrate into European markets' (Panitch et al. 2015: 123).

As Tooze (2018: 377) shows, swap lines provided 'easy access to short-term dollar funding', flushing dollars into the global system on a daily basis to offset the collapse of US money markets.[7] Absent this, foreign central banks faced two troubling options: they could either let firms manage their unfunded dollar exposures privately; or draw down their foreign exchange reserves to provide temporary liquidity. Either option would have crippled the transatlantic financial system, decimated major firms, and sparked a fire sale in the US domestic-international and Eurodollar bond markets, as firms and financial officials offloaded MBS and other dollar debt in a mad scramble to access dollars. But swap lines did more than just stabilize key dollar bond markets: they demonstrated the Fed's willingness to support offshore markets and established an institutional apparatus for supporting offshore liquidity, eliminating a key asymmetry between onshore and offshore markets: the lack of access to emergency dollar liquidity. This all represents a significant extension of the commitment US officials made in 1974, during the Franklin National crisis, to backstop offshore currency and dollar bond markets.

Blurring the distinction between onshore and offshore dollar markets in this way further supported the Eurodollar bond market, driving new issues and demand. As markets settled, European issuers returned, confident the Fed would support liquidity if conditions deteriorated. Even more importantly, Japanese savers and firms entered the market in a new way, reversing the traditional segmentation between Asian and European investment, whereby the former focused more on foreign official markets and the latter private issues, and extending the hub-and-spoke financial system. Following 2008, as 'the main imbalances in offshore dollar markets have migrated from the eurozone to Japan', major Japanese banks and insurance providers have swamped the market, attracted not only by higher yields but the additional layer of security offered by the Fed (Tett 2020).

THE POST-CRISIS EVOLUTION OF STATE MANAGEMENT

The crisis also exposed key regulatory and supervisory limitations and inspired significant adjustment in state policy. Crucially, such shifts demonstrate an important continuation of pre-crisis management, and a similar attempt to instrumentalize crisis conditions, at least in so far as they further tighten rules on US banks. This has further shifted the US financial system towards market-based patterns of intermediation, opening new opportunities for dollar denominated bonds – especially in the US domestic-international market – and the extension of US risk power. One marker of this shift, beyond the expansion of US international bonds discussed above, is the increase in corporate bonds as a percentage of non-financial borrowing in the US. This went from 49 per cent in 2007 to 67 per cent in 2017. While commercial and industrial loans have continued to increase in aggregate terms, these represent a rapidly declining share of total US credit, especially for the corporate sector. The liquidity created by QE, inasmuch as it drove investor demand for riskier assets and reduced credit risk premia, has played an essential role in the expansion of corporate bond markets. Low interest rates are a second important variable: these have impacted commercial bank profitability (by eroding 'the spread between lending and deposit rates') and had a 'detrimental' impact on lending (Campos 2019: 2, 3). Yet this explains only part of a more complex interactive dynamic. With the post-crisis re-regulation of the financial sector came the further consolidation of the banking system, led in particular by the decline of community banks.[8]

Such restrictions mainly took shape through the Dodd–Frank Act (DFA) and, perhaps more importantly, the Basel III Accord. The latter improved the risk control and measurement system devised under Basel II, making bank balance sheets less susceptible to common vulnerabilities. In terms of capital requirements, Basel III increased the amount of safe capital that banks must hold to protect against financial distress by creating a new 2.5 per cent capital conservation buffer and restricting the definition of core capital. These requirements raised the capital adequacy ratio for international banks to 10.5 per cent and made common shares and retained earnings 'the predominant form of Tier 1 capital' (BCBS 2010: 2). In forcing banks to set aside an additional 2.5 per cent of risk weighted assets during periods of financial expansion, the capital conservation buffer ensures they conserve a higher portion of their capital during the credit boom cycle to guard against 'deleveraging during times of stress' (Rogers 2018: 68). This reflects a greater awareness of the pro-cyclicality of financial markets and a shift in the direction of macroprudential risk management (ibid.). In fact, Baker (2013) argues that the capital conservation buffer signals how regulators have *openly* accepted the view that financial markets are cyclically inefficient and prone to endogenous failure, due to the natural over-extension of risk and the under-accumulation of safe assets during moments of market expansion.

Basel III also introduces new ratios for leverage and liquidity. The supplementary leverage ratio (LR) requires banks maintain a minimum ratio of 3 per cent between their Tier 1 capital (the capital measure) and on and off-balance sheet capital exposures (the exposure measure). By effectively 'capping the total amount of leverage banks can achieve', the LR limits their capacity to avoid capital requirements and 'provide[s] a simple non-risk based backstop' that controls the build-up of excessive leverage, even for those institutions that hold a 'large share of low risk weighted assets' (ECB 2015: 123; BIS 2017: 1). Both the Liquidity Coverage Ratio (LCR) and Net Stable Funding Ratio (NSFR) address the time dimension of financial stress. The LCR acts as a short-term stress test on bank balance sheets as it directs banks to 'hold a sufficient reserve of high-quality liquid assets (HQLA) to allow them to survive a period of significant liquidity stress lasting 30 calendar days' (BIS 2018a: 1). Under the LRC, internationally active banks must hold a 'stock of HQLA at least as large as expected total net cash outflows' arising in different stress scenarios combining 'elements of bank specific liquidity and market wide stress' (BIS 2018a: 1). The Net Stable Funding Ratio aims at 'creating incentives for banks to fund their activities with more stable sources of funding on an on-going basis', with the specific goal of limiting over-reliance on short-term wholesale funding channels (BIS 2018b: 1). The ratio requires a bank's total Available Stable Funding, the total 'portion of its capital and liabilities that will remain with the institution for more than one year', to be equal to or exceed its Total Required Stable Funding, the 'amount of stable funding a bank is required to hold' (BIS 2018b: 1). This means that funding structures must be developed around medium and long-term stable financing, such as long-term wholesale funding and consumer deposits, and that the additional accumulation of on or off-balance assets must be supported by 'a stable funding profile' (Deutsche Bank 2017: 78).

Overall, new rules have improved the loss-absorption capacity of financial firms, greatly increased core capital holdings, and reduced leverage rates. While this has in some ways stimulated lending, and pushed banks from trading and more complex activities, it has in other ways limited credit opportunities, as they must now often 'strengthen their capitalization and modify their balance sheet structures' to increase lending (Naceur et al. 2017: 4). Further, because loans are subject to higher risk weights than trading securities and qualify as semi-liquid or even illiquid assets under Basel III, there is a built-in incentive to invest in more marketable assets and to draw back from international lending (ibid.). As Jamie Dimon notes, the new rules have especially made it 'tougher for small players' and increased pressure towards consolidation, since smaller banks lack economies of scale and have higher operating costs (as quoted in Marsh and Norman 2013: 3). This has further standardized loan provision, closing opportunities for smaller or more specialized offerings. In addition, it has limited new lending in some sectors, since commercial and retail loans are driven more by small banks, due in part to their 'comparative advantage in producing soft information' (Naceur et al. 2017: 16). Thus even if the crisis raised doubts that market-based forms of intermediation dramatically improve stability, the tenor of post-crisis financial reform, with its focus on banks and minimal concern for risk outside the regular banking system, indicate a broad continuation of previous trends. At the very least, this helps to explain why, according to the BIS, 'non-bank finance and non-bank financial institutions have gained a greater role in financing economic activity in the aftermath of the crisis' and why corporate debt financing in particular 'has increasingly shifted to capital markets in advanced economics' (CGFS 2018: 10).

SUMMARY REMARKS

This chapter examined the complex relationship between US risk power and subprime management, noting three key points. First, the massive extension of government liquidity necessary to protect funding channels and key firms always required the tacit approval of global investors in the IBM, since it hinged on continued strong demand for US debt as well as the Fed's direct support for agency and Treasury markets. In this sense, the consistent demand for US dollar debt in the pre-crisis period served as the basis for the US state's continued management of financial volatility during the crisis, and reflected how the liquidity provided by the Fed's management was itself funnelled into dollar denominated debt in the IBM.

This management also bolstered US risk power and set the conditions for its further expansion in the post-crisis period. The US domestic-international market was a direct beneficiary of the Fed's quantitative easing programmes, and the bailout of Freddie and Fannie in September 2008 set a floor under US agency and Treasury markets. With the Fed's balance sheet backstopping these markets, ensuring liquidity and stability, the post-crisis period kickstarted a new wave of US financial hegemony, making the IBM ever more dependent on US denominated debt. The Fed's swap lines of credit extended these patterns to offshore markets, leading to the further expansion of Eurodollar bonds. This occurred because the new swap programmes devised during the crisis essentially extended the Fed's discount window to offshore markets, ensuring investors access to dollars through their domestic central banks. Moreover, as the Fed converted these into standing facilities, signalling its intent to continue managing Eurodollar liquidity, even beyond emergency situations, the credibility of US dollar bonds only expanded.

Third, post-crisis regulation mostly repeated earlier patterns of intervention. Previous regulatory programmes had already shifted banking strategies, giving shape to new patterns of market-based credit, which served to deepen US risk power in the IBM. The Dodd–Frank Act and Basel III extended these trends, initiating another process of consolidation that ultimately provoked new patterns of market-based intermediation. Whether or not these regulations were the main force in this respect, the critical point is that US credit markets have become ever more dependent on bond placements, opening new space for international demand. This all speaks to how the crisis was not just rooted in the special credibility of US bonds, but instrumentalized to extend US risk power. That the bank holding companies at the centre of this regulatory overhaul continued to augment their practices, while gaining market share,[9] indicates that this shift towards market-based intermediation was hardly a zero sum process, but rather a key part of an evolving system of US financial hegemony, of which US risk power is a constitutive element.

NOTES

1. According to the BIS, this relates to the specific way in which the Federal Reserve and Treasury Department managed the GSE crisis and how this left the 'ultimately government backing of the two agencies unresolved' (McCauley 2019).
2. For a full accounting see US Treasury Department, Treasury International Capital (TIC) System, historical data. Here again, foreign ownership as a percentage of publicly held federal debt is much higher.
3. See BIS, international bonds. See also Federal Reserve Economic Database.
4. According to the Bloomberg Barclays Euro Corporate Bond Index.
5. Through the Housing and Economic Recovery Act (2008) the Treasury also supported the agency market, effectively 'replacing agency securities with its own securities' (McCauley 2019: 8). This involved selling 'more of its debt than required to fund the federal government's deficit' and then using the extra money to purchase Freddie and Fannie MBS.

6.   Prior to the collapse of Lehman's, the Fed let a portion of its Treasury holdings expire in order to limit the total liquidity it provided (see Aquanno 2015).
7.   At the peak of the crisis in 2008, weekly swap credit reached nearly $1 trillion (Tooze 2018).
8.   Between 2010 and 2014, 14 per cent of US community banks failed, while the number of large banks increased by 6.3 per cent (Holmes 2018).
9.   Banks also succeeded in resisting new regulations on derivative markets and pushing against the so-called Volcker rule, which prohibited proprietary trading.

10. The future of risk in the era of authoritarian capitalism

This book offered a different way of viewing the post-Second World War history of financial markets, and explored the development of the international bond market over the last 75 years. It first explored key aspects of financial reason and advanced the concept of abstract risk to show that investment is conditioned by hegemonic imaginaries. This conceptualization of demand requires a closer examination and broader analysis of US financial power. It also cautions against reducing demand for dollar debt to US trade patterns or purely quantitative risk measurements. I argued that US risk power is rooted in – but emergent from – US material power, and that the demand for US Treasury debt in the IBM, which has always vastly exceeded the US's share of global GDP, has to be understood through the institutional and discursive properties organizing the financial system.[1]

The book also revisited the subprime crisis and put straight its historical origins. These were not analysable from the frameworks and starting points developed earlier. Ultimately, the internationalization of US subprime and securitized mortgage debt did not so much reflect a new model of financial engineering, regulatory restrictions, or interest rate spreads. Rather, it expressed a long-standing appetite for US debt obligations, constituted by the logic of capital accumulation and the norms of trust and confidence it operates through. As foreign investors and banks accumulated US mortgage debt, they were merely following the tracks of a long pattern of financial demand, reflective of the post-Second World War risk imaginary. In this respect, the crisis requires understanding the foreign, domestic-international, and offshore components of the IBM, even if this demand only 'caused' the crisis through its complex interaction with different social and financial rationalities and power processes.

It is also in this respect that US financial regulators gained the capacity to manage the crisis. From 2007 to 2009 officials at the Federal Reserve and Treasury Department engaged in more than a handful of innovative and complex financial arrangements to protect critical markets, with the basic goal of sustaining US financial privilege and reproducing the conditions laid down by the dollar standard in the 1970s. While this manoeuvring was no doubt messy, it prevented the complete seizure of global financial markets. It also deepened the shift to market-based intermediation and fostered a new wave of US risk power. The ability to act in this regard did not fall from the sky – here again the IBM comes into the limelight. Through this, US regulators gained the capacity to protect global financial markets and learned how to instrumentalize crisis conditions to further expand risk hegemony. Moreover, as the crisis swept through the transatlantic financial system, investors stockpiled Treasury debt, both to meet their unfunded dollar obligations and invest in safe portfolio assets, enabling US officials to expand operations, even as these same interventions reproduced US financial credibility.

Second, it was argued that US risk power shaped the development of global financial markets and was itself institutionally sedimented and reproduced. It is not just that historical patterns of risk showed up in the subprime crisis; these also traced out the institutional processes and mechanisms underpinning it. As US offshore bonds became ever more popular, the Eurodollar market itself became a nodal point for global investment, leading European interbank channels to become tightly correlated with dollar liquidity. European banks funded offshore US bonds with offshore dollar holdings available in interbank markets, and then rolled these bonds by tapping into the same source of liquidity, while the interest paid on US offshore bonds further contributed to the liquidity of Eurodollar markets. As a result, when the US MBS and subprime bond market collapsed, European interbank markets immediately seized, causing a broader crisis across Europe.

US firms and markets greatly benefited (even perhaps disproportionally) from the prevailing structure of risk. Foreign demand in the Yankee, offshore, and domestic-international markets meant that US investment and commercial banks became debt issuers to the world and established strong overseas operations and networks, integrating European firms into US markets. As European firms migrated across the Atlantic to gain from these same processes, the expansion of the IBM featured the development of a transatlantic financial system centred on Wall Street. It was through this hub-and-spoke system, and the privileged position of US debt, that new innovative financial practices were developed and extended: technological advancement and currency risk accelerated financial engineering, but so did US leadership in the IBM. At the very least, this laid down certain incentives and created space for regulatory and institutional experimentation, adaptation, and advancement.

This again relates back to state capacity and financial management. States support the general interests of the capitalist system and are not mere instruments of the ruling elite – as emergent institutional formations they act at a distance, often by responding to immediate problems through trial and error experimentation. The US state was no different in the post-Second World War period: risk power pressured officials to protect the dollar–gold link and extend the build-up of US bonds internationally. One outcome was the gradual development of a more market-based system of financial intermediation. Another was an ever more brittle distinction between Tier 1 and Tier 2 debt. Still another was the further extension of US risk power, the further dollarization of international bond markets.

THE FUTURE OF RISK AND THE ROLE OF INSTITUTIONS

Nothing that has been said weighs too heavily on the debate about imperial decay, or suggests the global economy is riveted to the dollar standard or the abstract risk emanating from it. This book has avoided the well-rehearsed debates about US decline and the role of financialization in secular stagnation, for example. So too, it avoided examining corporate investment patterns, shifts in productivity, and the growth of fictitious capital. It rather sought to abstract from these trends by examining US risk power in the IBM and its institutional and cultural roots, building from the work of Panitch and Gindin in *The Making of Global Capitalism*.

Ultimately, however, such patterns of demand and development cannot be viewed apart from the continuing dynamism of the US economy. As we have seen, risk imaginaries are tethered to deeper systems of political and material domination: the process of institutionalizing risk is always shot through political compromise, and the basic capacity to honour debt obligations rests on the ability to generate economic rents and harvest profit. Risk serves 'to mystify ... real relations in civil society' by imposing on society as a whole a world-view constituted 'under the aegis of the hegemonic classes' (Poulantzas 2008: 95–6). This takes us to an obvious question: To what extent will subsequent financial relations be influenced by the same unity of events? On this issue there is of course much to be said – the debate regarding the material basis of US hegemony is alone too much to confront. Still there is reason to believe US risk power will remain relatively stable in the near future, despite the legitimacy crisis consuming the US political system.

A Brief Note on Politics

Typically, arguments about the decline of US Treasury debt start with China. This is for two interconnected reasons, one being the ever-growing size of the Chinese economy, the other its foreign official holdings of US dollar debt. Since 1978, when Xiaoping initiated market reform, annual growth has hovered around 10 per cent. While growth has recently slowed, China's share of global aggregate demand continues to increase, indicating evolving economic sophistication, and important economic fundamentals – including the domestic savings rate, sovereign debt levels, and corporate productivity and profitability – continue to improve or remain strong. This has allowed China to become a key net external creditor to the world. As we saw, Japan emerged as a major support valve for US risk power in the 1980s, but from the Asian financial crisis onwards China played an increasingly significant role. From 2003 to 2007, China's holdings of US securities increased from $320 billion to $870 billion, representing about 15 per cent of total foreign ownership of long-term US debt (Morrison and Labonte 2009). Ten years later, even though this number slipped to 13 per cent, China overtook Japan as the largest holder of long-term US Treasury bonds.

Moreover, Chinese financial markets are continuing to develop and its economy is increasingly less dependent on bank credit. Liberalization of the Chinese onshore bond market began in 2002 with the Qualified Foreign Institutional Investor programme, which allowed access to Chinese renminbi denominated securities on a quota basis. This programme was expanded in 2010 to encourage greater international participation in domestic bond markets, including the emerging interbank bond market, and quotas were eventually removed in 2016 through the Interbank Direct Investment programme and the Bond Connect Initiative, giving investors wide access to China's $16 trillion onshore market. Chinese offshore markets were given a great boost in the mid-2000s with the creation of the so-called Dim Sum market operated through Hong Kong – Dim Sum bonds are a segment of the Eurobond market and include all renminbi denominated bonds issued outside mainland China (Ru and Chong 2018; Fung et al. 2014).[2] As demonstrated by China's 12th Five Year Plan, this was part of a wider strategy aimed at developing the RMB as an international reserve currency. Other steps in this direction include: 'promoting cross border trade settlement in RMB', allowing renminbi denominated foreign direct investment, and pegging the fixed rate against a basket of international currencies, rather than the dollar alone (Ru and Chong 2018: 3).

Nonetheless, as China has continued to build its massive portfolio of Treasury debt in the post-2008 period, these political ambitions can easily be overstated. Moreover, China's investment priorities are themselves shaped by US risk power. Recall that from 2007 to 2017, demand for dollar denominated bonds in the foreign and offshore markets increased by 89 per cent, and the dollar share of these markets rose from 31 per cent to 45 per cent. Likewise, foreign ownership of marketable US Treasury bonds increased by 180 per cent, despite the massive bond buying conditioned by the Fed through its QE programmes, bringing foreign ownership to 46 per cent of the total. In the market for US corporate debt, the 41 per cent increase in foreign holdings brought total foreign ownership from 23 per cent to 30 per cent.[3]

This strong demand for US Treasury debt – the continuation of the post-Second World War risk imaginary – means that Chinese demand has to be set in wider terms. Viewing the stability of the dollar and vibrancy of the

Treasury bond market simply in terms of the narrow political interests of the Chinese state obscures the deeper properties of international control driving demand and therefore both overstates and decontextualizes China's influence. Again, it is worth viewing this in terms of the post-crisis development of the US MBS market. Following the crisis, Chinese demand for US ABS declined steadily, partly reflecting a portfolio shift to US Treasury bonds, from $255 billion in 2006 to $184 billion in 2017. Meanwhile, total foreign ownership of US ABS remained virtually constant as other countries, namely Taiwan and Japan, eagerly absorbed excess capacity.

Moreover, though China's bond markets have grown considerably since the Asian financial crisis, they remain astonishingly inward-looking. As of 2018, foreign investors held only 2 per cent of China's onshore market, well below the average for developed and emerging economies (39 per cent), and even much less than Japan's 'domestically oriented' bond market (8 per cent) (ibid.: 5). While the Bank of China estimates that as much as 15 per cent of the market may eventually be foreign owned, even this represents a fraction of the US domestic-international market, and at any rate remains blocked by the panoply of onshore regulations restricting international access. Even in the most optimistic accounts, full liberalization is a long way from being realized (ibid.: 4). Further, the Dim Sum market has been slow to develop: despite its role in China's currency strategy, total issues barely exceed $80 billion. Instead, the most significant consequence of liberalization has been the expansion of the Eurodollar bond market, as Chinese companies have taken advantage of new opportunities to raise over $300 billion in offshore dollar markets.

This draws into question the validity of conceiving the renminbi as an alternative anchor in the IBM, or even a serious near-term threat to US dollar hegemony. Meanwhile, signs of instability also emanate from Europe, due to political fragmentation in the Eurozone. Until recently, there was some reason to argue that the euro would soon anchor global markets, not least of which was the strong performance of euro-linked obligations in the foreign and offshore bond markets, and the growth of the euro region economies in the period following 1999. Between 2000 and 2007, while US GDP as a percentage of the world total slipped from 31 per cent to 25 per cent, the countries of the euro monetary region increased their share of gross world economic output from 19 per cent to 22 per cent. Yet, as we saw with the emergence of US risk power in the antebellum period, it is important to be heedful of such short-term shifts.

The Eurozone crisis has shown, above all, that the economic and monetary policies supporting the euro remain fragmented and uncertain. Problems in Greece, Spain, and Portugal surrounding large national debts and the struggle to attract investment reveal broad concerns about the growth regimes in most of southern Europe (Atkins 2010). And although the crisis did not completely paralyse Europe's central economies, in large part due to the Fed's swap lines of credit, the continued mixture of budget cuts, austerity, and frozen credit channels has weakened the real economy throughout the region. Still more important, the fact that the ECB's lender-of-last-resort functions continue to appear politically fragile and too tightly conditioned by the Bundesbank's conservative ordoliberal guideposts, despite the rather massive QE programme started by Draghi in 2015, shows that the type of institutional capacity established by the Fed in the 1930s, prior to the development of the Bretton Woods system, is not yet fully formed (Neuger and Kennedy 2010; Panitch et al. 2015). As one financial executive put it: the subprime experience 'makes the euro area far less stable in any crisis than a traditional national union' (ibid.). A recent ruling by Germany's Constitutional Court that the ECB's QE policies were illegal under German law shows that these political fractures have not at all dissipated and will be decisive in shaping Europe's evolving monetary response to the COVID-19 pandemic, even if the recently announced European Recovery Programme[4] marks a small, yet grossly inadequate, step in the direction of fiscal unity.

In this context it may well be that the greatest immediate danger to US risk power comes not from beyond, but from within its borders.[5] At the present stage, neoliberal class rule has led to the fragmentation of American civil society: the top 1 per cent now owns as much or more as it did in the lead-up to the Great Depression and the patterns of class moderation established in the immediate postwar period, that informed adequate living conditions for segments of the working class, have been significantly eroded. This new gilded age has profoundly reworked the political landscape, as the elite have increasingly become disconnected from the disposed and dominated. The most obvious political consequence has been the increasing prominence of far right actors and ideas within the Republican Party. The continued success and empowerment of these political forces means growing inequality and social upheaval.

Yet though this speaks to the erosion of neoliberal sensibilities and a widening legitimation crisis, it does not appear to signal a wider political crisis, whereby the dominant power bloc fractures and has difficulty imposing its leadership (Poulantzas 1978). If anything, the 2008 crisis appears to have strengthened the linkages between different fragments of capital, as it has promoted a further fusion between financial and non-financial corporations (Maher and Aquanno 2021).[6] This has occurred as asset management firms, such as BlackRock and Vanguard, have deployed long-term investment strategies aimed at extracting value by influencing the action of their portfolio firms. If such changes signal important shifts in class power, and even the development of a new phase of capitalist development, they do not threaten US material domination and in fact seem to strengthen it. Moreover, the development of this new finance capital, is itself rooted in the continuing defeat of the working class. Absent a coherent challenge from the left – the inability of the Sanders campaign to draw sufficient support during the 2020 primaries is an indication that this movement, despite its remarkable gains, still requires considerable development – we can expect the further erosion of democratic processes, more aggressive forms of marketization, and a more concerted effort to foster racial and ethnic divisions. Biden's 'new deal' programs and sudden embrace of certain progressive policies may indeed temper some of these tendencies, but as these policy changes are not grounded in working class struggle, but rather pressures to restore global competitiveness, is it hard to say they will amount to a wide-ranging shift in the opposite direction.

Moreover, there are important institutional forces within the US state favouring continuation of the current system. Following the crisis, the Federal Reserve greatly developed its capacity to manage financial markets and support US risk power. This involved a wide process of institutional learning and adaptation that has played out in the development of new monetary and financial policy tools and programmes, including the New York Fed's Financial Institution Supervisory Group – which is responsible for overseeing the risk management operations of Wall Street firms – and the new system of paying interest on excess reserve balances held on account by depository institutions. These greatly expand the Fed's penetration into financial markets and its ability to supervise key firms. Such changes in institutional capacity have occurred as part of a wider regulatory overhaul, aimed at improving the resiliency of key markets: from 2008 to 2014 the number of restrictions and regulations imposed by the Federal Reserve Board increased by 70 per cent; this was accompanied by a dramatic increase in hiring for supervisory positions, and a new emphasis on tracking financial stability that saw the operating budget for supervision and regulation at the regional banks grow 80 per cent, from $641 million to $1.2 billion.

While the pace of change slowed during the Trump period, the Fed remains much more interventionist than before the crisis, and more capable of supporting key markets and firms. In fact, despite Trump's focus on financial deregulation, and his administration's dramatic attack on the Treasury Department, the Fed's supervision and regulation budget increased by 18 per cent from 2015 to 2019. Moreover, its management of systemically important financial institutions, as measured by onsite and offsite audits of large Tier 1 bank holding companies, has remained equally robust, and dramatically expanded as economic conditions deteriorated in 2019. The Fed's institutional capacity and renewed emphasis on financial oversight is also registered through its evolving network of regulatory training programmes, which serve to teach officials about new rules and financial practices. These too held steady during the Trump administration.

This insulation from outside political pressure and ability to continue developing its institutional knowledge allowed the Fed to further adjust its relationship to financial markets during the first wave of the COVID-19 pandemic. This included, above all, the resumption of quantitative easing and the development of new emergency spending facilities targeting commercial paper, municipal notes, and corporate bonds. The Fed's decision to purchase corporate debt – which effectively made the corporate market a subsidiarity of the Treasury market – almost immediately halved the yield on investment grade corporate bonds.[7] At the same time, the Fed reinstated unlimited swap lines of credit with key foreign central banks and further backstopped the Treasury bond market. The latter evolved in response to an unprecedented degree of chaos and dislocation caused by automatic trading and 'the frenzied dash for cash', and involved the most aggressive intervention into public markets on record (Wigglesworth 2020).

One can view such aggressive tactics as the culmination of the Bretton Woods risk standard – the fullest possible extension of US financial credibility to private dollar denominated international bonds. To be sure, while corporate bonds can still default, unlike Treasury and (presumably) GSE agency bonds, the market is now *generally* backstopped by the Fed's balance sheet, and linked to the US state in a way that ensures future worth – not just through underlying currency of denomination, but yields and market price. Any further extension, entailing the direct guarantee of specific bonds, would presumably mark a wider transformation of economic relations. Moreover, if history is any indication, such action will only draw international investors deeper into the US corporate market, either through onshore or offshore placements, demonstrating further how financial crises have been instrumental for the extension of US risk power.

Ironically, this all suggests that the neoliberal encasement of the Federal Reserve, which foremost involved linking central bank independence to inflation management and the free movement of capital, poses barriers for the authoritarian right as much as it does the democratic left. This institutional autonomy is obviously unfixed and has to be set against wider political debates and movements. It is no doubt significant that, since the collapse of the Soviet Union and rise of unipolarity, the US has steadily retreated from the multinational institutions erected in the postwar period, and that the populist right has further extended this programme in the name of promoting US interests. This poses clear threats to the Fed's interventionist mandate, especially as it continues blatantly to act as the world central bank, supporting offshore markets as much as domestic markets. Yet any attack on the Fed's autonomy presents unique problems, as it would elicit an immediate response from financial markets. Further, even if the Democratic Party is now more sceptical of globalization, as the *Wall Street Journal* has argued, the election of Joe Biden will surely suppress these tensions for the time being (Hilsenrath and Timiraos 2020).

The material basis of US risk power may very well be in doubt, with the legitimacy of the American empire increasingly fracturing and important questions about the functionality of its financial accumulation model still unresolved. But the state institutional mechanisms upholding this power seem firmly entrenched. The innovations and interventions of the last 10 years, which increasingly buried the dividing line between Tier 1 and Tier 2 debt, have bolstered dollar markets and cultivated extraordinary opportunities for institutional development, capable of reinforcing the decades-long spread of US risk power. This only further signals the essential risk dimensions of the subprime crisis.

NOTES

1. On this basis, the book supported both the cultural and institutional turn within IPE, while developing the IM framework presented by Panitch and Gindin (2012), Jessop (2010; 2014), and Maher and Aquanno (2018).
2. Since 2010, when Chinese companies were permitted to trade in renminbi with non-Chinese partners, a number of other international financial centres, including London, Frankfurt and Paris, have started issuing Dim Sum bonds.
3. See US Treasury Department, Treasury International Capital.
4. The European Recovery Programme is an $827 billion plan aimed at stimulating economic recovery from the COVID-19 pandemic. It involves the European Commission borrowing money and then allocating it in grants and loans to member countries based on a negotiated formula.
5. See also Albo et al. (2010).
6. For a further discussion of these trends and the rise of what has been called 'asset manager capitalism', see: Braun (2016); Fichtner et al. (2017); Bebchuk and Hirst (2019); and Jahnke (2019).
7. The decision to purchase corporate bonds also involved stockpiling exchange traded funds that track the corporate market.

References

Abolafia, Mitchell (1996) *Making Markets*, Cambridge, MA: Harvard University Press.

Adrian, T. and Shin, H.S. (2008) Financial Intermediaries, Financial Stability, and Monetary Policy, Staff Report, Federal Reserve Bank of New York, No. 346.

Aglietta, M. and Maarek, P. (2007) Developing the Bond Market in China: The Next Step Forward in Financial Reform, *Economie Internationale*, 3(111): 29–53.

Aitken, Rob (2002) The (Re)making of Prudential Masculinity: Culture Discourse and Financial Identity, paper presented at: *International Studies Association Convention*, New Orleans, LA.

Albo, Greg, Gindin, Sam and Panitch, Leo (2010) *In and Out of Crisis: The Global Financial Meltdown and Left Alternatives*, Oakland, CA: PM Press.

Aliber, R.Z. and Kindleberger, C.P. (2015) *Manias, Panics and Crashes: A History of Financial Crises*, 7th edn, New York, NY: Palgrave Macmillan.

Amira, Khaled and Handorf, William C. (2004) Global Debt Market Growth, Security Structure, and Bond Pricing, *The Journal of Investing*, 13(1): 79–90.

Aquanno, Scott M. (2008) US Power and the International Bond Market: Financial Flows and the Construction of Risk Value. In L. Panitch and M. Konings (eds), *American Empire and the Politics of International Finance*, 119–35, Toronto: Palgrave Macmillan.

Aquanno, Scott M. (2014) Contesting New Monetary Policy, *Contributions to Political Economy*, 33(1): 1–17.

Aquanno, Scott M. (2015) Crisis, Learning and Continuity: The Institutional Origins of Subprime Management at the Federal Reserve, *Competition and Change*, 19(1): 3–18.

Archer, Margaret (1995) *Realist Social Theory: The Morphogenetic Approach*, New York, NY: Cambridge University Press.

Arnoldi, Jakob (2004) Derivatives, Virtual Values and Real Risks, *Theory, Culture and Society*, 21(6): 23–42.

Arrighi, Giovanni (1994) *The Long Twentieth Century*, New York, NY: Verso.

Asami, Tadahiro (2003) Developing International Bond Markets in East Asia to Enhance Regional Monetary Cooperation, *The Institute for International Monetary Affairs*, no. 3.

Atkins, Ralph (2010) Debt Crisis is Dark Cloud over Europe, *Financial Times*, 22 June.

Ayres, I. and Braithwaite, J. (1992) *Responsive Regulation: Transcending the Deregulation Debate*, New York, NY: Oxford University Press.

Azahara, Luna and Gonzalez, Romo (2016) The Drivers of European Banks' US Dollar Debt Issuance: Opportunistic Funding in Times of Crisis, Banco de España, Working Paper, no. 1611.

Baker, A. (2013) The New Political Economy of the Macroprudential Ideational Shift, *New Political Economy*, 8(1): 112–39.

Baker, Dean (2009) *Plunder and Blunder: The Rise and Fall of the Bubble Economy*, Sausalito, CA: PoliPoint Press.

Balakrishnan, Gopal (2010) Speculations on the Stationary State, *New Left Review*, 59: 5–26.

Balder, John, Lopez, Jose A. and Sweet, Lawrence M. (1991) Competitiveness in the Eurocredit Market: International Competitiveness of US Financial Firms: Products, Markets and Conventional Performance Measures, *Federal Reserve Bank of New York*, Staff Study: 26–41.

Banham, Russ (1999) Kit and Caboodle: Understanding the Skepticism about Enterprise Risk Management, *CFO Magazine*, April.

Bank for International Settlements (2009) *BIS Quarterly Review*, June, Basel: Bank for International Settlements Monetary and Economic Department, International Debt Securities, A8.

Bank for International Settlements (2017) *Basel III Leverage Ratio Framework – Executive Summary*, Basel: BIS, 25 October.

Bank for International Settlements (2018a) *Liquidity Coverage Ratio – Executive Summary*, Basel: BIS, 30 April.

Bank for International Settlements (2018b) *Net Stable Funding Ratio – Executive Summary*, Basel: BIS, 28 June.

Bank of England (BOE) (1991) The International Bond Market. Quarterly Bulletin. Available at: https://www.bankofengland.co.uk/-/media/boe/files/quarterly-bulletin/1991/the-international-bond-market.

Barberis, Nicholas (1997) Markets: The Price May Not be Right, *Financial Times: Mastering Finance 7*, 23 June.

Basel Committee on Banking Supervision (BCBS) (2010) Basel III: A Global Regulatory Framework for More Resilient Banks and Banking Systems, *Bank for International Settlements*. Basel: BIS, December.

Bebchuk, Lucian A. and Hirst, Scott (2019) Index Funds and the Future of Corporate Governance: Theory, Evidence, and Policy, *Columbia Law Review*, 119(8): 2029–146.

Becker, Jo, Stolberg, Sheryl Fay and Labaton, Stephen (2008) Bush's Drive for Home Ownership Fueled Housing Bubble, *International Herald Tribune*, 21 December.

Bedell, Denise (2001) Beyond the Yankee/Global Debate, *Corporate Finance*, March, no. 196.

Bernanke, Ben (2015) *The Courage to Act: A Memoir of a Crisis and its Aftermath*, New York, NY: W.W. Norton.

Bernstein, Peter L. (1996) *Against the Gods: The Remarkable Story of Risk*, New York, NY: Wiley.

Best, Jacqueline (2005) *The Limits of Transparency*, New York, NY: Cornell University Press.

Bhaskar, Roy (1978) *A Realist Theory of Science*, 2nd edn, Brighton: Harvester Press.

Bhaskar, R. (1986) *Scientific Realism and Human Emancipation*, New York, NY: Verso.

Bhaskar, R. (1989) *Reclaiming Reality*, New York, NY: Verso.

Black, Fischer (1976) The Pricing of Commodity Contracts, *Journal of Financial Economics*, 3(1–2): 167–79.

Blackburn, Robert (2008) The Subprime Crisis, *The New Left Review*, March–April (50): 63–106.

Block, Fred L. (1977) *The Origins of International Economic Disorder: A Study of United States International Monetary Policy from World War II to the Present*, Los Angeles, CA: University of California Press.

Blyth, Mark (2013) *Austerity: The History of a Dangerous Idea*, New York, NY: Oxford University Press.

Bonefeld, Werner (1987) Reformulation of State Theory, *Capital and Class*, 33(1): 96–127.

Borden, William (1984) *The Pacific Alliance: United States Foreign Economic Policy and Japanese Trade Recovery, 1947–55*, Madison, WI: University of Wisconsin Press.

Braun, Benjamin (2016) From Performativity to Political Economy: Index Investing, ETF's and Asset Manager Capitalism, *New Political Economy*, 21(3): 257–73.

Brenner, Robert (2002) *The Boom and the Bubble: The US in the World Economy*, New York, NY: Verso.

Brenner, Robert (2004) New Boom or New Bubble?, *New Left Review*, January–February, no. 25: 57–100.

Brenner, Robert (2008) Devastating Crisis Unfolds, *Against the Current*, January–February, no. 132.

Brown, Wendy (2015) *Undoing the Demos: Neoliberalism's Stealth Revolution*, New York, NY: Zone Books.

Broz, Lawrence (1997) *The International Origins of the Federal Reserve System*, Ithaca: NY: Cornell University Press.

Bryan, Dick (2008) The Global Foreign Exchange Market: An Interpretation of the Bank of International Settlements' Survey of Foreign Exchange and Derivatives Market Activity, 2007, *Global Society*, 22(4): 491–505.

Burn, Gary (1999) The State, the City and the Euromarkets, *Review of International Political Economy*, 2(6): 225–61.

Burn, Gary (2006) *The Re-emergence of Global Finance*, London: Palgrave Macmillan.

Callinicos, Alex (1999) Capitalism, Competition and Profits: A Critique of Robert Brenner's Theory of Crisis, *Historical Materialism*, 4(1): 9–32.

Callinicos, Alex (2006) Making Sense of Imperialism: A Reply to Leo Panitch and Sam Gindin, *International Socialism*, no. 110. Available at: http://isj.org.uk/making-sense-of-imperialism-a-reply-to-leo-panitch-and-sam-gindin/.

Callon, Michel (1998) Introduction: The Embeddedness of Economic Markets in Economics. In Michel Callon (ed.), *The Laws of the Markets*, 1–57, Oxford: Blackwell.

Campos, Mauricio Ulate (2019) Going Negative at the Zero Lower Bound: The Effects of Negative Nominal Interest Rates, *Federal Reserve Bank of San Francisco*, Working Paper 2019-21.

Casey, William J. (1973) Internationalization of Capital Markets: Towards a New World Monetary System, Harriman, NY: The Committee for Monetary Research and Education, 10 March.

Chaplinsky, S. and Ramchand, L. (2004) The Impact of SEC Rule 144A on Corporate Debt Issuance by International Firms, *Journal of Business*, 77(4): 1073–98.

Chappe, Raphaele, Nell, Edward and Semmler, Willi (2015) Booms, Busts, and the Culture of Risk. In Bob Jessop, Brigitte Young and Christoph Scherrer (eds), *Financial Cultures and Crisis Dynamics*, 123–42, New York, NY: Routledge.

Chesnais, Francois (2016) *Finance Capital Today: Corporations and Banks in the Lasting Global Slump*, Boston, MA: Brill.

Chitu, Livia, Eichengreen, Barry and Mehl, Arnaud (2014) When did the Dollar Overtake Sterling as the Leading International Currency? Evidence from the Bond Markets, *Journal of Development Economics*, 111: 225–45.

Christophers, Brett (2015) Value Models: Risk Finance and Political Economy, *Finance and Society*, 1(2): 1–22.

Clark, Ephraim (2002) *International Finance*, 2nd edn, London: Thomson.

Clark, G.L. and Thrift, N. (2015) The Return of Bureaucracy: Managing Dispersed Knowledge in Global Finance. In K. Knorr and A. Preda (eds), *The Sociology of Financial Markets*, 229–49, New York, NY: Oxford University Press.

Clarke, Simon (1987) Capitalist Crisis and the Rise of Monetarism, *The Socialist Register*, 23: 393–427.

Cohen, Benjamin J. (1977) *Organizing the World's Money: The Political Economy of International Monetary Relations*, New York, NY: Basic Books.

Cohen, Benjamin J. (1998) *The Geography of Money*, New York, NY: Cornell University Press.

Cohen, Benjamin J. (2004) *The Future of Money*, Princeton, NJ: Princeton University Press.

Cohen, William D. (2009) *House of Cards: A Tale of Hubris and Wretched Excess on Wall Street*, New York, NY: Random House.

Collier, Andrew (1994) *Critical Realism: An Introduction to Roy Bhaskar's Philosophy*, New York, NY: Verso.

Committee on the Global Financial System (CGFS) (2018) Structural Changes in Banking after the Crisis, *Bank of International Settlements: CGFS Papers*, no. 60, January.

Congressional Research Service (2019) Foreign Holdings of Federal Debt, CRS Reports. Available at: https://fas.org/sgp/crs/misc/RS22331.pdf.

Country Studies Series (2005) Japan 1994, *Federal Research Division, Library of Congress*, Washington DC, 3 August.

Cowan, L. (2003) Hearing on Protecting Homeowners: Preventing Abusive Lending While Preserving Access to Credit: American Securities Forum, Washington DC: US House of Representatives, Subcommittee on Housing and Community Opportunity; Subcommittee on Financial Institutions and Consumer Credit, 5 November.

Craven, Barrie (1990) Debt Management in the United States of America. In David Gowland (ed.), *International Bond Markets*, 9–49, New York, NY: Routledge.

Creaven, Sean (2000) *Marxism and Critical Realism: A Materialistic Application of Realism in the Social Sciences*, New York, NY: Routledge.

Culpepper, Pepper D. (2005) Institutional Change in Contemporary Capitalism: Coordinated Financial Systems Since 1990, *World Politics*, 57(2): 173–99.

D'Arista, Jane W. (1994) *The Evolution of U.S. Finance Volume II: Restructuring Institutions and Markets*, Armonk, NY: M.E. Sharpe.

Das, Dilip K. (1993) Contemporary Trends in the International Capital Markets. In Dilip K. Das (ed.), *International Finance: Contemporary Issues*, 3–26, New York, NY: Routledge.

Davies, Glyn (2002) *A History of Money: From Ancient Times to the Present Day*, Cardiff: University of Wales Press.

Davies, Paul J. (2008) Trading in CDOs Slows to a Trickle, *Financial Times*, 11 February, A19.

de Goede, Marieke (2003) Beyond Economism in International Political Economy, *Review of International Studies*, 29(1): 79–97.

de Goede, Marieke (2005) Resocialising and Repoliticising Financial Markets, *Economic Sociology Newsletter*, 3(6): 19–28.

de Goede, Marieke (2006) Introduction: International Political Economy and the Promises of Poststructuralism. In M. de Goede (ed.), *International Political Economy and Poststructural Politics*, 1–20, New York, NY: Palgrave Macmillan.

Deutsche Bank (2017) Annual Report 2017: Risk Report. Available at: https://annualreport.deutsche-bank.com/2017/ar/risk-report/risk-and-capital-management/liquidity-risk-management/net-stable-funding-ratio.html.

DIHS (2008) Demographia International Housing Affordability Survey 2006, Christchurch: Pavletich Properties Limited, 14 August.

Doherty, N. (2000) *Integrated Risk Management: Techniques and Strategies for Reducing Risk*, New York, NY: McGraw Hill.

Duncan, Richard (2003) *The Dollar Crisis: Causes, Consequences, Cures*, Singapore: John Wiley and Sons.

Dymski, Gary A. (2010) From Financial Exploitation to Global Banking Instability: Two Overlooked Roots of the Subprime Crisis. In Martin Konings (ed.), *The Great Credit Crash*, 47–72, New York, NY: Verso.

Eatwell, John and Taylor, Lance (2000) *Global Finance at Risk: The Case for International Regulation*, New York, NY: The New Press.

Eichengreen, Barry (1996) *Globalizing Capital: A History of the International Monetary System*, Princeton, NJ: Princeton University Press.

Eichengreen, Barry (2008) *Globalizing Capital: A History of the International Monetary System*, 2nd edn, Princeton, NJ: Princeton University Press.

Eichengreen, Barry (2011) *Exorbitant Privilege: The Rise and Fall of the Dollar and the Future of the International Monetary System*, New York, NY: Oxford University Press.

Eichengreen, Barry and Flandreau, Mark (2009) The Rise and Fall of the Dollar, *European Review of Economic History*, 13(3): 377–411.

Eichengreen, Barry and Portes, Richard (1990) The Interwar Debt Crisis and its Aftermath, *The World Bank Research Observer*, 5(1): 69–94.

Eichengreen, B., Mehl, Arnaud and Chitu, Livia (2018) *How Currencies Work: Past, Present and Future*, Princeton, NJ: Princeton University Press.

Eisen, Arnold (1978) The Meanings and Confusions of Weberian Rationality, *British Journal of Sociology*, March, 29(1): 57–70.

Emanuel, Carlos J. (1976) The Expanding Eurobond Market, *Finance and Development*, 13(3), 33–35.

European Central Banks (2015) *Financial Stability Review*, Frankfurt: ECB, November.

Evans, John S. (1992) *International Finance: A Markets Approach*, Orlando, FL: The Dryden Press.

Evans, Peter, Rueschemeyer, Dietrich and Skocpol, Theda (eds) (1985) *Bringing the State Back In*, Cambridge: Cambridge University Press.

Federal Deposit Insurance Corporation (FDIC) (1997) *An Examination of the Banking Crises of the 1980s and Early 1990s, Volume 1*. FDIC.

Fichtner, Jan, Heemskerk, Eelke M. and Garcia-Bernardo, Javier (2017) Hidden Power of the Big Three? Passive Funds, Re-concentration of Corporate Ownership, and New Financial Risk, *Business and Politics*, 19(2): 298–326.

Fine, Ben and Saad-Filho, Alfredo (2017) Thirteen Things you Need to Know about Neoliberalism, *Critical Sociology*, 43(4–5): 685–706.

Fisher III, Frederick (1979) *The Eurodollar Bond Market*, London: Euromoney Publications.

Foster, John Bellamy (2006) The Household Debt Bubble, *Monthly Review*, 58(1): 1–11.

Foster, John Bellamy and Magdoff, Fred (2009) *The Great Financial Crisis: Causes and Consequences*, New York, NY: Monthly Review Press.

Fowler, Stephen A. (2014) Monetary Fifth Column: The Eurodollar Threat to Financial Stability and Economic Sovereignty, *Vanderbilt Journal of Transnational Law*, 47: 825–60.

Frieden, Jeffry (1987) *Banking on the World: The Politics of American International Finance*, New York, NY: Harper & Row.

Fritzdixon, Kathryn (2019) Bank and Nonbank Lending Over the Past 70 Years, *FDIC Quarterly*, 13(4): 31–39.

Fung, Hung-Gay, Ko, Glenn and Yau, Jot (2014) *Dim Sum Bonds: The Offshore Renminbi Denominated Bonds*, Hoboken, NJ: Wiley.

Gabor, Danelia (2016) The (Impossible) Repo Trinity: The Political Economy of Repo Markets, *Review of International Political Economy*, 23: 967–1000.

Gambau-Brisa, Fabia and Mann, Catherine L. (2009) Reviving Mortgage Securitization: Lessons from the Brady Plan and Duration Analysis, Federal Reserve Bank of Boston, *Public Policy Discussion Papers*, 09(3).

Global Marketing Network (2009) Expanding Homeownership Opportunities for all Americans, Washington DC: American Dream Down Payment Assistance: Informational Resource Guide, July.

Goodfriend, Marvin (1981) Eurodollars, *Economic Review Richmond Federal Reserve*, May/June, 12–18.

Goodfriend, Marvin (1998) Instruments of the Money Market, *Federal Reserve Bank of Richmond*. Available at: https://www.richmondfed.org/~/media/richmondfedorg/publications/research/special_reports/instruments_of_the_money_market/pdf/chapter_05.pdf.

Goodhart, William (1995) Injecting New Blood into Bunds, *Euroweek*, October.

Goodman, Laurie S., Li, Shumin and Lucas, Douglas L. (2008) *Subprime Mortgage Credit Derivatives*, Indianapolis, IN: John Wiley & Sons.

Gowa, Joanne S. (1983) *Closing the Gold Window: Domestic Politics and the End of Bretton Woods*, New York, NY: Cornell University Press.

Gowan, Peter (1999) *The Global Gamble: Washington's Faustian Bid for Global Dominance*, New York, NY: Verso.

Grabbe, Orlin J. (1996) *International Financial Markets*, 3rd edn, Englewood Cliffs, NJ: Prentice Hall.

Green, Jeremy (2016) Anglo-American Development, the Euromarkets, and the Deeper Origins of Neoliberal Deregulation, *Review of International Studies*, 42(2): 425–49.

Green, Stephen (2000) Negotiating with the Future: The Culture of Modern Risk in Global Financial Markets, *Environment and Planning D*, 18(1): 77–90.

Greenspan, Alan (1999a) Do Efficient Financial Markets Mitigate Financial Crises? Speech to the Financial Markets Conference of the Federal Reserve Bank of Atlanta, Sea Island, 19 October. Available at: https://www.federalreserve.gov/boarddocs/speeches/1999/19991019.htm.

Greenspan, Alan (1999b) Remarks by Chairman Alan Greenspan: Mortgage Markets and Economic Activity, Conference on Mortgage Markets and Economic Activity, 2 November. Available at: https://www.federalreserve.gov/boarddocs/speeches/1999/19991102.htm.

Hall, Peter and Taylor, Rosemary (1996) Political Science and the Three New Institutionalisms, *Policy Studies*, 44(5): 936–57.

Hall, Rodney Bruce (2009) *Central Banking as Global Governance: Constructing Financial Credibility*, Cambridge: Cambridge University Press.

Harman, Chris (2009) The Slump of the 1930s and the Crisis Today, *International Socialism*, Winter, 121.

Harvey, David (2005) *A Brief History of Neoliberalism*, New York, NY: Oxford University Press.

Hasselstrom, Anna (2000) Can't Buy Me Love: Negotiating Ideas of Trust, Business and Friendship in Financial Markets. In Herbert Kaltoff, Richard Rottenburn and Hans Wagener (eds), *Facts and Figures: Economic Representations and Practices*, 257–76, Marburg: Metropolis Verlag.

Hawley, James P. (1987) *Dollars and Borders*, Armonk, NY: M.E. Sharpe.

Hayes III, Samuel L. and Hubbard, Philip M. (1990) *Investment Banking: A Tale of Three Cities*, Boston, MA: Harvard Business School Press.

Helleiner, Eric (1994) *States and the Reemergence of Global Finance: From Bretton Woods to the 1990s*, Ithaca, NY: Cornell University Press.

Helleiner, Eric (2003) *The Making of National Money: Territorial Currencies in Historical Perspective*, New York, NY: Cornell University Press.

Helleiner, Eric (2009) Enduring Top Currency, Fragile Negotiated Currency. In Eric Helleiner and Jonathan Kirshner (eds), *The Future of the Dollar*, 69–87, New York, NY: Cornell University Press.

Helleiner, Eric (2010) A Bretton Woods Moment? The 2008 Crisis and the Future of Global Finance, *International Affairs*, 86(3): 619–36.

Henning, Randall C. (1994) Currencies and Politics in the United States, Germany and Japan, Washington DC: Institute for International Economics.

Hertz, Ellen (1998) *The Trading Crowd: An Ethnography of the Shanghai Stock Market*, Cambridge: Cambridge University Press.

Hilferding, Rudolf ([1905] 2017) Karl Marx's Formulation of the Problem of Theoretical Economics. In R.B. Day and D.F. Gaido (eds), *Responses to Marx's Capital: From Rudolf Hilferding to Isaak Illich Rubin*, 362–77, London: Brill.

Hilsenrath, Jon and Timiraos, Nick (2020) Biden's Economic Team Charts a New Course for Globalization, With Trumpian Undertones, *Wall Street Journal*, 1 December.

Ho, Thomas S.Y. and Lee, Sang Bin (2004) *The Oxford Guide to Financial Modeling*, New York, NY: Oxford University Press.

Holmes, Frank (2018) With Rollback Dodd–Frank is now Officially a Dud, *Forbes*, 19 March.

Hooper, Charlotte (2001) *Manly States: Masculinities, International Relations and Gender Politics*, New York, NY: Columbia University Press.

Hoschka, Tobias C. (2005) ERD Working Paper: Developing the Market for Local Currency Bonds by Foreign Issuers: Lessons from Asia, Manila: Asian Development Bank, February.

Hudson, Michael (2003) *Super Imperialism: The Economic Strategy of American Empire*, 2nd edn, London: Pluto Press.

Humpage, Owen F. and Shenk, Michael (2008) Economic Trends: SWAP Lines, *Federal Reserve Bank of Cleveland*, 9 October.

Ingham, Geoffrey (1996) Money is a Social Relation, *Review of Social Economy*, Winter, 54(4): 507–29.

Ingham, Geoffrey (1998) On the Underdevelopment of the Sociology of Money, *ACTA Sociologica*, 41(1): 3–18.

Ingham, Geoffrey (2001) Fundamentals of a Theory of Money: Untangling Fine, Lapavitsas and Zelizer, *Economy and Society*, August, 30(3): 304–23.

Ip, Greg (2005) Federal Reserve Chairman Warns on Reliance on Housing Loans, *The Wall Street Journal*, 28 September.

Jackson, Patricia, Furfine, Craig, Groeneveld, Hans, Hanncock, Diana, Jones, David, Perraudin, William, Radecki, Lawrence and Yoneyama, Masao (1999) Capital Requirements and Bank Behaviour: The Impact of the Basle Accord, *Basle Committee on Banking Supervision*, Working Papers, N1.

Jahnke, P. (2019) Ownership Concentration and Institutional Investors' Governance Through Voice and Exit, *Business and Politics*, 21(3), 327–350.

James, Harold (2009) The Enduring International Preeminence of the Dollar. In Eric Helleiner and Jonathan Kirshner (eds), *The Future of the Dollar*, 24–44, New York, NY: Cornell University Press.

Japanese Ministry of Finance (2005) Securities Issuance – Historical Data, Tokyo: Japanese Ministry of Finance.

Jefferis, Richard H. (1990) The High Yield Debt Market: 1980–1990, Federal Reserve Bank of Cleveland, Economic Commentary, 1 April.

Jessop, Bob (1988) Regulation Theory, Post Fordism and the State: More than a Reply to Werner Bonefeld, *Capital and Class*, 34(1): 147–68.

Jessop, Bob (2001) Institutional Re(turns) and the Strategic Relational Approach, *Environment and Planning A: Economy and Space*, 33(7): 1213–35.

Jessop, Bob (2010) Cultural Political Economy and Critical Policy Studies, *Critical Policy Studies*, 3(3–4): 336–56.

Jessop, Bob (2014) Cultural Semiotic Analysis and Cultural Political Economy, *Worldpress.com*, 15 December. Available at: https://bobjessop.wordpress.com/2014/12/15/critical-semiotic-analysis-and-cultural-political-economy/.

Jessop, Bob (2015) Cultural Political Economy and Critical Political Studies, *Worldpress.com*, 15 December. Available at: https://bobjessop.wordpress.com/2015/01/26/cultural-political-economy-and-critical-policy-studies/.

Jessop, Bob and Oosterlynck, Stijn (2008) Cultural Political Economy: On Making the Cultural Turn without Falling into Soft Economic Sociology, *Geoforum*, 39: 1155–69.

Jessop, Bob and Scherrer, Christoph (2015) Introduction, In Bob Jessop, Brigitte Young and Christoph Scherrer (eds), *Financial Cultures and Crisis Dynamics*, 1–24, New York, NY: Routledge.

Kamin, Steven B. and DeMarco, Laurie Pounder (2010) How Did a Domestic Housing Slump Turn into a Global Financial Crisis, Board of Governors of the Federal Reserve System, *International Finance Discussion Papers*, 994.

Kaminska, Izabella (2016) A Global Reserve Requirement for all those Eurodollars, *Financial Times*, 15 April.

Kapstein, Ethan Barnaby (1992) Between Power and Purpose: Central Bankers and the Politics of Regulatory Convergence, *International Organization*, Winter, 46(1): 265–87.

Kapstein, Ethan Barnaby (1994) *Governing the Global Economy: International Finance and the State*, Cambridge, MA: Harvard University Press.

Karger, Howard (2007) The Homeownership Myth, *Dollars and Sense*, Spring i(270). Available at: http://www.dollarsandsense.org/archives/2007/0507homeownership.html.

Kenen, Peter B. (1995) Capital Controls, the EMS and EMU, *The Economic Journal*, January, 105(428): 181–92.

Keynes, John Maynard (1936) *The General Theory of Employment Interest and Money*, London: Macmillan and Co..

Kim, Alvin K. (1998) The S&L Crisis Revisited: Exporting an American Model to Resolve Thailand's Banking Problems, *Duke Journal of Comparative and International Law*, 9: 343–82.

Kindleberger, Charles P. (1968) *International Economics*, 4th edn, Homewood, IL: Richard D. Irving.

Kirchhoff, Sue and Keen, Judy (2007) Minorities Hit Hard by Rising Costs of Subprime Loans, *USA Today*, 25 April.

Kirshner, Jonathan (2000) The Study of Money, *World Politics*, April, 52(3): 407–36.

Kirshner, Jonathan (2001) The Political Economy of Low Inflation, *Journal of Economic Surveys*, 15(1): 41–70.

Kirshner, Jonathan (2003) Money is Politics, *Review of International Political Economy*, November, 10(4): 645–60.

Kliman, Andrew (2008) A Crisis at the Center of the System, *International Socialism*, Autumn, no. 120.

Knight, Jerry (1990) The S-L-Junk Bond Link, *The Washington Post*, 18 February.

Kobrak, Christopher and Troege, Michael (2015) Forty Years of International Attempts to Bolster Bank Safety, *Financial History Review*, 22(2): 133–56.

Kolb, Robert W. and Overdahl, James A. (2003) *Financial Derivatives*, 3rd edn, Hoboken, NJ: John Wiley and Sons.

Konings, Martijn (2008) The Institutional Foundations of US Structural Power in International Finance: From the Re-emergence of Global Finance to the Monetarist Turn, *Review of International Political Economy*, 15(1): 36–61.

Konings, Martijn (2011) *The Development of American Finance*, New York, NY: Cambridge University Press.

Konings, Martijn (2018) *Capital and Time: For a New Critique of Neoliberal Reason*, Stanford, CA: Stanford University Press.

Konings, Martijn and Panitch, Leo (2009) The Politics of Imperial Finance. In Leo Panitch and Martijn Konings (eds), *American Empire and the Political Economy of Global Finance*, 225–52, New York, NY: Palgrave.

Kothari, Vinod (2006) *Securitization: The Financial Instrument of the Future*, Toronto: John Wiley & Sons.

Kregel, Jan (2008) Using Minsky's Cushions of Safety to Analyze the Crisis in the US Subprime Mortgage Market, *International Journal of Political Economy*, Spring, 37(1): 3–23.

Krippner, Greta (2007) The Making of US Monetary Policy: Central Bank Transparency and the Neoliberal Dilemma, *Theory and Society*, 36: 477–513.

Krugman, Paul (2008) Fannie, Freddie and You, *The New York Times*, 14 July.

Langley, Paul (2002) *World Financial Orders: An Historical International Political Economy*, London: Routledge.

Lapavitsas, Costas (2003) *Social Foundations of Markets, Money and Credit*, New York, NY: Routledge.

Lapavitsas, Costas (2009) Working Paper: Financialised Capitalism: Crisis and Financial Expropriation, London: SOAS Research Online, Money and Finance, 15 February.

Lapavitsas, Costas (2014) *Profiting without Producing: How Finance Exploits Us All*, New York, NY: Verso.

Levine, Ross (2012) The Governance of Financial Regulation: Reform Lessons from the Recent Crisis, *International Review of Finance*, 12(1): 36–56.

Lipietz, Alain (1986) *Mirages and Miracles: The Crises in Global Fordism*, London: New Left Books.

Lipuma, Edward and Lee, Benjamin (2004) *Financial Derivatives and the Globalization of Risk*, Durham, NC: Duke University Press.

Liu, Henry C.K. (2008) Debt Capitalism Self-Destructs, *Asia Times Online*, 22 July.

Maher, Stephen and Aquanno, Scott M. (2018) Conceptualizing Neoliberalism: Foundations for an Institutional Marxist Theory of Capitalism, *New Political Science*, 40(1): 33–50.

Maher, Stephen and Aquanno, Scott M. (2021) A New Finance Capital? Theorising Corporate Governance and Financial Power. In Judith Dellheim and Otto Frieder Wolf (eds), *Rudolf Hilferding: What Do We Still Have to Learn from His Legacy?*, London: Palgrave Macmillan, 129–154.

Mailander, Christopher (1997[1998]) Financial Innovation, Domestic Regulation and the International Marketplace: Lessons on Meeting Globalization's Challenge Drawn from the International Bond Market, *The George Washington Journal of International Law and Economics*, 31(3): 341–92.

Makin, John H. (1971) Swaps and Roosa Bonds as an Index of the Cost of Cooperation in the Crisis Zone, *The Quarterly Journal of Economics*, May, 85(2): 349–56.

Markose, Sheri, Giansante, Simone and Shaghaghi, Rais Ali (2012) 'Too Interconnected to Fail' Financial Networks of the US CDS Market: Topological Fragility and Systemic Risk, *Journal of Economic Behavior & Organization*, 83: 627–46.

Markose, Sheri M., Oluwasegun, Bewaji and Giansante, Simone (2015) Multi Agent Financial Network Model of US Collateralized Debt Obligations. In Information Resources Management Association (ed.), *Banking, Finance and Accounting*, 561–91, Hershey, PA: Business Science Reference.

Markowitz, Harry Max (1959) *Portfolio Selection*, New Haven, CT: Yale University Press.

Marsh, Tanya D. and Norman, Joseph (2013) Reforming the Regulation of Community Banks after Dodd–Frank. Available at: https://www.stlouisfed.org/~/media/files/pdfs/banking/cbrc-2013/marsh_norman_reforming_regulation.pdf.

Martino, Enrique (2018) Irrationality and Speculation in Finance, *Journal of Ethnographic Theory*, 8(3): 467–73.

Marx, Karl ([1852] 2006) *The 18th Brumaire of Louis Bonaparte*, Project Gutenberg.

Marx, Karl ([1867] 1976) *Capital, Volume 1*, London: Penguin Books.

Marx, Karl ([1894] 1972) *Capital, Volume 3*, London: Lawrence and Wishart.

Maurer, Bill (2002) Repressed Futures: Financial Derivatives' Theological Unconscious, *Economy & Society*, 31(1): 15–36.

McCauley, Robert (2018) The 2008 Crisis: Transpacific or Transatlantic?, *BIS Quarterly Review*, December: 39–58.

McCauley, Robert (2019) Safe Assets: Made, Not Born. *BIS Working Papers*, 769: February.

McKinnon, Ronald (1993) The Rules of the Game: International Money in Historical Perspective, *Journal of Economic Literature*, March, 31(1): 1–44.

McKinnon, Ronald (2007) Why China Should Keep its Dollar Peg, *International Finance*, 10(1), 43–70.

McLean, Bethany (2005) The Fall of Fannie Mae, *Fortune*, 24 January.

McNally, David (2008) From Financial Crisis to World Slump: Accumulation, Financialisation and the Global Slowdown, *Historical Materialism*, 17(2): 35–83.

McNally, David (2010) *Global Slump: The Economics and Politics of Crisis and Resistance*, Los Angeles, CA: PM Press.

Mehrling, Perry (2011) *The New Lombard Street: How the Fed Became the Dealer of Last Resort*, Princeton, NJ: Princeton University Press.

Melamed, Leo (2003) *Leo Melamed on the Markets*, Toronto: John Wiley & Sons.

Melamed, Leo (2009) *For Crying Out Loud: From Open Outcry to the Electronic Screen*, Hoboken, NJ: John Wiley & Sons.

Mensbrugghe, Jean (1964) Foreign Issues in Europe, *IMF Staff Papers*, July.

Merrill Lynch (1994) Yankee Bonds, *Asiamoney*, July/August.

Miliband, Ralph (1969) *The State in Capitalist Society*, New York, NY: Basic Books.

Miliband, Ralph (1970) The Capitalist State: Reply to Nicos Poulantzas, *New Left Review*, 59: 59–60.

Miller, Merton H. and Scholes, Myron S. (1978) Dividends and Taxes, *Journal of Financial Economics*, 6(4): 333–64.

Millman, Gregory (1995) *The Vandals' Crown: How Rebel Currency Traders Overthrew the World's Central Bank*, New York, NY: Free Press.

Minsky, Hyman (1972) *Financial Instability Revisited: The Economics of Disaster*, Washington DC: US Federal Reserve.

Minsky, Hyman (1980) Money Financial Markets and the Coherence of a Market Economy, *Journal of Post-Keynesian Economics*, Fall, 3(1): 21–31.

Minsky, Hyman (1992) Working Paper No. 74: The Financial Instability Hypothesis, Annandale-on-Hudson: The Jerome Levy Economics Institute.

Mirochnik, Michael (2010) The Financial Crisis, Financial Markets and Official Interventions, Columbia University, Academic Commons. Available at: http://hdl .handle.net/10022/AC:P:11061.

Mohan, Rakesh, Patra, Michael Debabrata and Kapur, Muneesh (2013) The International Monetary System: Where are We and Where Do We Need to Go?, *International Monetary Fund*, Working Paper 13/224.

Montoriol-Garriga, Judit (2016) Bank Globalization and the International Transmission of Monetary Policy, CaixaBank, 7 September.

Morrison, Wayne M. and Labonte, Marc (2009) China's Holding of US Securities: Implications for the US Economy, Washington DC: Congressional Research Service.

Moseley, Fred (1999) The Decline in the Rate of Profit in the Post-War US: Due to Increased Competition or Increased Unproductive Labour, *Historical Materialism*, 4(1): 131–48.

Muolo, Paul and Padilla, Mathew (2008) *Chain of Blame: How Wall Street Caused the Mortgage and Credit Crisis*, Hoboken, NJ: John Wiley & Sons.

Naceur, Sami Ben, Pepy, Jeremy and Roulet, Caroline (2017) Basel III and Bank Lending: Evidence from the United States and Europe, International Monetary Fund, Working Paper 17/245.

Nesvetailova, Anastasia (2007) *Fragile Finance: Debt, Speculation and Crisis in the Age of Global Credit*, London: Palgrave Macmillan.

Nesvetailova, Anastasia and Palan, Ronen (2008) A Very North Atlantic Credit Crunch: The Geopolitics of the Global Liquidity Meltdown, *Journal of International Affairs*, 62(1): 165–85.

Neuberger, Jonathan A. (1988) Tax Reform and Bank Behavior, *FRBSF Weekly Letter*, Federal Reserve Bank of San Francisco, 16 December.

Neuger, James G. and Kennedy, Simon (2010) Founding ECB Vision Eclipsed by European Debt Crisis, *Bloomberg Businessweek*, 24 May.

New York University (2005) Currency Composition of Foreign Exchange Reserves, New York, NY: New York University: Leonard N. Stern School of Business, 28 June.

Nurisso, George C. and Prescott, Edward S. (2017) The 1970s Origins of Too Big To Fail, Economic Commentary, Federal Reserve Bank of Cleveland, October (17).

O'Brien, Richard (1992) *Global Financial Integration: The End of Geography*, London: Royal Institute of International Affairs, Printers Publishers.

Obstfeld, Maurice (1985) Floating Exchange Rates: Experience and Prospects, *Brookings Papers in Economic Activity*, 2: 369–464.

O'Connor, James (1973) *The Fiscal Crisis of the State*, New York, NY: St. Martin's.

Oehmke, Martin and Zawadowski, Adam (2016) The Anatomy of the CDS Market, Columbia Business School. Available at: https://www0.gsb.columbia.edu/faculty/moehmke/papers/OehmkeZawadowski_CDS.pdf.

Okuda, M. and James, Stephen (1990) The Japanese Bond Market. In David Gowland (ed.), *International Bond Markets*, 50–78, New York, NY: Routledge.

O'Malley, Brian (2015) *Bonds Without Borders: A History of the Eurobond Market*, New York, NY: John Wiley.

Organisation for Economic Co-operation and Development (OECD) (1992) International and Foreign Bond Markets, *Financial Market Trends*, 52.

Organisation for Economic Co-operation and Development (OECD) (1994) International and Foreign Bond Markets, *Financial Market Trends*, 57.

Organisation for Economic Co-operation and Development (OECD) (1998a) International Bond Markets, *Financial Market Trends*, 69.

Organisation for Economic Co-operation and Development (OECD) (1998b) International Financial Markets: Overview, *Financial Market Trends*, 69.

Panitch, Leo (1981) Dependency and Class in Canadian Political Economy, *Studies in Political Economy*, 6(1): 7–33.

Panitch, Leo (1999) The Impoverishment of State Theory, *Socialism and Democracy*, 13(2): 19–35.

Panitch, Leo and Gindin, Sam (2004) Global Capitalism and American Empire, *The Socialist Register*, 40: 1–42.

Panitch, Leo and Gindin, Sam (2005) Finance and American Empire, *The Socialist Register*, 41: 46–81.

Panitch, Leo and Gindin, Sam (2006) 'Imperialism and Global Political Economy' – a Reply to Alex Callinicos, *International Socialism*, Winter, vol. 109.

Panitch, Leo and Gindin, Sam (2012) *The Making of Global Capitalism: The Political Economy of American Empire*, New York, NY: Verso.

Panitch, Leo and Konings, Martijn (2009) Demystifying Imperial Finance. In Leo Panitch and Martijn Konings (eds), *American Empire and the Political Economy of Global Finance*, 1–13, New York, NY: Palgrave Macmillan.

Panitch, Leo, Gindin, Sam and Aquanno, Scott M. (2015) American Empire and the Relative Autonomy of European Capitalism, *Competition and Change*, 19(2): 113–28.

Panitch, Leo, Konings, Martijn, Gindin, Sam and Aquanno, Scott M. (2009) The Political Economy of the Subprime Crisis. In Leo Panitch and Martijn Konings (eds), *American Empire and the Political Economy of Global Finance*, 253–92, New York, NY: Palgrave Macmillan.

Pauly, Louis (1997) *Who Elected the Bankers? Surveillance and Control in the World Economy*, New York, NY: Cornell University Press.

Peagam, Norman (1992) Yankee Issuers Make a Splash, *Euromoney*, April.

Peterson, Spike (2006) Getting Real: The Necessity of Critical Poststructuralism in Global Political Economy. In M. de Goede (ed.), *International Political Economy and Poststructural Politics*, 119–38, New York, NY: Palgrave Macmillan.

Pierson, Paul (2000) Increasing Returns, Path Dependence and the Study of Politics, *American Political Science Review*, 92(4): 251–67.

Pigeoon, Marc-Andre (2000) Working Paper No. 303: It Happened, but Not Again: A Minskian Analysis of Japan's Lost Decade, Annandale-on-Hudson, NY: Jerome Levy Economics Institute.

Porter, Tony (2005) *Globalization and Finance*, Cambridge: Polity Press.

Posner, R.A. (2009) *A Failure of Capitalism: The Crisis of '08 and the Descent into Depression*, Cambridge, MA: Harvard University Press.

Poulantzas, Nicos (1976) The Capitalist State: A Reply to Miliband and Laclau, *New Left Review*, 95: 63–83.

Poulantzas, Nicos (1978 [2014]) *State, Power, Socialism*, New York, NY: Verso.

Poulantzas, Nicos (2008) *The Poulantzas Reader: Marxism, Law and the State*, New York, NY: Verso.

Power, Michael (2015) Enterprise Risk Management and the Organization of Uncertainty in Financial Institutions. In K. Knorr and A. Preda (eds), *The Sociology of Financial Markets*, 250–68, New York, NY: Oxford University Press.

Preda, Alex (2001) Sense and Sensibility: Or How Social Science Studies of Finance Should Be(have)? A Manifesto, *Economic Sociology Newsletter*, 2(2).

Preda, Alex (2002) Financial Knowledge, Documents and the Structures of Financial Activities, *Journal of Contemporary Ethnography*, 31(2): 207–39.

Rattner, Steven (1982) The Comeback in Eurobonds, *The New York Times*, 2 March. Available at: www.nytimes.com/1982/03/02/business/the-comeback-in-eurobonds .html.

Roberts, Chris (2002) *Harnessing Competition? The UAW and Competitiveness in the Canadian Auto Industry, 1945–1990*, PhD Dissertation, Faculty of Graduate Studies, York University.

Robinson, Kenneth J. (2013) Savings and Loan Crisis, *Fed History, Federal Reserve Bank of Dallas*, 22 November.

Rogers, Chris (2018) Global Finance and Capital Adequacy Regulation, *Review of Radical Political Economics*, 50(1): 66–81.

Roubini, Nouriel (2007) Why China Should Abandon its Dollar Peg, *International Finance*, 10(1): 71–89.

Ru, Peter and Chong, Ian (2018) White Paper: Welcome to the Real China Bond Market, *Neuberger Berman*, April.

Rubin, Robert (1998a) Address on the Asian Financial Situation to Georgetown University, Department of Treasury, 21 January.

Rubin, Robert (1998b) Remarks Before the Institute of International Bankers, Department of Treasury, 2 March.

Ruggie, John G. (1992) Multilateralism: The Anatomy of an Institution, *International Organization*, 46(3): 561–98.

Sachs, Jeffrey D. (1988) International Policy Coordination: The Case of the Developing Country Debt Crisis. In Martin Feldstein (ed.), *International Economic Cooperation*, 233–78, Chicago, IL: University of Chicago Press.

Sachs, Jeffery and Huizinga, Harry (1987) US Commercial Banks and Developing-Country Debt Crisis, *Brookings Papers on Economic Activity*, 2: 555–606.

Sastry, Parinitha (2018) The Political Origins of Section 13(3) of the Federal Reserve Act, *FRBNY Economic Policy Review*, September.

Savona, Paolo and Sutija, George (1985) *Eurodollars and International Banking*, London: Palgrave Macmillan.

Sayer, Andrew (1992) *Method in Social Science: A Realist Approach*, New York, NY: Routledge.

Sayer, Andrew (2000) *Realism and Social Science*, London: Sage Publications.

Schenk, Catherine R. (2002) International Financial Centers 1958–1971: Competitiveness and Complementary. In Stefano Battilossi and Youssef Cassis (ed.), *European Banks and the American Challenge*, 71–102, New York, NY: Oxford University Press.

Schwartz, Herman M. (n.d.) Down the Wrong Path: Path Dependence, Increasing Returns and Historical Institutionalism, University of Virginia, Department of Politics. Available at: http://people.virginia.edu/~hms2f/Path.pdf.

Schwartz, Herman M. (2009a) *Subprime Nation: American Power, Global Capital and the Housing Bubble*, New York, NY: Cornell University Press.

Schwartz, Herman M. (2009b) Housing Finance, Growth, US Dollar's Surprising Durability. In Eric Helleiner and Jonathan Kirshner (eds), *The Future of the Dollar*, 88–115, New York, NY: Cornell University Press.

Schwartz, Herman M. (2019) *States Versus Markets: Understanding the Global Economy*, 4th edn, London: Red Globe Press.

Seabrooke, Leonard (2001) *US Power in International Finance: The Victory of Dividends*, New York, NY: Palgrave Macmillan.

Seabrooke, Leonard (2006) *The Social Sources of Financial Power: Domestic Legitimacy and International Financial Orders*, New York, NY: Cornell University Press.

Selden, George C. (1912) *Psychology of the Stock Market: Human Impulses Lead to Speculative Disasters*, New York, NY: Ticker Publishing.

Senior, Nassau (1938) *An Outline of the Science of Political Economy*, London: Allen and Unwin.

Setser, Brad (2007) Foreign Holdings of US Debt: Is Our Economy Vulnerable? Hearing Before the Committee on the Budget, *House of Representatives*, Washington DC, 26 June.

Sewell, Martin (2010) Behavioral Finance, University of Cambridge, April.

Shafer, Jeffrey R., Loopesko, Bonnie E., Bryant, Ralph C. and Dornusch, Rudiger (1983) Floating Exchange Rates after Ten Years, *Brookings Papers on Economic Activity*, 1: 1–86.

Shan, Susan Chenyu et al. (2014) The Effects of Credit Default Swaps on Bank Capital, Lending, Risk and Return, Available at: http://moore.sc.edu/UserFiles/moore/Documents/ExecEd/CDSBanking_ShanTangYan_11April2014.pdf.

Shedlock, Michael (2007) Banks Worldwide Engage in Global Coordinated Panic, *Seeking Alpha*, 14 December.

Shiller, Robert (2000) *Irrational Exuberance*, Princeton, NJ: Princeton University Press.

Shiller, Robert (2008) *The Subprime Solution: How Today's Global Financial Crisis Happened and What We Can Do about it*, Princeton, NJ: Princeton University Press.

sifma (2019) Capital Markets Fact Book. Available at: https://www.sifma.org/wp-content/uploads/2019/09/2019-Capital-Markets-Fact-Book-SIFMA.pdf.

Simon, Brady (1995) Opportunities in the Yankee Market, *Corporate Finance*, July.

Sims, Jocelyn and Romero, Jessie (2013) Latin American Debt Crisis of the 1980s, *Federal Reserve*. Available at: https://www.federalreservehistory.org/essays/latin_american_debt_crisis.

Sinclair, Timothy J. (2005) *The New Masters of Capital: American Bond Rating Agencies and the Politics of Creditworthiness*, New York, NY: Cornell University Press.

Sooklal, J. (2012) Funding and Liquidity Risk Considerations: The Federal Reserve in the 21st Century, 19–20 March, New York, NY: New York Federal Reserve.

Spero, Joan E. (1988–1989) Guiding Global Finance, *Foreign Policy*, Winter, 73: 114–34.

Spiro, David (1999) *The Hidden Hand of American Hegemony*, New York, NY: Cornell University Press.

Strange, Susan (1997) *Casino Capitalism*, Manchester: Manchester University Press.

Strange, Susan (1998) *Mad Money: When Markets Outgrow Governments*, Manchester: Manchester University Press.

Streeck, W. (2014) *Buying Time: The Delayed Crisis of Democratic Capitalism*, New York, NY: Verso.

Stulz, Rene M. (2009) Financial Derivatives: Lessons from the Subprime Crisis, *The Milken Institute Review*, First Quarter.

Stulz, Rene M. (2010) Credit Default Swaps and the Credit Crisis, *Journal of Economic Perspectives*, 24(1): 73–92.

Sum, Ngai-Ling and Jessop, Bob (2013) *Towards a Cultural Political Economy: Putting Culture in its Place in Political Economy*, Cheltenham, UK and Northampton, MA, USA: Edward Elgar Publishing.

Tames, George (2019) Paul A. Volcker, Fed Chairman Who Waged War on Inflation, is Dead at 92, *New York Times*, 9 December.

Tett, Gillian (2020) Federal Reserve's Swaps Intervention will Preserve Dollar's Reach, *Financial Times*, 21 May.

Thelen, Kathleen (1999) Historical Institutionalism in Comparative Politics, *Annual Review of Political Science*, 2: 369–404.

Thompson, E.P. ([1978] 2008) *The Poverty of Theory*, New York, NY: Monthly Review Press.

Tobin, James (1958) Liquidity Preference as Behaviour Towards Risk, *Review of Economic Studies*, 73(3): 420–27.

Tooze, Adam (2017) The Secret History of the Banking Crisis, *Prospect Magazine*, 14 July.

Tooze, Adam (2018) *Crashed: How a Decade of Financial Crises Changed the World*, New York, NY: Viking.

Torres, Greg and Adam, Shamim (2008) US Fed Agrees to $30 Billion Swap with Four Central Banks, *Bloomberg*, 24 September.

Triffin, Robert (1978) The International Role and Fate of the Dollar, *Foreign Affairs*, Winter, 57(2): 269–86.

Underhill, Geoffrey R.D. (2003) States, Markets and Governance for Emerging Market Economies: The Public Good and the Legitimacy of the Development Process, *International Affairs*, 4(79): 755–81.

University of Houston (2005) International Bond Markets, Houston: University of Houston: C.T. Bauer College of Business, 26 June.

US Census Bureau (1976) Statistical Abstracts of the United States, 1975, Washington DC: The National Data Book: Banking, Finnace and Insurance.

US Census Bureau (2004) Statistical Abstracts of the United States, 2003, Washington DC: The National Data Book: Banking, Finance and Insurance.

US Census Bureau (2006) Statistical Abstracts of the United States, 2005, Washington DC: The National Data Book: Banking, Finance and Insurance.

US Census Bureau (2007) Statistical Abstracts of the United States, 2006, Washington DC: The National Data Book: Banking, Finance and Insurance.

US Census Bureau (2008) Statistical Abstracts of the United States, 2007, Washington DC: The National Data Book: Banking, Finance and Insurance.

US Federal Reserve (1967) Memorandum of Discussion, Washington DC: Federal Reserve Open Market Committee.

US Treasury (2009) Exchange Stabilization Fund, Washington DC: US Department of Treasury.

Versluysen, Eugene (1981) *The Political Economy of International Finance*, New York, NY: St Martin's Press.

Wade, Robert (2008) Financial Regime Change, *New Left Review*, 53: 5–21.

Wallich, Henry C. (1979) Testimony before the Committee on Banking, Finance and Urban Affairs, House of Representatives, 96th Congress. In *The Eurocurrency Market Control Act of 1979*. Washington: US Government Printing Office.

Walmsley, Julian (1991) *Global Investing: Eurobonds and Alternatives*, London: Macmillan Press.

Walrus, Leon (1984) *Elements of Pure Economics*, New York, NY: Orion Editions.

Walter, T. and Wansleben, L. (2019) How Central Banks Learned to Love Financialization: The Fed, the Bank, and the Enlisting of Unfettered Markets in the Conduct of Monetary Policy, *Socio-Economic Review*, 1–29.

Weaver, Karen (2008) US Asset-Backed Securities Market: Review and Outlook. In *Global Securitization and Structured Finance*, Deutsche Bank.

Weber, Max (1978) *Economy and Society: An Outline of Interpretive Sociology*, Guenther Roth and Claus Wittich (eds), Los Angeles, CA: University of California Press.

Weicher, John (2006) Homeownership: Patterns, Trends and Policies, Washington DC: Hudson Institute: Center for Housing and Financial Markets, 16 May.

Weston, Fred J. (1981) Developments in Finance Theory, *Financial Management*, 10(2): 5–22.

White, William (2008) Globalization and the Determinants of Domestic Inflation: BIS Working Paper 250, Basel: Bank of International Settlements Monetary and Economic Department, March.

Wigglesworth, Robin (2020) US Treasury Market's Brush with Disaster must Never be Repeated, *Financial Times*, 21 September.

Wilsher, Peter (1970) *The Pound in your Pocket*, London: Camelot Press.

Yates, Charlotte (1993) *From Plant to Politics: The Autoworkers Union in Postwar Canada*, Philadelphia, PA: Temple University Press.

Young, Terry, McCord, Linnea and Crawford, Peggy (2010) Credit Default Swaps: The Good, The Bad and the Ugly, *Journal of Business and Economics Research*, 8(4): 29–36.

Zaloom, Caitlin (2004) The Productive Life of Risk, *Cultural Anthropology*, 19(3): 365–91.

Zandi, Mark (2009) *Financial Shock: A 360 Degree Look at the Subprime Mortgage Implosion and How to Avoid the Next Financial Crisis*, Upper Saddle River: NJ: FT Press.

Zelizer, Viviana A. (1997) *The Social Meaning of Money: Pin Money, Paychecks, Poor Relief and Other Currencies*, Princeton, NJ: Princeton University Press.

Zysman, John (1983) *Governments, Markets, and Growth: Financial Systems and Politics of Industrial Change*, Ithaca, NY: Cornell University Press.

Index